# Critical Essays on
# Gary Snyder

# Critical Essays on
# Gary Snyder

## Patrick D. Murphy

G. K. Hall & Co. • Boston, Massachusetts

First published 1990.
10  9  8  7  6  5  4  3  2  1

**Library of Congress Cataloging-in-Publication Data**

Critical essays on Gary Snyder / [edited by] Patrick D. Murphy.
    p.  cm. — (Critical essays on American literature)
    Includes bibliographical references and index.
    ISBN 0-8161-8900-5 (alk. paper)
    1. Snyder, Gary—Criticism and interpretation. I. Murphy,
Patrick D., 1951-   . II. Series.
PS3569.N88Z625    1990
811'.54—dc20                     90-41684
                                           CIP

The paper used in this publication meets the minimum requirements of American National Standard for Information Sciences—
Permanence of Paper for Printed Library Materials, ANSI Z39.48-
1984. ∞™

Printed and bound in the United States of America

# CRITICAL ESSAYS ON AMERICAN LITERATURE

This series seeks to anthologize the most important criticism on a wide variety of topics and writers in American literature. Our readers will find in various volumes not only a generous selection of reprinted articles and reviews but also original essays, bibliographies, manuscript sections, and other materials brought to public attention for the first time. *Critical Essays on Gary Snyder* contains the most comprehensive collection of criticism ever published on this contemporary writer. It contains both a sizable gathering of early reviews and a broad selection of more modern scholarship as well. Among the authors of reprinted reviews and articles are Sherman Paul, Laszlo Géfin, Jody Norton, and Julia Martin. In addition to a substantial introduction by Patrick D. Murphy, there are also five original essays commissioned specifically for publication in this volume, new studies by Thomas J. Lyon, Katsunori Yamazato, Jack Hicks, David Robertson, and Murphy. We are confident that this book will make a permanent and significant contribution to the study of American literature.

JAMES NAGEL, GENERAL EDITOR

*Northeastern University*

*For Michael J. Hoffman, Mentor and Friend*

# CONTENTS

# INTRODUCTION

By age twenty-five Gary Snyder had begun to write mature poems in a form recognizably his own,[1] ones that would later be highly praised by fellow poets and academic critics alike. Yet, five years would pass before people would see such work published in a volume of Snyder's poetry.[2] And it would take another eight years for critics to take note. But since 1968, critics have increasingly analyzed and praised Snyder's work. In 1975 he was awarded the Pulitzer Prize for *Turtle Island*,[3] published the previous year, and in 1987 he was elected to the American Academy and Institute of Arts and Letters. In addition to his poetry, he has published several volumes of prose, as well as essays in a variety of environmental magazines and other publications. As a result, he has been recognized both as one of the most significant contemporary poets alive today and as a serious thinker, an important spokesperson for American Buddhism, international environmentalism, and bioregional politics. It should not be surprising, then, to discover that Snyder's life and poetry are more inextricably entwined than that of virtually any other modern American writer. The literary criticism of his work reflects this interpenetration of the personal and the public.

Given the views he holds and the poetics he practices, controversy remains a prominent feature of the critical scrutiny of the life and the work. Supporters and detractors alike have resorted to hyperbole. While in the late 1960s one critic would claim that Snyder had founded a new culture, another would lump Snyder and his varied readership together and dismiss them as a fringe band of "the young and the dropped out who cling on and make do, chanting mantras at the social margins."[4] In contrast, a few years later a fellow poet and critic would claim that "Snyder has for two dozen years been hewing out the guidelines along which the greening of America must proceed," while another on the heels of Snyder's receiving the Pulitzer would argue that "in order to gain a public effect Snyder is unfaithful to the basic terms of his vision."[5] And in the 1980s, one would praise his commitment to long-range change and his optimism

1

for human and planetary survival, while another would label his work one of the "extensions of early iconic modernism" that obscure "the destructive sources of the primary thrust of the postmodern literary imagination."[6]

Snyder's biography remains to be written, and those works that do detail aspects of his life, such as David Kherdian's *Six Poets* and Bob Steuding's *Gary Snyder*,[7] are out of date and too sketchy to serve the needs of a sophisticated criticism. That task cannot be undertaken here, but some biographical information needs to be shared as part of the framework for understanding the essays that follow. The rest of this introduction, then, will attend to its main purpose: giving an overview of the history of Snyder criticism.

Gary Snyder was born in 1930 in San Francisco, and shortly thereafter his family moved to Washington State to try and make a go of farming during the Depression. Snyder remembers these early years in terms of both the incessant chores that attended such a life and the experience of growing up in a rural area, close to forested mountain wilderness and a large Native American population. During World War II, he lived in Portland, but he spent his summers outside the city working at a camp on Spirit Lake. In 1947 he enrolled in Reed College on a scholarship, and he spent the next summer as a galley boy on an oceangoing ship. In 1950 he married Allison Gass, but the marriage lasted only six months. The following year, after producing an undergraduate honors thesis that was eventually published,[8] he graduated with a degree in anthropology and literature and, having received a fellowship, hitchhiked out to Indiana University for graduate school. He stayed six months, then abandoned the promise of an academic career in order "to sink or swim" as a poet. But his days as a student were far from over. He returned to San Francisco, the place of his birth, and in 1953 worked as a lookout on Sourdough Mountain and wrote some of the poems that would eventually constitute *Myths & Texts*.[9] The following year he worked as a "choker," someone who attaches cables to downed trees, for a lumber company, and in 1955 he worked on a trail crew in Yosemite, where he began writing the bulk of the poems that would go into *Riprap*, his first published collection. That fall he participated in the Six Gallery reading that gained nationwide attention for the Beat Generation when Allen Ginsberg first performed "Howl." All three of his labor experiences, as lookout, logger, and "riprapper"—laying cobbled rock on mountain trails—would appear repeatedly throughout his writing, while the experience of that reading would shift his attention from publication to performance. "I realized," states Snyder, "that poetry reading was the most interesting place for poems to happen, and that the poem is embodied in the reading, not in the book,"[10] a realization reflected in Snyder's continuous attention to the performance of poetry, both through live readings and through typographical "scoring." In 1956 while studying Oriental languages at Berkeley he shared a cabin with Jack Kerouac, which led to Snyder's immortalization as Japhy Ryder in *The Dharma Bums*.[11]

In 1956, after delays in obtaining permission to leave the country because of blacklisting, Snyder set out for Japan to study at the First Zen Institute of America in Japan. This trip, the first of several that would result in his not returning permanently to the United States until 1968, as well as the year he spent as a wiper in the engine room of an oil tanker, the *Sappa Creek*, account in part for the delay in the publication of *Myths & Texts*, which he had finished in 1955 but did not see in print until 1960.[12] Then in 1959, the year *Riprap* appeared, Snyder returned to Japan with Joanne Kyger—the two of them were married there under pressure from the Zen Institute— and remained in Japan through the 1960 publication of *Myths & Texts* until 1964. At the very point at which Snyder's career as a poet was poised to take off, he was out of the country. Yet Snyder's reputation grew both in terms of attention given to his first two books by other poets and reviewers and in terms of their recognition of the seriousness with which he was pursuing his study of Buddhism, particularly Rinzai Zen. During his brief return to Berkeley in 1964, he participated in the now famous Bread and Poetry radio talk and reading with Philip Whalen, a former Reed classmate, and Lew Welch, another close friend, that drew 800 people.[13]

In 1965, *Riprap and Cold Mountain Poems*, adding his translations of Han-shan to the earlier volume, and *Six Sections from "Mountains and Rivers without End,"* a portion of the long sequence described idealistically by Kerouac in *The Dharma Bums*, were published.[14] He and Kyger—already separated—finally divorced, and Snyder returned to Japan on a Bollingen grant. The next year *A Range of Poems*, a British collection of his previously published work, appeared.[15] In 1967 he lived at Banyan Ashram, a Japanese commune on a volcanic island, and married Masa Uehara on the lip of an active volcano. That year Fulcrum Press brought out a British edition of *The Back Country*, which was published in somewhat different form two years later in the United States by New Directions.[16] The following year Masa bore their son Kai, Snyder received a Guggenheim grant, and the new family moved to the United States. In 1969 his first prose work, the journal entries and essays of *Earth House Hold*, was published and their second son Gen was born.[17] The following year *Regarding Wave* was published, marking a significant shift in the focus of Snyder's poetry toward home and family.[18] In 1971 he built a house on land he had previously purchased on San Juan Ridge north of Nevada City, California. The following two years witnessed the publication of some small limited-edition works, most significantly *The Fudo Trilogy*,[19] as well as Snyder's attendance at the UN Conference on the Human Environment in Stockholm.

His growing recognition as a spokesperson for environmental concerns solidified with the publication of *Turtle Island* by New Directions in 1974, which contained a more militant environmental message than any of his previous volumes. The following year he won the Pulitzer Prize and the Modern Language Association convention devoted a special session to his poetry. In 1977 his focus on environmentalism continued with the publication of a series of talks and essays, particularly ones on the Gaia hypothesis and ethnopoetics, *The Old Ways*.[20] Three years later a collection of interviews appeared, called *The Real Work*,[21] providing valuable insights into Snyder's poetics. And another three years later *Axe Handles* was published by North Point Press,[22] incorporating a number of limited-edition pieces, as well as new poems, and expressing a less militant, more long-range perspective on environmental and political change and the continuity of culture. That same year *Passage through India*, containing more journal entries, was published.[23] And, finally, in 1986 Snyder brought out *Left Out in the Rain: New Poems 1947–1985*, published by North Point Press, which collects nearly all of the poems he has previously written but never included in any of his other books. Not only a fine collection in its own right, it also provides a valuable critical tool for scholars seeking to analyze Snyder's poetic and thematic development through nearly forty years of writing. Now a member of the American Academy and Institute of Arts and Letters, Snyder is also a part-time member of the faculty of the University of California at Davis. He is working primarily on a prose book, although he continues to write new sections of *Mountains and Rivers*, which remains in process despite numerous promises over the years to complete it. Like a number of other major poetic sequences written in this century, it is turning into a life's work. But as Snyder reaches sixty, he remains vigorous, healthy, and extremely active, so that those promises may yet be fulfilled with a volume that could only enhance his position as a significant contributor to the development of posthumanist ecological thought in America.

The history of Snyder criticism is far briefer than his biography but no less varied. The titles of the journals in which criticism and reviews have appeared suggest the breadth and complexity of attention bestowed on Snyder's writings, ideas, and life: *Codex Shambala, Iowa Review, Snowy Egret, Poetry, Wetlands Magazine, Parnassus, Not Man Apart, Kansas Quarterly, Poetry Nippon, Western American Literature, East/West Journal, American Poetry, Mountain Gazette, Sagetrieb, Living Wilderness*, and an entire issue of the *Okanogan Natural News*, to name just a few. But while fellow poets, Beats, and reviewers were quick to recognize Snyder's promise as a major contemporary poet, academic critics were somewhat slower in risking an evaluation.

Only a handful of reviews and essays appeared between 1960 and 1962 in response to Snyder's first two books, but all of these suggested that Snyder should be looked at very seriously as a promising new poet. Dell Hymes, for example, remarks of *Myths & Texts* that "future historians of the role of folklore in our literature may find this book to have had a significant cultural role."[24] James Wright, writing under the pseudonym of "Crunk," provides the first overview of Snyder's work by another poet. He begins by stating that "Gary Snyder is an original man. He has written a poetry which is quite unusual and very different from most poetry written in the last years."[25] But then, with Snyder out of the country and no new volumes appearing, silence descended until *A Range of Poems* sparked a spate of primarily British reviews, including the praise of poet Thom Gunn who had endorsed the volume's publication.[26] Meanwhile, in the United States, the recognized senior spokesperson for the Beats, Kenneth Rexroth, remarked that "I recently polled a wide representation of colleagues of all ages and conditions of poetude, seeking our best poets under thirty-five. The *Abou ben Adhem* turned out to be Gary Snyder, one of the most remarkable young men ever to show up in American literature. . . . I think he, more than any other contemporary poet, has lived a life of eventfulness."[27]

The year that Snyder returned permanently to the United States, 1968, was the year that Snyder criticism truly began, both in and out of the academy. With four volumes in print, plus numerous chapbooks, broadsides, and journal publications, Snyder already had a substantial body of work and a repertoire demonstrating development, change, and sophistication. Thomas Parkinson, in an essay reprinted here, kicked off the academic recognition with his essay in the *Southern Review*. Parkinson is clearly an enthusiast, and he makes claims that seem today hyperbole, but his views also reflect the general wave of optimism that arose in the United States as the flower children of Berkeley became not only a national phenomenon but also part of a rising force, allied with the civil rights and antiwar movements, calling for and believing in rapid radical change. People believed history was being made and culture remade, and in that context Parkinson's belief that Snyder "has effectively done something that for an individual is extremely difficult: he has created a new culture" is really not so surprising, even if it is naively idealistic. Snyder himself would never have made such a claim, although he had clearly identified himself with the need to create a new culture as early as his honor's thesis in prose and *Myths & Texts* in poetry. Like Wright and Rexroth before him, Parkinson did recognize that "when one thinks of Snyder, the personal and biographical obtrude in a way they do not with Duncan or with Levertov." Without explicitly stating it, Parkinson not only promotes biographical and cultural approaches for Snyder criticism but also attacks those who would continue to apply New Critical methods of close textual analysis disregarding cultural and biographical details to a new kind of poetry, the politics and aesthetics of which deny the very dissociations required of high modernism and its attendant analysis. The emphasis on a cultural approach was effectively reiterated the same year by Thomas J. Lyon in the pages of *Western American Literature.*[28]

With the general groundwork now laid for treating Snyder in the academic journals, three extremely important essays appeared in 1970. Two of these are reprinted here in their entirety, as well as excerpts from the third. In "The Ecological Vision of Gary Snyder," Thomas J. Lyon argues that not only does Snyder participate in a growing movement in the West to forsake "progress-domination theory" but also "as Snyder begins to emerge as an important force in the ideas and art of America, he shows signs of embodying the Western ecological vision in a culturally viable form." Two key points appear here: first, Snyder's work should not just be critiqued aesthetically but also thematically—he is an important thinker as well as poet; second, Snyder's vision is "culturally viable," rather than simply utopic or esoteric. The second point remains far more controversial than the first one. Lyon concludes his essay by defining Snyder as a "bard-seer" and stating that the "more fundamental requirement for such a figure is that his work, thought, and life be of a piece" and "it is almost inevitable that this be true of the ecological vision." In "Gary Snyder's Lyric Poetry: Dialectic as Ecology," Charles Altieri continues the focus on the ecological dimensions of the poetry, but he concerns himself more with Snyder's poetics: "one might even claim that Snyder is preeminent among the literary figures concerned with ecology because he has developed a lyric style which itself embodies a mode of consciousness leading to a state of balance and symbiotic interrelation between man and his environment." Unlike Lyon, Altieri draws almost entirely upon the poems in *The Back Country*, examining individual poems and poetics in greater detail.

In "From Lookout to Ashram: The Way of Gary Snyder," which is excerpted in this volume, Sherman Paul focuses on Snyder's prose writings, specifically *Earth House Hold*. He begins with a statement that would seem like nothing more than the exaggeration of a devotee until one stops to consider the source, a recognized Thoreau scholar: "I know of no one since Thoreau who has so thoroughly espoused the wild as Gary Snyder—and no one who is so much its poet." He then equates in terms of "import" Snyder's "Poetry and the Primitive" and Thoreau's "Walking" before launching into a discussion of Snyder's journal entries and essays. Paul's essay unearths valuable correlations between the autobiographical elements of Snyder's prose and his development as a poet and ecologist. Paul does not ignore the poetry but relates each of Snyder's volumes to the journal entries for the years in which those poems were produced, and in the process he gives penetrating interpretations of a number of the poems in *Riprap*, *Myths & Texts*, and *Regarding Wave*.

The following year three very interesting and different works appeared that are of value to Snyder criticism. One is *Some Notes to Gary Snyder's "Myths & Texts,"*[29] which contains a series of brief definitions, explanations, and sources for allusions, particularly the Asian ones in Snyder's sequence. Developed with Snyder's assistance, it contains many brief direct quotations on various points. The introductory note also indicates that Snyder did not think it necessary to track down every specific source for the use of Native American material. "It is enough," he writes, "if the reader be told that the poem's use of Indian material is authentic." Also in 1971 a long essay by a Welsh critic, titled "Poetry and the Tribe," appeared in *Raster*, an Amsterdam review, providing one of the first detailed analyses of Snyder's work by a critic outside of the United States. This essay, in somewhat different form, was reprinted a few years later as *The Tribal Dharma*.[30] Kenneth White begins with a brief overview of the "San Francisco Renaissance" and then turns to a discussion of "Rules of Poetic Wandering." "The Indian Background" places Snyder in the tradition of literary overtures to Native American cultures, while the next section takes up the Eastern influences on Snyder before turning to readings mainly of *Myths & Texts* and *Earth House Hold*. The final section demonstrates that White is mainly concerned with revitalizing the concept of "tribe," and sees Snyder as a leading thinker in that movement. This monograph proves most valuable not for the conclusions it reaches but for all of the connections White outlines but does not develop. The third item of 1971 is Bert Almon's "The Imagination of Gary Snyder,"[31] which appears to be the first doctoral dissertation on this poet accepted in the United States. Snyder managed to go from academic oblivion to suitable subject for theses in three short years.

The link between Snyder and the Orient—already biographically treated by previous critics but not analyzed in a way that breaks out of a Western literary model—and the need to research it further— not just in relation to Japan but also to China—were suggested in 1972 by a collection of Chinese poems in translation. In the introduction to *Hiding the Universe: Poems by Wang Wei*, translator Wai-lim Yip uses one part of the concluding section of *Myths & Texts* to demonstrate the Chinese style of poetry practiced by Wang Wei.[32] Yip goes on to discuss Snyder in greater detail a couple of years later in "Classical Chinese and Modern Anglo-American Poetry,"[33] and by then it had become recognized that one could not talk about Snyder and Oriental influences by restricting the discussion to his experiences in Japan.

William Jungels, on the other hand, completed a dissertation in 1973 at the State University of New York at Buffalo, "The Use of Native American Mythologies in the Poetry of Gary Snyder," that sheds valuable light on Snyder's indebtedness to Native American cultures. Jungels's work is a valuable resource, but as a critical work in its own right it devotes too little attention to interpreting the significance of Snyder's various allusions and adaptations. Similarly, Julian Gitzen's "Gary Snyder and the Poetry of Compassion" develops an excellent thesis but reveals flaws in its summaries of the tenets of Zen Buddhism.[34] Later critics would display a more careful discrimination between types of Buddhism and those sects that most deeply influenced Snyder (see, for instance, Katsunori Yamazato's original essay printed in this volume). Alan Williamson, in "Language against Itself," focuses instead on Snyder's position within what he defines as the "middle generation of contemporary poets," placing Snyder among Galway Kinnell, Robert Bly, W. S. Merwin, and others. Analyzing their recognition of the limitations and problematic nature of language itself, Williamson asserts that language tends "to simplify and conventionalize any complex inner state . . . that it plays an active role in socializing and repressing us," and he observes that "Gary Snyder is the most remarkable personality among these poets, and the most famous, having become, in America, a kind of patron saint of ecology. . . . In sound, too, Snyder is perhaps the subtlest craftsman of his generation."[35] Williamson extended this appreciation of Snyder in another piece published two years later.[36] While Williamson stresses the generational, William Everson emphasizes the geographical, placing Snyder in the tradition of western American (especially Californian) authors in his essay titled "Archetype West," which has a much more sweeping scope than Lyon's earlier essay.[37]

In 1974, the year that Snyder published *Turtle Island,* the collection that would win him the Pulitzer Prize, the critics were relatively quiet, producing only two essays of note on Snyder's work. Nathan Mao discusses the influence of Zen once again, adding to readings of a few poems but not providing any major new insights, while Rudolph Nelson approaches Snyder not simply in terms of religious dimensions but also in terms of contemporary theology, particularly the breakdown of the "Platonic-Cartesian dualisms between subject and object, mind and body, man and nature, natural and supernatural" that he notes have never been a problem for Zen.[38] Nelson distinguishes between religious dimensions in poetry and religious poems, and he warns that Snyder and other poets mentioned should not be seen "as crypto-religionists" but as contributors to a new definition of the "religious," "affirming transcendent values which endure even in a culture that takes for granted the absence of a transcendent God."[39]

The high point of 1975 for Snyder criticism was surely the special session held at the Modern Language Association convention in December. Out of it came greater academic attention to Snyder, as well as a balanced but negative essay by Charles Altieri, who found himself less satisfied with *Turtle Island* than with previous Snyder collections. In "Gary Snyder's *Turtle Island:* The Problem of Reconciling the Roles of Seer and Prophet," Altieri concludes that Snyder fails to resolve this problem and advises him to stick with being a "seer" rather than attempting to prophesy about the future of America. Specifically, he says that he believes that many of the poems of *Turtle Island* fail because they contain "ideological resonance"—but what seems more likely, as suggested in an endnote, is that Altieri fears that he hears an acceptance of apocalypse in some of Snyder's conclusions: "One must be careful to see that Snyder is torn between two audiences—one a remnant that must 'learn the flowers' in order to survive the coming apocalypse and the other a general public that might prevent the apocalypse."[40] It remains unclear, however, why Snyder cannot be granted the right to address some poems to the first audience and others to the second, while at the same time collecting them into a single volume. In the same year, interestingly enough, an essay on Orientalism in Snyder's poetry by Yao-fu Lin concludes that "in the wilderness, indeed, is the preservation of the world. Snyder's poetry, with its program for recreating the wilderness in the mind, is finally a poetry for human survival."[41] The key publication of 1976, however, is Bob Steuding's *Gary Snyder,* published in the Twayne Series; it is the first full-length study of the poet. Space does not permit detailing Steuding's various interpretations. Suffice it to say that it provides the most detailed biographical information up to that time, as well as extended discussions of all of the published volumes and a number of the chapbooks. Its primary shortcoming today is that Snyder has accomplished much since the book was written, and a secondary weakness is that Steuding did not understand the Oriental influences in Snyder's work as well as he might have. This remains a valuable work but one that badly needs updating, either by Steuding or another author.

In the spring of 1977 Ling Chung focused on Snyder's translations of Han-shan, the Chinese hermit poet.[42] Initially, this might seem a tangential subject, but it turns out to be a valuable source of information regarding Snyder's poetics, particularly his field composition, ellipses, and avoidance of articles, all of which can be traced to Chinese poetry. Although Snyder did the translations in 1955, first published his "Cold Mountain" poems in 1958 (Han-shan translates as "Cold Mountain"), and added them to the 1965 edition of *Riprap*, they did not receive much attention until Ling Chung's essay. Since then, a number of essays have discussed the translations in their own right or utilized them for discussions of poetics.[43]

Also in this year, Robert Kern published two essays focusing on Snyder's poetics in relation to modernism. In "Clearing the Ground," he claims that "Snyder emerges from these discussions as the eco-logical poet *par excellence*, the writer who not only wants to recall us to nature 'as the ultimate ground of human affairs' but who has developed a poetic style embodying and promoting a mode of con-sciousness with which to do it, a mode that eliminates the problem of relationship between man and nature, subject and object, by assuming their unity a priori or supporting it with the evidence of ecology itself."[44] He pays particular attention to Snyder's strong use of metonymy instead of metaphor throughout his poems, a feature that many structuralists would associate with prose fiction rather than poetic language. In some ways Kern's essay can be read as an early poststructuralist critique of Snyder recognizing that "the focus is on the differences, and the distance, between language as a concep-tualizing medium and the reality which it conceptualizes, so that language is defined as the absence or displacement of that to which it refers. . . . That is why, for Snyder, language cannot be a substitute for reality and why these poems do not participate in the modernist pursuit of the thing itself."[45] This raises the question that Kern had perhaps not yet conceptualized, and which remains as yet inadequately answered, of whether or not Snyder should be considered a "post-modernist" poet. Kern's other essay, focusing on recipes and cata-logues, attempts at the end to address the question of the importance of the autobiographical reality as each poet uses it in his or her poems and forces or expects the reader to know that reality in order to shape the interpretive experience. Kern concludes that form and content interpenetrate and points out that "one's life, in effect, is not one's own. . . . The sequence aspires instead toward a liberating anonymity (for both reader and writer), a transpersonal sense of life that carries with it a greatly expanded definition of human possi-bility."[46]

An essay reprinted in this volume, "Buddhism and Energy in the Recent Poetry of Gary Snyder," focuses on a different aspect of the relationship of Snyder's Buddhist influences and his poetics: narrative. Bert Almon claims *Turtle Island* reverses the previous stylistic trend toward lyricism because "social criticism and the desire to come to terms with Western America take precedence over the dancing grain of things." He also explains how Snyder can express denunciation and wrath without violating basic Buddhist principles. It soon becomes clear that at a number of points Almon is responding to Altieri's earlier criticism of *Turtle Island*.

Interviews have always been and remain a valuable source of critical material for Snyder readers. Ekbert Faas, in 1979, combined interview and essay as part of his larger study of contemporary American poetics.[47] Faas treats Snyder alongside Charles Olson, Robert Duncan, Robert Creeley, Robert Bly, and Allen Ginsberg, and he begins each section with his own interpretation of the development of each one's poetics as well as the similarities, differences, and mutual influences among them. This is followed by a lengthy interview, usually conducted after the essay was actually written, to allow the poet's responses to be compared to Faas's own views. Both parts remain extremely useful. In another more general study of poets, Charles Altieri returns with a more positive reading of Snyder than the one he gave *Turtle Island*. In "Process as Plenitude: The Poetry of Gary Snyder and Robert Duncan," Altieri calls Snyder a postmodern writer: "Now I want to concentrate on the careers of Gary Snyder and Robert Duncan in order to clarify pure or naive (in Schiller's sense) poetic visions that assert a radical faith in the aesthetics of presence as the ground for a postmodern religious attitude."[48] Along the way, Snyder is compared with Dante, Donne, Yeats, and Eliot, among others. While predominantly affirmative, Altieri still denies Snyder any immediate political or cultural relevance, confessing that he can only achieve "a really deep participation in and commitment to the poet's work" by "abstracting from his specific dramatic contexts and his social positions to concentrate exclusively on his treatment of epistemological and metaphysical themes and strategies,"[49] thereby dismissing as insignificant, exotic, or utopian such themes as ecological survival, opposition to nuclear power, and bioregional and community activism.

Also in 1979, Bert Almon published *Gary Snyder* as part of the Boise State University Western Writers Series, which sketches Snyder's life and work in fewer than fifty pages up through the publication of *The Old Ways*. David Robbins also contributed to Snyder criticism, focusing on *Regarding Wave*, which had not received as much attention as either *Riprap*, *The Back Country*, or *Turtle Island*. In "Gary Snyder's 'Burning Island,' " reprinted in this volume, he analyzes a single Snyder poem that constitutes the beginning turn toward family and marriage that is celebrated throughout that volume. He also discusses the biographical specifics of the time the poem describes, Snyder's days on Suwa-no-Se Island and his marriage to Masa Uehara.

By the beginning of the 1980s controversy had arisen over the issue of "white shamanism," that is, the use of shamanistic concepts and even the term *shaman* by white poets drawing on Native American and other aboriginal cultures. Tom Henighan addresses this issue in

"Shamans, Tribes, and the Sorcerer's Apprentices," an essay that includes discussion of the ways in which Snyder "assumes the tribal and shamanistic role."[50] A few years later, in "Snyder and the Emergence of Indian Poets: Restoring Unity," chapter 7 of *Interpreting the Indian*, Michael Castro would defend Snyder against criticism by some Native American writers, such as Leslie Marmion Silko, that he was exploiting shamanism rather than defending and adapting it. (Portions of Castro's chapter 6, treating Snyder's Native American borrowings, are reprinted in this volume.) Also, in 1980, two essays on Snyder appeared in *Western American Literature*. In the summer issue, L. Edwin Folsom examines Snyder's rooting himself in the American land—rather than his Oriental influences—as a fundamental element of his more recent poetry, in an essay titled "Gary Snyder's Descent to Turtle Island: Searching for Fossil Love." And in the fall issue, Anthony Hunt performs an excellent close reading in " 'Bubbs Creek Haircut': Gary Snyder's 'Great Departure' in *Mountains and Rivers without End*." Few critics have analyzed the individual sections as poems, preferring to wait for the complete sequence, still not finished after thirty years. While conclusions about individual parts of *Mountains and Rivers* must necessarily remain tentative, nothing stands in the way of reading the published parts as individual works in accordance with their actual publication history. Hunt's explication provides an excellent model for just such an undertaking.

Two essays reprinted in this volume that appeared in 1981 and 1982 respectively turn attention once again to prosody. Robert Kern adds to his earlier analyses with "Silence in Prosody: The Poem as Silent Form." Laszlo Géfin studies the impact of the Chinese ideogram on Snyder, which he would have encountered both directly through his study of Chinese language and poetry and indirectly through Pound's adaptations via imagism, in a chapter of *Ideogram: History of a Poetic Method*.[51] The same year Géfin's book appeared, Lee Bartlett published one of the rare essay-length studies devoted exclusively to *Myths & Texts*, the few other lengthy treatments of it appearing as parts of books or dissertations. Bartlett utilizes a theory of Apollonian and Dionysian conflicts in modern poetry, claiming that *Myths & Texts* "traces the overthrow of the Apollonian tendencies toward culture, education, and the ego by the Dionysian impulses toward the primitive, ecstasy, and the unconscious," as well as Joseph Campbell's Jungian theory of the monomyth: "separation—initiation—return."[52] While it is an interesting reading, with some valuable insights on specific passages, Bartlett's Apollonian/Dionysian conflict theory is viewed by Snyder as a false dichotomy; and my essay, "Alternation and Interpenetration: The Structure of Gary Snyder's *Myths & Texts*," included in this volume, argues that the monomyth triad is inadequate to explain the intricacies of the resonating structure of the sequence.

After a nine-year period in which Snyder only published limited-edition chapbooks of poetry and the slim prose volume, *The Old Ways* (*He Who Hunted* and *The Real Work* also appeared but those projects were initiated by others), 1983 saw the publication of *Axe Handles* and *Passage through India*. It also saw the publication of the second full-length study of Snyder's work, Charles Molesworth's *Gary Snyder's Vision*, a small segment of which is reprinted in this volume. Like Steuding, Molesworth organizes his study chronologically, but he also groups various volumes thematically under the general headings of "Contexts," "Figures," and "Mediations," capped by "Some Closing Thoughts." Perhaps most interesting and controversial is Molesworth's interpretation of Snyder's politics by means of Hannah Arendt's *The Human Condition*.

The following year, *American Poetry*, which is coedited by Lee Bartlett, devoted a large part of its fall issue to material on Snyder, including: two pieces by Snyder published in Japanese translation in 1960, written to introduce the Japanese intelligentsia to the Beats; David Robertson's essay "Gary Snyder Riprapping in Yosemite, 1955," which provides valuable biographical background on the composition of the *Riprap* poems; and my essay "Two Different Paths in the Quest for Place: Gary Snyder and Wendell Berry," which concludes that "the reader who finds himself attracted to their alternatives to the self-destructive character of modern life can choose both Snyder and Berry as sources of inspiration for seeking a new identity with the earth; but, he cannot, in the final analysis, agree with both poets because their conflicting conceptions of man's proper place in nature lead the reader down very different paths."[53] I continued this comparison with "Penance or Perception: Spirituality and Land in the Poetry of Gary Snyder and Wendell Berry," which was published a few years later.[54] That same year Woody Rehanek devoted an entire issue of *Okanogan Natural News* to a discussion of *Axe Handles*.[55] And in 1985, following Anthony Hunt's lead, my analysis of two sections of *Mountains and Rivers* in terms of their mythic and fantastic elements appeared in *Extrapolation*.[56]

In 1986, the year *Left Out in the Rain* appears, Sherman Paul published another volume of his meditative, journal-entry-style criticism with a third of it devoted to Snyder. Not only does it provide readings of various poems, including *Myths & Texts* through the focus of human sexuality, but it also includes two responses from Snyder to Paul's interpretations.[57] David Wyatt's *The Fall into Eden: Landscape and Imagination in California*, published by Cambridge University Press, also contains a long chapter on Robinson Jeffers and Snyder. Wyatt also teamed up with Robert Schultz to publish in the same year an up-to-date survey of Snyder's career, which is reprinted in this volume, while Woon-ping Chin Holaday added to criticism of *Mountains and Rivers,* focusing on its structure. What is most interesting about this essay is not the discussion of sources and influences, but rather the ecological and poststructuralist conclusion that Holaday reaches: "The anti-teleological nature of *Mountains and Rivers without End,* thus, may be seen as a way for the poet to lead the reader to an anti-teleological, trans-historical, relativist view of Totality, in which the operational values are those of wisdom and compassion for all sentient beings."[58] The ecological dimension of Snyder's work is also emphasized in a dissertation completed in 1986 at the University of Hawaii, James W. Kraus's "Gary Snyder's Biopoetics: A Study of the Poet as Ecologist."

Two essays from the following year are reprinted in this volume, Jody Norton's "The Importance of Nothing: Absence and Its Origins in the Poetry of Gary Snyder" and Julia Martin's "The Pattern Which Connects: Metaphor in Gary Snyder's Later Poetry." While Norton rehearses topics treated by previous critics, such as the poetics of silence and spaces in the poems, as well as the importance of ideograms and haiku on prosody, he treats them from a more overtly poststructuralist method, including references to Wittgenstein and Derrida along the way. Similarly, Julia Martin uses feminist theory, as well as Roman Jakobson's definition of metaphor, to analyze the sophistication of Snyder's metaphoric complexes, as well as to note that "the post-feminist reader is likely to ask," in regard to Snyder's Gaia metaphor, "whether it is possible to associate woman and nature metaphorically without calling up the patriarchal-technological viewpoint which made this connection an exploitative one. Although I do find Gaia an effective metaphor, I think that the poetry shows very little self criticism on this subject, and little sense of the problems inherent in making such connections."[59]

Since a number of essays on Snyder must have appeared in 1988, and more will appear in the time between the completion of this introduction and its publication, it is not possible to indicate safely the major ones at this time. As for this volume, in addition to the original essays already cited—my essay on *Myths & Texts* and Katsunori Yamazato's on cross-cultural vision—Jack Hicks has contributed one on Snyder's last collection, "Poetic Composting in Gary Snyder's *Left Out in the Rain,*" and David Robertson has provided an interview with Snyder, conducted 6 July 1989, at Davis, California. There is also other significant work in progress, some of which may be published by the time this volume goes to print. In 1987, Peter Georgelos completed a very sophisticated master's thesis, "Post-Structural 'Traces' in the Work of Gary Snyder," and while doctoral exams prevented his contributing part of that to this volume, I hope that, unlike so much other Snyder criticism in theses and dissertations, much of it will see print in the near future. Also, British critic Tim Dean has recently completed a manuscript titled *Gary Snyder and the American Unconscious: Inhabiting the Ground,* forthcoming from Macmillan. Scott McLean, the editor of *The Real Work,* is working on a study of Snyder's poetics, while Jon Halper is currently editing a *festschrift* of essays and reminiscences to honor Snyder on his sixtieth birthday, with a wide range of contributors, including personal friends ranging from his adolescence to his present life on San Juan Ridge. And I will begin my next work, *Understanding Gary Snyder,* once this introduction is completed. What the beginning of the 1990s promises, then, is a new level of scholarship in Snyder studies, the writing of full-length critical works, of which only two have been previously published, while attention to Snyder in essays and multiauthor studies, as well as dissertations and theses, will no doubt continue apace. What remains to be written is a biography that is as definitive as possible given Snyder's continued energy and productivity, as suggested by the plans he outlines to David Robertson.

While the flaws in this introduction and any weaknesses in the book due to the arbitrary character of critical selection are surely my sole responsibility, the book's strengths result from the combined energies of a number of people, without whom I would not have initiated this project or completed it. First of all, I wish to thank Michael J. Hoffman who accepted me as his research assistant not so long ago and taught me the fundamentals of the art of editing through his assembling of *Critical Essays on Gertrude Stein,* also in this series. I also owe thanks to Gary Snyder, who listened politely and attentively when I first outlined my ideas for a volume such as this, and who provided me with sound advice, gave me quick replies, and introduced me to some of the essays appearing in this volume. I feel very fortunate to have made his personal acquaintance. I would like to thank James Nagel also, who was willing to approve a volume proposal from someone with a very meager track record. Finally, I will thank Bonnie Iwasaki-Murphy, the woman to whom I am married, for being far more sensible than I am about work loads and when it's time to turn off the computer and take a rest.

PATRICK D. MURPHY

*Indiana University of Pennsylvania*

## Notes

1. See David Robertson, "Gary Snyder Riprapping in Yosemite, 1955," *American Poetry* 2 (1984): 52–58.

2. Gary Snyder, *Riprap* (Ashland, Mass: Origin Press, 1959; printed in Japan).

3. Gary Snyder, *Turtle Island* (New York: New Directions, 1974).

4. Thomas Parkinson, "The Poetry of Gary Snyder," reprinted in this volume. See also Theodore Roszak, "Technocracy: Despotism of Beneficent Expertise," *Nation* 209 (1 September 1969): 182. Bibliographical data relating to all works reprinted in this volume will be found in notes accompanying those essays.

5. William Everson, "Archetype West," in *Regional Perspectives: An Examination of America's Literary Heritage*, ed. John Gordon Burke (Chicago: American Library Association, 1973), 295. See also Charles Altieri, "Gary Snyder's *Turtle Island:* The Problem of Reconciling the Roles of Seer and Prophet," *boundary* 2 4 (1976): 770.

6. Charles Molesworth, *Gary Snyder's Vision: Poetry and the Real Work* (Columbia: University of Missouri Press, 1983), 120–27. Another portion of this book is reprinted in this volume. See also Wm. V. Spanos, *Repetitions: The Postmodern Occasion in Literature* (Baton Rouge: Louisiana State University Press, 1987), 44–45. This essay was originally written in 1972 and revised in 1976, but since Spanos did not revise his evaluation of Snyder, he apparently considers it still true in 1987.

7. David Kherdian, *A Biographical Sketch and Descriptive Checklist of Gary Snyder* (Berkeley, Calif.: Oyez, 1965); repr. in *Six Poets of the San Francisco Renaissance, Portraits and Checklists* (Fresno, Calif.: Giligia Press, 1967), 47–70. See also Bob Steuding, *Gary Snyder*, Twayne's United States Authors Series, no. 274 (Boston: Twayne, 1976).

8. Gary Snyder, *He Who Hunted Birds in His Father's Village: The Dimensions of a Haida Myth* (Bolinas, Calif.: Grey Fox Press, 1979).

9. Gary Snyder, *Myths & Texts* (New York: Totem Press, Corinth Books, 1960; New York: New Directions, 1978).

10. Katherine McNeill, *Gary Snyder: A Bibliography* (New York: Phoenix Bookshop, 1983), xi. This is the most reliable and exhaustive bibliography of both primary and secondary materials but, unfortunately, stops at 1976. After that only selective lists are available and tend to focus on academic, particularly literary, criticism, thereby neglecting much valuable work.

11. Jack Kerouac, *The Dharma Bums* (New York: Viking, 1958).

12. According to Snyder, "In the Spring of 1956, before I went to Japan, I had given a complete manuscript of it to Robert Creeley, who had been carrying it around the country in the trunk of his car. Carried it around for a long time" (McNeill, 9). LeRoi Jones actually arranged its initial publication, contacting Snyder in Japan.

13. See *On Bread and Poetry: A Panel Discussion with Gary Snyder, Lew Welch, and Philip Whalen*, ed. Donald Allen (Bolinas, Calif.: Grey Fox Press, 1977).

14. Gary Snyder, *Riprap & Cold Mountain Poems* (San Francisco: Four Seasons Foundation, 1965); reprinted as *Riprap, & Cold Mountain Poems* (San Francisco: Grey Fox Press, 1980). A new edition is forthcoming from North Point Press, also of San Francisco. *Riprap* was first published separately in 1959 by Origin Press, Ashland, Mass.; "Cold Mountain Poems" was originally published in *Evergreen Review* 2 (Autumn 1958): 69–80. See also Gary Snyder, *Six Sections from Mountains and Rivers without End* (San Francisco: Four Seasons Foundation, 1965), repr. in *Six Sections from Mountains and Rivers without End Plus One* (San Francisco: Four Seasons Foundation, 1970).

15. Gary Snyder, *A Range of Poems* (London: Fulcrum Press, 1966).

16. Gary Snyder, *The Back Country* (London: Fulcrum Press, 1967). The New Directions edition published in 1968 contains a fifth section not in the British edition, "Miyazawa Kenji," translations of poems from the Japanese that had appeared in *A Range of Poems* but had not been previously published in the United States, as well as some emendations by Snyder (McNeill, 35).

17. Gary Snyder, *Earth House Hold: Technical Notes and Queries to Fellow Dharma Revolutionaries* (New York: New Directions, 1969).

18. Gary Snyder, *Regarding Wave* (New York: New Directions, 1970). The first three parts of this volume appeared in a limited edition with the same title (Windhover Press: Iowa City, 1969).

19. Gary Snyder, *The Fudo Trilogy* (Berkeley, Calif.: Shaman Drum, 1973).

20. Gary Snyder, *The Old Ways: Six Essays* (San Francisco: City Lights Books, 1977).

21. *The Real Work: Interviews and Talks, 1964–1979*, ed. William Scott McLean (New York: New Directions, 1980).

22. Gary Snyder, *Axe Handles* (San Francisco: North Point Press, 1983).

23. Gary Snyder, *Passage through India* (San Francisco: Grey Fox Press, 1983); originally published in *Caterpillar* 19 (Spring 1972).

24. Dell Hymes, Review of *Myths & Texts*, *Journal of American Folklore* 74 (April–June 1961): 184.

25. James Wright, "The Work of Gary Snyder," *Sixties* 6 (Spring 1962): 25; repr. in James Wright, *Collected Prose*, ed. Anne Wright (Ann Arbor: University of Michigan Press, 1983), 105–19.

26. Thom Gunn, "Interpenetrating Things," *Agenda* 4 (Summer 1966): 39–44.

27. Kenneth Rexroth, "A Hope for Poetry," *Holiday* 39 (March 1966): 149, 151.

28. Thomas J. Lyon, "Gary Snyder, a Western Poet," *Western American Literature* 3 (1968): 207–16.

29. Howard McCord, *Some Notes to Gary Snyder's "Myths & Texts"* (Berkeley, Calif.: Sand Dollar, 1971). The copyright page indicates that this volume was "first published for private distribution by the Tribal Press," apparently in 1968, the date appended to the introduction.

30. Kenneth White, *The Tribal Dharma: An Essay on the Work of Gary Snyder* (Llanfynydd, U.K.: Unicorn Bookshop, 1975).

31. Bert Almon, "The Imagination of Gary Snyder" (Ph.D. diss., University of New Mexico, 1971).

32. Wai-lim Yip, "Wang Wei and Pure Experience," intro. to Wang Wei, *Hiding the Universe: Poems by Wang Wei*, ed. and trans. Wai-lim Yip (New York: Grossman Publishers, Mushinsa Books, 1972), vii–viii. This introduction was actually written in 1970.

33. Wai-lim Yip, "Classical Chinese and Modern Anglo-American Poetry: Convergences of Language and Poetry," *Comparative Literature Studies* 11 (1974): 21–47.

34. Julian Gitzen, "Gary Snyder and the Poetry of Compassion," *Critical Quarterly* 15 (1973): 341–57.

35. Alan Williamson, "Language against Itself: The Middle Generation of Contemporary Poets," in *American Poetry Since 1960: Some Critical Perspectives*, ed. Robert B. Shaw (Cheshire, UK: Carcanet Press, 197), 55, 61–62.

36. Alan Williamson, "Gary Snyder: An Appreciation," *The New Republic* (1 November 1975): 28–30.

37. See Everson, "Archetype West," 292–98.

38. Nathan Mao, "The Influence of Zen Buddhism on Gary Snyder," *Tamkang Review* 5 (1974): 125–33. See also Rudolph L. Nelson, " 'Riprap on the Slick Rock of Metaphysics': Religious Dimensions in the Poetry of Gary Snyder," *Soundings* 57 (1974): 210.

39. Nelson, "Riprap on the Slick Rock of Metaphysics," 220.

40. Altieri, "Gary Snyder's *Turtle Island*," 770 and 777.

41. Yao-fu Lin, " 'The Mountains Are Your Mind': Orientalism in the Poetry of Gary Snyder," *Tamkang Review* 6–7 (1975–1976): 389.

42. Ling Chung, "Whose Mountain Is This?—Gary Snyder's Translation of Han Shan," *Renditions* 7 (Spring 1977): 93–102.

43. See, for example, Dan McLeod, "Some Images of China in the Works of Gary Snyder," *Tamkang Review* 10 (1980): 369–83; Lee Bartlett, "Gary Snyder's Han-shan," *Sagetrieb* 2 (1983): 105–10; and Jacob Leed, "Gary Snyder, Han-shan, and Jack Kerouac," *Journal of Modern Literature* 11 (1984): 185–93.

44. Robert Kern, "Clearing the Ground: Gary Snyder and the Modernist Imperative," *Criticism* 19 (1977): 158.

45. Kern, "Clearing the Ground," 171.

46. Robert Kern, "Recipes, Catalogues, Open Form Poetics: Gary Snyder's Archetypal Voice," *Contemporary Literature* 18 (1977): 196.

47. Ekbert Faas, *Towards a New American Poetics: Essays & Interviews* (Santa Barbara, Calif.: Black Sparrow Press, 1979), 91–142.

48. Charles Altieri, *Enlarging the Temple* (Lewisburg, Pa.: Bucknell University Press, 1979), 128.

49. Altieri, *Enlarging the Temple*, 150.

50. Tom Henighan, "Shamans, Tribes, and the Sorcerer's Apprentices: Notes on the Discovery of the Primitive in Modern Poetry," *Dalhousie Review* 59 (1979–80): 613; also see 612–15.

51. By the beginning of the 1980s there had developed a proliferation of multiauthor studies that included discussion of Snyder, such as Géfin's and Castro's already mentioned, and Beonghchen Yu's *The Great Circle: American Writers and the Orient* (Detroit, Mich.: Wayne State University Press, 1983), Sanehide Kodama's *American Poetry and Japanese Culture* (Hamden, Conn.: Archon Books, 1984), John Elder's *Imagining the Earth: Poetry and the Vision of Nature* (Urbana: University of Illinois Press, 1985), and others mentioned later in this introduction.

52. Lee Bartlett, "Gary Snyder's *Myths & Texts* and the Monomyth," *Western American Literature* 17 (1982): 138.

53. Patrick D. Murphy, "Two Different Paths in the Quest for Place: Gary Snyder and Wendell Berry," *American Poetry* 2 (1984): 60.

54. Patrick D. Murphy, "Penance or Perception: Spirituality and Land in the Poetry of Gary Snyder and Wendell Berry," *Sagetrieb* 5 (1986): 61–72.

55. Woody Rehanek, "The Shaman Songs of Gary Snyder," *Okanogan Natural News* 19 (1984): 1–13. In 1987 *Columbiana* replaced this newsletter as the journal of the bioregion that ranges from the Cascades to the Selkirks Okanagan area in Washington State.

56. Patrick D. Murphy, "Mythic and Fantastic: Gary Snyder's *Mountains and Rivers without End*," *Extrapolation* 26 (1985): 290–99.

57. Sherman Paul, *In Search of the Primitive: Rereading David Antin, Jerome Rothenberg, and Gary Snyder* (Baton Rouge: Louisiana State University Press, 1986).

58. Woon-ping Chin Holaday, "Formlessness and Form in Gary Snyder's *Mountains and Rivers without End*," *Sagetrieb* 5 (1986): 51.

59. For further discussion, see my essay, "Sex-Typing the Planet: Gaia Imagery and the Problem of Subverting Patriarchy," *Environmental Ethics* 10 (1988): 155–68.

# ARTICLES
## AND ESSAYS

# The Poetry of Gary Snyder
Thomas Parkinson°

## I

The poetic pantheon keeps changing for the young. They cannot look on Yeats, Eliot, even Pound as their parents and teachers did—the world before the atomic bomb is as remote to them as Ovid's Rome, and Yeats and Eliot are literature, what is studied in school, artifacts in anthologies, only rarely live books carried into the heart by passion. A new order is established of the living gods, contemporary legends, stars in active influence. The way of the world. Some poets, Allen Ginsberg, Vozneshensky, Robert Duncan, Denise Levertov, or Robert Lowell, have the status of such celebrities as Norman Mailer and Stokely Carmichael.

Gary Snyder has not had so much public exposure, having spent most of the past decade in Japan, where he writes and studies. He has become a legend for several reasons: First, he is not merely interested in Buddhism but has studied Japanese and Chinese so thoroughly that he is fluent in conversational Japanese and translates easily from both languages. When he taught freshman English at Berkeley for a year, he was vaguely troubled by the problem of fitting Andrew Marvell's "The Garden" into the history of Chinese poetry. The Western world with its dualisms and antinomies he has made alien to himself. His knowledge of Zen Buddhism is not that of a dilettante but, insofar as this is possible for an occidental, of an adept. He is at present completing a study of the history of Zen rituals for the Bollingen Foundation, based on records that have not been available to an occidental nor systematically studied by anyone. Second, he is skilled in the use of his hands. If he were put down in the most remote wilderness with only a pocket knife, he would emerge from it cheerfully within two weeks, full of fresh experience, and with no loss of weight. There is a physical, intellectual, and moral

° Reprinted from *Southern Review* 4 (1968): 616–32, by permission of the author. This essay has been brought up to date and is available in Thomas Parkinson, *Poets, Poems, Movements* (Ann Arbor, Mich.: UMI Research Press, 1987), 285–97.

sturdiness to him that is part of each movement he makes and each sentence he phrases. He is gracious, soft-spoken, incisive, and deeply intelligent. Third, he is an extraordinarily skillful poet, and his work develops steadily toward more thorough and profound insight. If there has been a San Francisco renaissance, Snyder is its Renaissance Man: scholar, woodsman, guru, artist, creatively maladjusted, accessible, open, and full of fun.

This is no way to start a critical essay. I should have a problem, a critical problem, but these introductory notes are personal and biographical—perhaps that is the problem. For when one thinks of Snyder, the personal and biographical obtrude in a way they do not with Duncan or with Levertov—their work remains intelligible within the traditions of European poetry; Snyder presents a different set of references and beings. It is necessary to call on different habits of thought, and to think of the poetry as creating a different set of human possibilities. Nor is it a simple matter—insofar as such matters are simple—of translating Eastern into Western nomenclature; Snyder is Western in many direct and palpable ways. He has effectively done something that for an individual is extremely difficult: he has created a new culture.

The culture was there in potential for anyone who cared to seize upon it; to paraphrase Trotsky, Pacific Basin Culture was lying in the streets and no one knew how to pick it up. The paintings of Mark Tobey (pre-white paintings) and of Morris Graves and the sculpture of Richard O'Hanlon prefigured what Snyder would do, and Kenneth Rexroth had an intuitive grasp. But the peculiar blending of Zen Buddhism with IWW political attitudes, Amerindian lore, and the mystique of the wilderness was Snyder's special articulation. He had associates—Phil Whalen, Lew Welch, Jack Kerouac, Allen Ginsberg— and he has followers, especially James Koller. Along with Creeley and Lowell, he is a primary influence on the writing of young people now, though as a spiritual rather than technical force. His voice is so clear and firm that it is fatally easy to imitate, so that the Gary Snyder poem that his apprentices discover and write has a certain mechanical quality—a reference to Coyote or Bear, a natural (preferably wilderness) setting, erotic overtones, plain colloquial language, firm insistence on an objective imagery, an anecdotal frame, short lines modeled on the Chinese Cantos of Ezra Pound with much internal rhyme and alliteration, very little dead weight (the prepositional phrase held in abomination). The sources of the style are Pound and Rexroth, Pound technically, Rexroth for general political orientation and stress on beach and high country—the segment of *A Range of Poems* called "The Back Country" is dedicated to Rexroth. The proximity to Pound and Rexroth comes partly from genuine indebtedness to them but more largely from immersion in the same origins: he started from the older poets but returned to their sources to see and shape them in a special form.

## II

*Riprap* is Snyder's first book. The title means "a cobble of stone laid on steep slick rock / to make a trail for horses in the mountain." In a later poem he wrote of "Poetry a riprap on the slick rock of metaphysics," the reality of perceived surface that grants men staying power and a gripping point.

> Lay down these words
> Before your mind like rocks.
>> placed solid, by hands
> In choice of place, set
> Before the body of the mind
>> in space and time:
> Solidity of bark, leaf, or wall
>> riprap of things:
> Cobble of milky way,
>> straying planets,
> These poems . . .

The body of the mind—this is the province of poetry, a riprap on the abstractions of the soul that keeps men in tune with carnal eloquence. The notorious dislike of abstractions in modern poetic theory is here seen in a fresh perspective. Poets are entitled to dislike all abstractions except one, and that is language. For Yvor Winters is entirely right in pointing out that poetry is necessarily abstract because its elements are words. The words may be like rocks, but only in the sense that they are so placed, so composed that the action of placement is carried by the syntax and prosody of the poem. Their gravity depends on their placement, as does their capacity for bearing human weight; Snyder's equation is one of proportion, poetry being to metaphysics as riprap to slick rock. Things and thoughts are not then in opposition but in parallel:

> . . . ants and pebbles
> In the thin loam, each rock a word
>> a creek-washed stone
> Granite: ingrained
>> with torment of fire and weight
> Crystal and sediment linked hot
>> all change, in thoughts,
> As well as things.

The final and title poem of *Riprap* is programmatic for subsequent work as well, and the program seems to be to deny or transcend or go back of the famous dissociation of sensibility that Eliot identified. The aim is not to achieve harmony with nature but to create an inner human harmony that equals to the natural external harmony. There is not then an allegorical relation between man and natural reality but an analogical one; a man does not identify with a tree nor does he take the tree to be an emblem of his own psychic condition; he establishes within himself a state of being that is equivalent to that of the tree, and there metaphysics rushes in. Only poetry can take us through such slippery territory, and after *Riprap* Snyder tries to find a guide in his *Myths & Texts.* The basic guide should be style, a style of movement that will account for the solidity, denseness, and relations of phenomena.

I am not sure that Snyder has, even in his most recent work, found such a style. He has a personal voice but that is not, except for moments in printed segments of *Mountains and Rivers without End,* enough; certainly not enough for a poetics that claims, in effect, that poetry is not the expression of order but the basis. The distrust of metaphysics and of ethical schemes forces Snyder to that position. The problem is further complicated by the picaresque structure of the poetry, literally the poetry of a picaro, the roguishness of the verse being related to the roguish wit of Zen masters, the tricksterism of Coyote, the travel records of Bashō, and the wanderings of bindlestiffs: "Down 99, through towns, to San Francisco / and Japan." Some of the poetry's pleasure derives from its anecdotal narrative structures, so that reading a sizable body of the poetry puts the reader in touch with an amusing cultivated mind, a lovely harsh landscape, and a capricious movement through experience. The result is rather like reading a good novel. As early as *Riprap* these qualities are evident, in "The Late Snow and Lumber Strike," "Milton by Firelight," and the title poem. The crucial poem, "A Stone Garden," shows why Snyder's style cannot accept the standard line of English poetry, for in that poem he tries to accept the norm of the five-stress lines, and can't hold to it; can't, not because he doesn't want to but because of the inherent tendency of that line toward reminiscent meditation. For all its subject matter it sounds oddly British and New England:

> But with the noble glance of I Am Loved
> From children and from crones, time is destroyed.
> The cities rise and fall and rise again . . .
> The glittering smelly ricefields bloom,
> And all that growing up and burning down
> Hangs in the void a little knot of sound.

The entire poem moves from the kind of standard movement seen here to occasional destruction of the line by the intervention of

abstraction that is not controlled: "Because impermanence and destructiveness of time" is a mouthful; or toward the kind of ellipse
that later marks the poetry distinctively: "The oldest and nakedest
women more the sweet." The kind of trouble that grows from the
beat of tradition against his not totally comprehended subject matter
upsets the movement of many poems:

> A few light flakes of snow
> Fall in the feeble sun;
> Birds sing in the cold,
> A warbler by the wall . . .

All right, up to the point of the last line. Then it becomes, in the
pejorative sense, poetic, too much attention to the alliteration and
internal rhyme, not enough momentum in the motivation. The poem
continues in an almost nineteenth-century form: ". . . The plum /
Buds tight and chill soon bloom." This is both clumsy and archaic,
the inversion not necessary to the style, the heavy closing internal
rhyme. The ambiguity of "buds" (verb or noun?) is not controlled
and doesn't function, so that the appearance of modernity, the typical
Williamsean trick of using line breaks to create functioning syntactic
ambiguity, gets held down by the habits of an irrelevant syntax. Often
lines move, as they do in Robert Lowell's recent verse, in designs
that give and withhold the promise of conventional prosody:

> Beneath the roofs of frosty houses lovers part,
> From tangle warm of gentle bodies under quilt
> And crack the icy water to the face and wake
> And feed the children and grandchildren that they love.

This is hexameter, in my printing, but it is broken hexameter in
Snyder's printing:

> . . . Beneath the roofs
> Of frosty houses
> Lovers part, from tangle warm
> Of gentle bodies under quilt
> And crack the icy water to the face
> And wake and feed the children
> And grandchildren that they love.

This is not in any sense free verse, nor is it hacked-up prose; it is
the product of a mind that moves naturally in traditional meters and
then tries to deny the movement. The contention is interesting; the
subject matter is compelling; the sensibility is engaged in what it
perceives; with *Riprap* alone Snyder's work is an uneasy wedding of
European forms with attitudes that threaten and try desperately to
break those forms. But it is surprising how many standard lines appear,
and at crucial points such as the end of a poem: ". . . & salvage

only from it all a poem." Or the beginning: "Old rusty-belly thing
will soon be gone / Scrap and busted while we're still on earth. . . ."
"It started just now with a hummingbird. . . ." Or at a moment of
thematic resolution: "The noise of living families fills the air."

## III

*Myths & Texts* is a different matter. Although some of the poems
were printed as early as 1952 and Snyder gives its date of completion
as 1956, it is a world away from the first book. It has a genuine
informing principle and coherence of purposeful movement, and the
line has a life that is particular to its subject. The first two sections
of the book are on Logging and Hunting, what men do to the earth;
the third on Fire, why they do it. In this book appear in complex
form the issues that compel the verse at its base. He wants to reach
a prehuman reality, the wilderness and the cosmos in which man
lives as an animal with animals in a happy ecology. This precivilized
reality he finds embodied in Amerindian lore, especially of the Pacific
Northwest and of California, and in Buddhist myth. He occupies the
uneasy position of understanding this mode of perception and of
acting, as logger and hunter, against its grain. This realization is the
dramatic core of the book and holds it from sentimentality, granting
it a kind of tension and prophetic force (evident in the pro-Wobbly
poems) that *Riprap* and much of his later work lacks. *Myths & Texts*
is an elegy of involvement: to have witnessed, it was necessary to
be one of the destroyers. His sense of involvement keeps him from
invective, except against those exploiters who ordered the destruction
of nature and at the same time denied rights to the workers who
had the hard nasty labor. The world that Snyder treats is part of his
total fabric, and he cannot falsely externalize it. He cannot point
with awe to the objects of his experience because they have become
attached to him through touch and action. It is not even necessary
for him to lament this world which, through his poetry, he has
preserved. He moves fluently through this world as a local spirit
taking the forms of Coyote and Han-shan and a ghostly logger. In
these poems action and contemplation become identical states of
being, and both states of secular grace. From this fusion wisdom
emerges, and it is not useless but timed to the event. The result is
a terrible sanity, a literal clairvoyance, an innate decorum. This poetry
does not suffer from cultural thinness. The tools, animals, and processes are all interrelated; they sustain the man; he devours them.
But the author of the book and the poet in the book are nourished
by a web of being, a culture. To have the support of a culture you
have to work in and respect your environs, not as one respects a
supermarket (thanks for the grapefruit wrapped in plastic) but as one

respects a farm, knowing what labor went into the fruit, what risks were accepted and overcome, what other lives (moles, weasels, foxes, deer) were damaged or slighted in the interests of your own.

One of the touchstone lines for modern poetry is Pound's "Quick eyes gone under earth's lid." It holds its unity partly through the internal rhyme of first and final word, partly through the unstrained conceit of random association between eyelid and coffin lid, and the earth as dead eye and graveyard. Mainly, though, it has no waste, no void spaces, none of the flab that English invites through the prepositional phrase designs of a noninflected language. Solid poetry in English manages compressions that keep up the stress, and relaxations from that motive have their justification in the larger poetic unit of poem or book. The temptation of composition in serial form, the method of *Myths & Texts,* is vindicating the relaxed line in the name of a higher motive, the world view of the poet, the personal relevance. Snyder doesn't fall back on such flimsy supports. Sometimes, straining to maintain the stress he loses control: ". . . fighting flies fixed phone line . . ." This is not only pointlessly elliptical but meaninglessly ambiguous and far too clogged. But in its excesses it demonstrates the basic prosodic motive, full use of consonant and vowel tone as organizing devices, reduction of connective words having merely grammatical function and no gravity.

Snyder himself thinks of this prosody as deriving from classical Chinese forms, and both he and Pound make severe and interesting variations on that line. But variations, and since Pound's Cathay and the Chinese Cantos, people like Snyder are compelled toward Pound's brilliant invention of a line using the Anglo-Saxon alliterative line in conjunction with a line of four and two main centers of stress divided by cesura or by line break.

I talk at such length of prosody because it is the main factor ignored in most recent discussion of poetry. Thanks to Donald Davie and Josephine Miles, attention has very rightly been turned toward poetic syntax, with fine results, and the extension to prosody is inevitable and right. New criticism (old style) placed heavy weight on suggestion and symbolic reference; now as our poetry stresses drama and syntactic movement, vocality, it seems necessary to supplement the notion, and a pernicious one, that poetry functions through symbol mainly. Language functions symbolically and metaphorically, but poetry makes more precise and delimiting use of syntax through its prosodic measure. This is after all what Pound and Williams were agitated about: the dance of language. I don't want to hang everything on syntactic and metric effects and take a plunge into providing new mechanical vocabulary that will deaden poetic study from yet another perspective. What poets like Snyder, Duncan, and Creeley ask is that readers take the poem as indicator of physical weight. Until the day, not far off, when poems are related to taped performances as musical scores now are, the poem on the page is evidence of a voice and the poetic struggle is to note the movement of that voice so that it can be, as is music, followed.

> The groves are down
> > cut down
> Groves of Ahab, of Cybele
> Pine trees, knobbed twigs
> > thick cone and seed
> > Cybele's tree this, sacred in groves
> Pine of Seami, cedar of Haida
> Cut down by the prophets of Israel
> > the fairies of Athens
> > the thugs of Rome
> > > both ancient and modern;
> Cut down to make room for the suburbs
> Bulldozed by Luther and Weyerhaeuser
> Crosscut and chainsaw
> > squareheads and finns
> > high-lead and cat-skidding
> Trees down
> Creeks choked, trout killed, roads.

The procedures of the line here are largely halving and coupling, and the variations are relaxations that reach out semantically to other results:

> Crosscut and chainsaw
> > squareheads and finns
> > high-lead and cat-skidding
> Trees down
> Creeks choked, trout killed, roads.

The violence of the first four linear divisions creates a tension that is cumulative; the dangers of the catalogue are diminished by the prosody so that it is not a simple matter of adding item to item but of seeing each item as part of design and pattern, a concert of yoked energies. The final line leaves a single word uncoupled, a result, a relaxation into barrenness. The poem is a perversion of religious ceremony, the text of life against the myth of natural sacredness.

This book thus creates and denies one of the greatest of American experiences, that of a wild ecology. But it is not merely American; the human race really is on the way to destroying the planet, if not by some mad outrageous single explosion then by steady careless greedy attrition of all those qualities that have over the centuries kept men as sane as they have been. Curiously, although this has been the overriding historical fact of the past generation, only one extensive book of poetry has tried to tackle this problem as subject and come to some prophetic stance. Yet there is nothing pompous or portentous about *Myths & Texts;* it is genuinely contemplative. It has received no prizes, but over the years it may well become, for those men who care, a sacred text.

Many poems have followed *Myths & Texts* but no book with the unity and impact that Snyder is capable of. The *Six Sections from Mountains and Rivers without End* have the mark of Snyder's style, the same tough placement of words in an order that makes the language articulate. There is in this book a kind of boyishness that is engaging but not up to the best of his possibilities. Simplicity should not seem, as it does in so complex a poet, an affectation. What most tempts Snyder is the anecdotal mode, the candid snapshot, the reduction of perception to objects merely, wondering at the simple. There is an insistence on youthfulness that I find embarrassing— perhaps because of my own great age. In the "Hymn to the Goddess San Francisco in Paradise" he speaks for the Chamber of anti-Commerce with contempt for the tourists because they are too old. Hatred of tourists (did you ever see such a bunch of freaks) is an honorable tradition of all San Franciscans from restaurateurs to bohemians (one of San Francisco's best restaurants does not accept credit cards because, according to the owner, "I don't want a bunch of Texans in here."). But Snyder's "Hymn" is kiddish, a bohemian version of Herb Caen. His attitude toward cities remains that of a young logger from the provinces, as his "This Tokyo" indicates. There is a healthy side to this attitude, that of the Jeremiad; and yes, of all American cities, only New York and San Francisco have managed to work into poetic idiom with any strength. If Gloucester and Paterson become mythical, it will be because of highly individuated local spirits rather than because of any inherent quality. But Snyder seems to be playing on external and sentimental associations, something that poets like Jack Spicer and Ron Loewinsohn have not allowed to happen in their work.

Then there is the hitchhiking poem. Some day a man will write a great novel using the frame of hitchhiking—it is the only way for a current American to do a Don Quixote, Tom Jones, or Pickwick. Consider the varieties of chance associations, mistakes, lures, and wanderings by the way. A modern Chaucer would make his *Canterbury Tales* from such possibilities; a Homer, an *Odyssey.* Snyder's poem is short, as are the presentations of characters met along the way:

Oil-pump broken, motor burning out      *Salem*

Ex-logger selling skidder cable
    wants to get to San Francisco,
    fed and drunk                                      *Eugene*

Guy just back from Alaska—don't like
    the States, there's too much law        *Sutherlin*

A woman with a kid & two bales of hay.  *Roseburg*

Some of the episodes might cover as much as eight lines, but the characters
remain thin: ". . . a passed-out LA whore / glove compartment full of booze, /
the driver a rider, nobody cowbody, / sometime hood . . . ." The places
are given brief play:

Snow on the pines & firs around Lake Shasta
    —Chinese scene of winter hills & trees
    us "little travellers" in the bitter cold

six-lane highway slash & DC twelves
bridge building   squat earth-movers
—yellow bugs

I speak for hawks.

It's a poem of around four hundred lines, intimate and panoramic,
but one thing after another. It lacks conceptual force, and as narrative
remains facile drift, with some witty or engaging observation. So the
great opportunity of the hitchhiking subject remains sketched, em-
bryonic, waiting its full development.

Other poems from these six sections of what may become a life-
work have starker and more concentrated force growing out of Snyder's most passionate apprehension of life. Snyder has spoken often
of the importance of the rhythms of various kinds of work for his
poetry, and his sense of experience is largely a sense of work, of
measured force exerted on the world. When he sees a second-growth
forest, he wonders, looking at the stumps, what they did with all the
wood; a city evokes in him the tough brutal labor involved, the
carpentry and plumbing and simple excavating. His world is a world
of energy constantly reformulating itself, and most often a world of
human energy, exploited, misdirected, and full of pathos—he can't
take it for granted but sees at its base the wilderness and fundamental
man, and the products generated through history. This is why "The
Market," full of dangers of sentimentality in tone, and mere cata-
loguing in technique, has an inner vigor that the hitchhiker poem
lacks. This is not entirely a matter of mood but of conviction and of
consequent drive. Technical considerations aside, poetry like all art
comes out of courage, the capacity to keep going when reason breaks
down. The equivalences established in "The Market" are equivalences
of energy very roughly estimated.

seventy-five feet hoed rows equals
one hour explaining power steering

equals two big crayfish=
    all the buttermilk you can drink
=twelve pounds cauliflower
=five cartons greek olives=hitch-hiking
    from Ogden Utah to Burns Oregon
=aspirin, iodine, and bandages
=a lay in Naples=beef
=lamb ribs=Patna
     long grain rice, eight pounds
equals two kilogram soybeans=a boxwood
     geisha comb.
equals the whole family at the movies
equals whipping dirty clothes on rocks
  three days, some Indian river
=piecing off beggars two weeks
=bootlace and shoelace
  equals one gross inflatable
  plastic pillows
=a large box of petit-fours, chou-cremes—
  barley-threshing
  mangoes, apples, custard apples, raspberries
=picking three flats strawberries
=a christmas tree=a taxi ride
carrots, daikon, eggplant, greenpeppers,
oregano, white goat cheese
  =a fresh-eyed bonito, live clams
a swordfish
a salmon

And the close of the second section shows the melancholy and weariness that accompanies the breakdown of reason before all this relentless, pointless, back-breaking labor:

> I gave a man seventy paise
> In return for a clay pot
> of curds
> Was it worth it?
> how can I tell

The terrible concluding section leaves us with a vision of a totally human world, a world of monstrosity:

> they eat feces
>   in the dark
>   on stone floors.
> one legged animals, hopping cows
>   limping dogs   blind cats
>
>   crunching garbage in the market
>   broken fingers

cabbage
head on the ground.

who has young face.
   open pit eyes
between the bullock carts and people
head pivot with the footsteps
               passing by
dark scrotum spilled on the street
   penis laid by his thigh
         torso
turns with the sun
I came to buy
   a few bananas by the ganges
      while waiting for my wife

Contemporaneous with this long-projected series of poems like an enormous Chinese scroll are other poems, more lyric and brief, and many of these have been collected and published this year by New Directions under the title *The Back Country*. Characteristically, the first two sections are called "Far West" and "Far East"; and Snyder's most recent essay is called "Passage to More Than India." The synthesis he is working towards, that obsesses his being, maintains its momentum:

> We were following a long river into the mountains.
> Finally we rounded a bridge and could see deeper in—
> the farther peaks stony and barren, a few alpine
> trees.
> Ko-san and I stood on a point by a cliff, over a
> rock-walled canyon. Ko said, "Now we have come to
> where we die." I asked him, what's that up there,
> then—meaning the further mountains.
> "That's the world after death." I thought it looked
> just like the land we'd been travelling, and couldn't
> see why we should have to die.
> Ko grabbed me and pulled me over the cliff—
> both of us falling. I hit and I was dead. I saw
> my body for a while, then it was gone. Ko was
> there too. We were at the bottom of the gorge.
> We started drifting up the canyon, "This is the
> way to the back country."

## IV

Snyder has already written, published, read aloud, and generally made available a large and remarkable body of work. He is distinguished not only as poet but as prose expositor—he has a gift for

quiet, untroubled, accurate observation with occasional leaps to genuine eloquence. He has taken to himself a subject matter, complex,
vast, and permanently interesting, a subject so compelling that it is
not unreasonable to assert that he has become a center for a new
set of cultural possibilities. There are two kinds of trouble that readers
experience with this impressive accomplishment.

The first is the Gary Snyder poem. I have already described this
short, anecdotal, erotic, concrete poem set in the wilderness with
Zen masters and Amerindian mythological creatures commenting on
each other and on nature. There comes a time when tedium sets in,
when the personal style seems to be carrying along for no particular
reason except to carry along, keep busy in the act of writing. The
poems then exist all at exactly the same level and seem to have
interchangeable parts. Objects from one could be moved to another
without loss or gain. The prosody retains the same tone. The surfaces
are attractive and monotonous. Even though there are variations from
high rhetoric to self-deprecating humor, the unanimity of the poems
is restrictive. Too much goes along the surface, gliding. And often I
get the impression that Snyder doesn't care about the art, that poetry
for him is only one of a set of instruments in a spiritual quest, that
the act of construction is not something that requires its own special
resolutions. Like most writers with a coherent world view, he sometimes refuses to let his material be intractable, there is no sense of
contention between subject and object, no dramatic struggle toward
a new form. Then the poems do not seem *forms* but *shapes.*

I don't think this happens often or that it is a totally crippling
defect; otherwise I shouldn't have troubled to write this extended
essay. The complaints here registered could have been made against
Blake, Whitman, and Lawrence. The second complaint, one that I
have heard from students, especially those from large urban areas,
is that Snyder does not face the problems of modern life. In this
view, the great bulk of Americans live in cities and in an age of
anxiety verging on total panic. The wilderness exists only in a mythical
past or in the lives of those privileged by money (for pack animals
and guides) or skills based on specialized work in areas remote from
normal experience. Hence Snyder's poetry doesn't answer to the
tensions of modern life and depends on a life no longer accessible
or even desirable for men. A mystique of the wilderness based on
the humane naturalism of the highly limited Zen Buddhism sect and
the primitive insights of American savages can't satisfy the existential
*Angst* of modern man. Everything is too simple, too easy, too glib,
a boy's book in verse, Huck Finn on the Skagit, Innocents in Japan.
The poetry is archaic, not in the sense that all poetry is, but out of
tune with life in the 1960s.

It's tempting to reply that only Lyndon Johnson and Barry Goldwater are in tune with life in the 1960s and let it go at that. But the argument that a poet must speak to the problems of the bulk of the people seems to me to support rather than undermine Snyder's work. Properly understood, Snyder's poetry does *speak to* basic current problems, but it does not simply embody them. A usually sensible critic recently praised a poet for writing what he decided was "The poem of the 60's." Now this is a mentality that I understand and abominate. It is the mentality that runs and ruins museums of modern art. Who would think of calling Catullus *the* poet of the sixties (B.C.)? At present commentators and curators seem intent on timely masterpieces, by which they mean representative documents. Qualitative judgments, relevance not to the contemporary limited box but to the continuously human—these do not seem pertinent. Prepackaged history, projected museums, anticipatory anthologies for survey courses are all silly and pointless enterprises, admired and supported by people who pride themselves on being, of all things, antiacademic.

Snyder's work is not part of that academy. It is rather part of another academy, an ill-defined and perhaps undefinable group of people, including historians, novelists, poets, artists, various scholars, and many others, who are seriously seeking some proper answer or at least a set of questions appropriate to the world in its current stage of history, but seeing that world against the vast background of all human possibilities. At present, human power, pure brute controlled energy, threatens the entire planet. Some norms have to be found and diffused that will allow men to check and qualify their force. Snyder makes this large effort: "As poet I hold the most archaic values on earth. They go back to the late Paleolithic: the fertility of the soil, the magic of animals, the power-vision in solitude, the terrifying initiation and re-birth, the love and ecstasy of the dance, the common work of the tribe. I try to hold both history and wilderness in mind, that my poems may approach the true measure of things and stand against the unbalance and ignorance of our times." He is calling upon the total resources of man's moral and religious being. There is no point in decrying this as primitivism; it is merely good sense, for the ability to hold history and wilderness in the mind at once may be the only way to make valid measures of human conduct. A larger and more humble vision of man and cosmos is our only hope, and the major work of any serious person. In that work, Snyder's verse and prose compose a set of new cultural possibilities that only ignorance and unbalance can ignore.

# The Ecological Vision
# of Gary Snyder

Thomas J. Lyon°

There are some positive signs—more than straws in the wind—that a significant number of Western minds are forsaking the progress-domination theory inherent in the political view which has ruled and conquered for so long, in favor of a more relaxed and open way with the world founded on ecological sensitivity. The political mind, based ultimately on bossmanship in theology and bent on converting world matter into exclusively human use with efficient if violent technology, seems to be giving way to a gentler feeling of mutuality. We are coming, many think, to a great verge: Pisces then, now Aquarius . . . or Vico's fourth stage in cyclical history, returning to awe of the supernatural . . . or Yeats's "Second Coming." Whatever it is called, the apparently dawning age seems not to give its allegiance to hierarchies of dominance and power, nor to profane Growthmanship, but to a steady-state interdependence with all the world, its trees, rocks, rivers, and animals. The enormous expansion and deepening of the conservation movement, the new interest in the ecological sciences, and the wide search for cooperative, sacral, communal forms are all evidence that we seem to be trying to raise our sights to a holy vision of the world as a unity.

The eternal dream of the peaceable kingdom, if it can be called a dream now and not the only sane hope for survival—escape from the self-doom of ecological sin—is also emerging as a force in contemporary writing. Not as outright prophecy, Jeremiad, or prescription, but as theme growing from massive contact with natural particulars—viz., Ginsberg's important "Wales Visitation"—this kind of writing gives promise of transcending conventional romanticism to the same degree that Wordsworthian ecstasy transcended the rational optimism that went before it.

The literature of the new ecology has apparent roots in Romantic writing, certainly, as well as in Oriental thinking and in the contemporary subculture's opening of the "doors of perception" to the realization of endless interrelatedness. But perhaps the most important roots—direct apprehension of wild nature and perception of the primitive reference point in human (Indian) terms—are not so obvious, and it is here that the student of Western American literature can draw on the traditions of his regional field for insights.

Before the West had produced a great writer on its own ground, Henry David Thoreau had mapped it out as the great mother-center

° Reprinted by permission from *Kansas Quarterly* 2 no. 2 (Spring 1970); 117–24.
©*Kansas Quarterly.*

of wilderness and the place to learn ecological truth—"The West of which I speak is but another name for the Wild; and what I have been preparing to say is, that in Wildness is the preservation of the World"—and most of the best Western writers from later years have lived on Thoreau's map. John Muir, Robinson Jeffers, Walter Van Tilburg Clark, and Frank Waters, just to name four, have built on direct experience of elemental and often violent Western nature, working toward a post-humanist, post-technological world-view in which man fits into natural patterns rather than simply following his greed into the city of ecological imbalance and poisoning. This is not really to be wondered at; nature in the West has been primary, sometimes even overwhelming. It is not, except for the tourist industry, leisure-time beauty; garden-variety, escapist romantics have not grown well here. Jeffers wrote of the California coast as "crying out for tragedy," speaking of the great forms and space and immense changes in sea and sky that became his poetic world; one of the dimensions of his total work is the tragedy of Western civilization's drive to render the wild world tame . . . leaving finally only "introverted man," "taken up / Like a maniac with self love." Jeffers said he stood "west of the west"; his "Inhumanism" is nothing more shocking than the ecological vision looking back on the strictly "humanist" westward movement of plunder and destruction.

The limitations of White / Western thought have also been limned, for serious Western writers, by the presence of the Indian, who lasted long enough in the West to be the model of primitive ecology and religious responsibility to earth. But the critique has not been simple-minded. Frank Waters, to name perhaps the deepest student of the Indian among writers, has long been recommending a supra-rational, supra-emotional synthesis between cultures, making finally an ecologically responsible civilization and psychically whole persons; the Western writer's ability to take the Indian seriously has resulted in real trailbreaking.

It may be—I almost believe it—that the West's great contribution to American culture will be in codifying and directing the natural drive toward ecological thought: a flowering of regional literature into literally worldwide attention and relevance. Now, after all this prologue, I come to my subject, the poet Gary Snyder, for as Snyder begins to emerge as an important force in the ideas and art of America, he shows signs of embodying the Western ecological vision in a culturally viable form. His writing is popular, certainly, and as I hope to show, it is valid in deeper, permanent ways.

The first thing that strikes one about Snyder's poetry is the terse, phrase-light and article-light diction, the sense of direct *thing*-ness. In common with most of the poetic generation that has rebelled against the formulaic Eliot rhetoric and intellectual abstraction, Snyder writes a solid line, but the special quality in his diction, the personal voice, lies in his knowledgeable selection of objects. They are things he has worked with and felt the grain of, and thus known better than good-sounding "poet's" catalogs:

> Rucksack braced on a board,
>     lashed tight on back.
> sleeping bags, map case, tied on the
>     gas tank
> sunglasses, tennis shoes, your long tan
>     in shorts
> north on the west side of Lake Biwa
> Fukui highway still being built,
>     crankcase bangd on rocks—
>     pusht to the very edge by a
>         blinded truck
> I saw the sea below beside my knee:
> you hung on and never knew how close.

Experience is not elaborately prepared for, in the Snyder poetics, just handed over: "Woke once in the night, pissed, / checkt the coming winter's stars / built up the fire" opens a poem and puts the reader in the mountains without any pastoral-tradition framing. This is the "near view" of the Sierra that John Muir wanted so much and knew that conventional art didn't give. Snyder's open directness moves toward solving one of Muir's and other transcendentalists' great dilemmas: how to talk about things, especially wild ones, without harming their integrity by language; how to preserve and communicate suchness without falling into an arch aesthetic distance between subject and object, a romantic decoration that destroys the very wholeness, which is wildness, one loved and wanted to convey somehow. The thin line of poetic truth between overstatement and private code requires first of all respect for things, letting them stand free instead of being marshaled into line for a mental performance. Snyder apparently recognizes the lover's paradox in writing ("each man kills the thing he loves"), and turns back on his own mind with good humor:

> foxtail pine with a
> clipped curve-back cluster of tight
>     five-needle bunches
>     the rough red bark scale
> and jigsaw pieces sloughed off
>         scattered on the ground.
> —what am I doing saying "foxtail pine"?

The comment might be on alliteration and rolling rhythm, as well as on the general deceit of naming: the poem moves beyond nature love to a focus on relation, among Snyder and his poem and the tree, and the ironic mode of the final question enters dimensions of richness quite beyond simple appreciation, if such a thing is simple. The openness of Snyder's seemingly casual presentation of objects, then, should not be mistaken for naïvete. The freshness of youth in his perceptions seems to be the result of having passed through a midstage of poeticizing and returned to the primal, simultaneous brotherhood-in-separateness of all objects. This is the wild world which Thoreau intuitively saw great poetry aiming at. Leaving it in integrity requires only pointing, and here Snyder's long Zen training provides the exact discipline needed. But the poet can also bring himself in and show the paradoxical nature of knowledge (and the poignant human con-sciousness of separateness) by levels of irony. So we have Snyder writing,

> When
> Snow melts back
>     from the trees
> Bare branches   knobbed pine twigs
>     hot sun on wet flowers
> Green shoots of huckleberry
> Breaking through the snow.

on the one hand, and

> A clear, attentive mind
> Has no meaning but that
> Which sees is truly seen.
> No one loves rock, yet we are here.

on the other. The inclusiveness resulting is literally "part" and "par-cel" of the ecological vision. Tingeing the Zen core with irony, though it is far from his only technique, is one of Snyder's singular contri-butions to modern poetry, a byproduct of the connection he has knitted in his life between East and West. In a sense, Snyder is moving westward in the way that Whitman meant for us to do, the total effect of his final synthesis being, to use one of his essay titles, a "Passage to More Than India."

Snyder shows his naturalness and American-West roots most ob-viously in his colloquial, object-laden language, but another and perhaps more important consonance with the wilderness world can be felt in his verse rhythms. "I've just recently come to realize that the rhythms of my poems follow the rhythm of the physical work I'm doing and the life I'm leading at any given time,"[1] he wrote in 1959, and many of his poems are tuned so closely to muscular and breath paces that they seem quite as spontaneous as his analysis implies. A bit of "Riprap," which grew out of building trails on slick granite in the Sierra, will illustrate this:

> Lay down these words
> Before your mind like rocks.
>                 placed solid, by hands
> In choice of place, set
> Before the body of the mind
>                 in space and time:
> Solidity of bark, leaf, or wall
>                 riprap of things:
> Cobble of milky way,
>                 straying planets,
> These poems, people,
>                 lost ponies with
> Dragging saddles—
>                 and rocky sure-foot trails.

There are some fine rhythms starting from non-human wilderness, too, where the birds and other animals seem almost to have written the poem by themselves.

> Birds in a whirl, drift to the rooftops
> Kite dip, swing to the seabank fogroll
>
> . . . . . . . . . . . . . . . . . . . . . . . . . . . . .
>
> The whole sky whips in the wind
> Vaux Swifts
> Flying before the storm
> Arcing close hear sharp wing-whistle
> Sickle-bird

Snyder flirts with meter and with internal rhyme and alliteration, clearly, but the forming principle is not external. He once described formal poetry as "the game of inventing an abstract structure and then finding things in experience which can be forced into it,"[2] identifying this kind of writing with the rationalistic philosophy-culture of the West—of civilization—and then stated his preference for wilderness: "the swallow's dip and swoop, 'without east or west.' " The basic direction of his prosody is that of his image-selection: to go beyond the midstage to the consciously primitive, where there is no "east or west." Since we are both an unconscious, animal process and a conscious intellect, Snyder's poetics can be seen as an attempt at continuous self-transcendence, a leading through ego-borders into the wild. Self, ego, is at work in nature-love, as it is more obviously in nature-hate, as it is also in cultural typologies and forms for poetry. The ultimate meanings in Snyder's poetry, deeply revolutionary meanings in the sense of consciousness-changers, putting man in a different place from where he thought he was all these years, can be sensed very clearly in his formal poetics alone. His work is therefore organic rather than contrived, and although this can be said of many contemporary poets and indeed marks the fundamental direction of modern American poetry, the special virtue in Snyder's work is that he has created or allowed to develop a form that grows so rightly out of *wild* things, and which leads the reader uncannily ahead to a wild point of view. This is the technique of the ecological sense which goes past both the primitive and primitiv*ism*, into something else, in certain poems the ecstatic ecology of wholeness. Then to keep the sense of mind—"all the junk that goes with being human," as Snyder wrote once—alive along with the transparent eyeball, is art. Snyder's best poems, in my opinion, are the ones that move through these levels of apprehension, keeping the whole thing alive and total, finally conveying the great molecular interrelatedness, yet not as a static "thing," not even as a "poem," sweated out, but with the rhythmic feel of the unworded wild truth. "Wave," a recent poem, simultaneously perceives, creates, and leaps over form in this way:

> Grooving clam shell,
>     streakt through marble,
>   sweeping down ponderosa pine bark-scale
>     rip-cut tree grain
>         sand-dunes, lava
>         flow
>
> Wave   wife.
>         woman—wyfman—
> "veiled; vibrating; vague"
>   sawtooth ranges pulsing;
>             veins on the back of the hand.
>
> Forkt out: Birdsfoot-alluvium
>         wash
>
>       great dunes rolling
> Each inch rippld, every grain a wave.
>
> Leaning against sand cornices til they blow away
>
>   —wind, shake
>   stiff thorns of cholla, ocotillo
>   sometimes I get stuck in thickets—
>
> Ah, trembling spreading radiating wyf
>             racing zebra
>   catch me and fling me wide
> To the dancing grain of things
>             of my mind!

The solidity in Snyder's writing, which is often commented on, results from the fact that his ideas, like the verse rhythms, flow from close attention to wilderness, unmediated perception of grain and wave. The total structure appears in startling systematic clarity, once one gets used to the point of view. Thing / rhythm / idea, over and over, so that the meanings are inextricable from the settings. The contrasting point of view, where there is always the anthropocentric splitting which prevents things from expressing completely their innate rhythms, and which keeps things from entering our heads in fullness, should immediately be more familiar in our unpoetic culture. We tend to mark everything according to its vulnerability. But this grasping approach seals itself off from authentic experience by refusing the integrity or self-nature of things: rocks, trees, people . . . anything. This integrity is what is meant by wildness; according to Snyder, it takes a consciously primitive sensibility to know it and respect it, that is, one not overlaid with the programmed covetousness our culture seems to demand. Poets have to deal from authentic experience in order to communicate the wild truth of the matter, which is, Snyder holds, "at deep levels common to all who listen." He describes the moment of connection between feeling and making, in *Earth House Hold:* "The phenomenal world experienced at certain pitches is totally living, exciting, mysterious, filling one with a trembling awe, leaving one grateful and humble. The wonder of the mystery returns direct to one's own senses and consciousness: inside and outside, the voice breathes, 'Ah!' "

So far, our culture has managed to include this untamed poetic mind as a kind of occasional delight or relief, thus blotting up its power. As Herbert Marcuse and many others since *One-Dimensional Man* have commented, it has been the peculiar strength of the instrumental, technological culture to be able to make tame commodities out of potentially revolutionary states of consciousness. The taming of the mind has kept even pace with the taming of the outer wilderness; conventional-romantic nostalgia is a good example of the parallelism I am suggesting. It is perfectly powerless to regain its lost paradise, its noble savage or gentle woods-bowers, because its civilized formulations are only half real. There have been writers from Blake onward, to be sure, who have seen that we stand to lose immensely by conquering the world; but very few—Thoreau, Jeffers, Snyder, perhaps alone—have made the connection between outer and inner wilderness, and have dared to suggest that a primitive mind can understand it most clearly. The direct link between the two sides of wild integrity is the ground of the ecological values. Perceiving the link enables one to stand with and among, yet retaining and developing the consciousness of membership—or the ironies of mental separateness. Either way, this sort of perception calls into question the major assumptions of Western civilization. By going beyond both techno-humanist instrumentalism and cutely impotent romanticism, this approach builds a whole new mind. "Poets," Snyder writes, "as few others, must live close to the world that primitive men are in . . ." and poetry itself, in this world, becomes "an ecological survival technique."

It is perhaps expectable that Snyder contrasts the primitive / poetic mind with the world of "nationalism, warfare, heavy industry and consumership," which are "already outdated and useless," but what is not so expectable is that he has developed a forthrightly revolutionary system of ideas on his poetic perceptions. With the exceptions again of Thoreau, and possibly Jeffers, most of our wilderness poets have been rather passive regretters of the destruction closing in on them. But Snyder speaks, almost millenially, of healing. There are ways to the ecological mind, and they can be shown; people are more ready than ever. "The traditional cultures are in any case doomed, and rather than cling to their good aspects hopelessly it should be remembered that whatever is or ever was in any other culture can be reconstructed from the unconscious [our inner side of the vast pool of wilderness], through meditation. In fact, it is my own view that the coming revolution will close the circle and link us in many ways with the most creative aspect of our archaic past."

It might be argued that this progressivism, reversed as it is, shows Snyder's American heritage. In an outward, ideological sense, yes; but the core of it is the ecological understanding, the primitive (primal) sense of things. In turn, the chief ingredients of the ecological understanding seem to me to be Snyder's American West wilderness experience—he has worked as a logger, fire lookout, and trail crewman, and has backpacked and climbed extensively in California, Oregon, and Washington, working on the actual skills of primitive ecology and developing close ties to several Indian tribes—on the one side, and his formal, disciplined study of Buddhism on the other, beginning in 1956 in Kyoto.

Although it is somewhat tempting to read Snyder's going to the Zen temple in Kyoto as a resolution for tensions generated during 1952–56, when he worked part of the time as a tool of the anthropocentric culture (as a logger), and when he came to the end of conventional graduate-school climbing, I think Snyder's intellectual history is not a simple move from West to East. On the early end, he had been disenchanted with Christianity since childhood. "Animals don't have souls," he had been told as a child; making the connection between this pronouncement and the general Western ethos had been his intellectual work for years before 1956. This, along with positive motivations, resulted in a kind of textual Buddhism, especially when Snyder became reasonably expert in Chinese while at Berkeley, and one can see the going to Kyoto as merely putting theory into practice. On the other end, after the Zen training, Snyder has repeatedly shown his independence of traditional structures. His Buddhism is not programmatic. "Institutional Buddhism has been conspicuously ready to accept or ignore the inequalities and tyrannies of whatever political system it found itself under," he wrote in 1961, showing that left-anarchist, IWW ideas from working in the logging industry were not abandoned in favor of quietism. And the wild, original reference point, the special Snyder flavor, is shown in comments like this one from *Earth House Hold:* "The Far Eastern love of nature has become fear of nature: gardens and pine trees are tormented and controlled. Chinese nature poets were too often retired bureaucrats living on two or three acres trimmed by hired gardeners. The professional nature-aesthetes of modern Japan, tea-teachers and flower-arrangers, are amazed to hear that only a century ago dozens of species of birds passed through Kyoto where today only swallows and sparrows can be seen; and the aesthetes can scarcely distinguish those." My point is that Snyder has not been susceptible to either gross cultural influences or temporary currents, but has always seemed to measure things according to a primal standard of wild ecology. The basic materials of this he learned in the West. The Buddhist training has been extremely important, I do not doubt, and the steeping in Oriental writing, particularly Chinese poetry, has helped Snyder as a poet; but I am suggesting that he is now into something like a world-relevant fusion, a planetary consciousness, both in ideas and techniques. Berkeley Professor Thomas Parkinson writes, "He has effectively done something that for an individual is extremely difficult: he has created a new culture,"[3] and I think this may very well be the case. At the least, Snyder has provided the articulation, both in his poems and now in *Earth House Hold,* that can shape the generalized, inchoate desire for an ecological life.

As a cultural figure, his durability is evidenced by his fame having outlasted all three of the major movements in the American West since World War II—the Beat Generation, the Zen interest of the 50's, and the Hippies of the 60's. The strong points of these currents—creative alienation from robotlife, purified mind, and gentle community, respectively—had been present in Snyder's work from the start, and his steady focus on wilderness clarity helped him avoid the well-publicized pitfalls along the way. Thus he has always seemed ahead of the times, which is essential for a popular American bard-seer. Another, more fundamental requirement for such a figure is that his work, thought, and life be of a piece; as I hope I have shown, it is almost inevitable that this be true of the ecological vision. In our accelerating re-examination of civilization in the light of enduring perceptions and longings, it is not too much to suggest that Gary Snyder's insights can be extremely valuable.

## Notes

1. Quoted in Donald M. Allen, ed., *The New American Poetry* (New York: Grove Press, 1960), p. 420.

2. "Some Yips and Barks in the Dark," in Stephen Berg and Robert Mezey, eds., *Naked Poetry* (Indianapolis: Bobbs-Merrill, 1969), p. 357.

3. Thomas Parkinson, "The Poetry of Gary Snyder," *Southern Review* 4 (1968), 617.

# Twenty Years Later—A Coda    Thomas J. Lyon°

The first thing that strikes me upon rereading "The Ecological Vision of Gary Snyder" is its tone of confidence, even expectancy. It must have seemed, in 1969, that some sort of general, human corner had been turned. Instrumental, dominionist culture had come to the end of its road, but somehow, within it, the power to love and to reconnect with the earth still stirred. Energy was in the air—perhaps we were in a true renaissance! This must have been what Concord felt like in the time of Emerson and Thoreau, with all of human possibility in the open, discussable. We knew that in 1930 Newton Arvin had written of Emerson's assuredness that no one would ever speak that way again, but now we were speaking that way.

Naturally, we spoke a lot of unprovable things, wishful things, and wrong things, and I think we knew even at the time that there would have to be a filtering. What was so attractive about Gary Snyder's work, to many of us, was that he seemed to have both the energy and the filter, already. He had sounded back into deep, old resilient ways. Buddhism had given him a tried theory of human psychology; contact with wilderness in the modern time, and study of anthropology, had shaped him into a different kind of American pragmatist, one who could take seriously the practice of "primitive" cultures. He seemed to be in touch with what would last. Clearly the best-grounded, most classical of the Beats—he was in truth a kind of scholar—he had the approval of seasoned academics like Thomas Parkinson and Sherman Paul. He also had an enthusiastic following of young people, most of whom, perhaps, had not heard

° This essay was written specifically for this volume and appears here for the first time by permission of the author.

of these critics. His readings were dramatic events with a strong overtone of tribal solidarity.

With so much of the energy of the sixties having been stunted or diverted in these last two decades, one might ask how much of Snyder has come through. I now wonder about a favorite idea of Snyder's, the Whitman-like proposal that poetry, specifically its public reading or speaking, has important social power. In the late sixties or early seventies, at a Gary Snyder reading, one had the unmistakable feeling of windows and doors opening—possibly even doors being taken from their jambs. When Snyder, or Bly, or Stafford read, what was happening seemed greater than poetry. Alas, a generation of non–Whitmans seems to have taken the stage; too many readings do not suggest anything more than poetry or, worse, a code society of poets. The apparent decline may be only temporary, and it may not be as pervasive or serious as I think it is, certainly; but it does touch on an important, or at least often-stated, aspect of Snyder's thought. Scott McLean, editor of *The Real Work*, writes in summary, ". . . poetry is seen more and more by Snyder to be a binding force in the fabric of community life."[1] As an analytic or general proposition, and over the long run, if we do make a long run, the idea may of course prove valid. But at the moment, it appears that poetry's relevance to community life is at least in question.

"At-the-moment" criticism, however, may not really speak to Gary Snyder's basic intentions as a writer. When the *Fessenden Review*, for example, recently scoffed at Snyder on the grounds that his 1975 Pulitzer had become "hoary," the jab seemed to fly wild and irrelevant; the reviewer's scene of prizes and preferments appeared paltry, somehow, alongside Snyder's poetic preoccupations.[2] Indeed, the depth and import of his commitments, interests, and ideas—looking outward to nothing less than the general patterning of life on the planet and back over evolutionary time—may not be entirely reachable by contemporary fashion.

I think it continues to be true that Snyder's attempt to incorporate principles of evolutionary ecology gives his work weight and scope and separates it decisively from the current solipsism—indeed, from the "inturnedness" marking Western, anthropocentric culture for many centuries. The relationship of species diversity to the stability of biotic communities, for instance, and the important role of recycling in natural processes, are key concepts to him. These ecological truths are not simply interesting analytically; they are for Snyder ethically instructive. He noted in a 1977 interview that "almost half of the energy that flows in [a climax] system does not come from annual growth, [but] from the recycling of dead growth."[3] Maturity, in ecological terms, is signaled by a complexity of relations developed in place, a network of usings and reusings of materials; such is characteristic of old-growth or "virgin" forests. The relevance of this to human, social life seems obvious to Snyder: what we call civilization (that is, progressive, Western, frontier-minded society) "is analogous to a piece of scraped-back ground that is kept perpetually scraped back so that you always get a lot of grass quickly every year—monoculture, rapid production, a few species, lots of energy produced, but no recycling to fall back on."[4] The principle of Snyder's analysis is that if we know how to look at nature we can see what to do. He sets forth this perhaps not-so-obvious derivation in one of his most ambitious poems, "Toward Climax," in which approximately three billion years of life on earth are covered in ninety-eight lines. The key section of the poem, for the present discussion, begins with the general statement that "science walks in beauty," and after suggesting imagistically that humankind has in the past gained significant insights from watching nature's ways, Snyder moves to an ethical exhortation based on the recycling that characterizes climax ecosystems:

> maturity. stop and think. draw on the mind's
> stored richness. memory, dream, half-digested
> image of your life. "detritus pathways"—feed
> the many tiny things that feed an owl.
> send heart boldly travelling,
> on the heat of the dead & down.[5]

Clearly, wisdom is seen to originate in perceiving the utter continuousness of humanity and nature, and it must be said again that in holding this position, Snyder stands well outside the main tradition of the West. For him, the world's wilderness is not an "area," as legally defined, and "man" is not "a visitor who does not remain," to use the oddly revealing terms of the Wilderness Act of 1964. Snyder's vision is fundamentally nondualistic, and this stance of his may be founded as much in the concepts of ecology as in Buddhist metaphysics. Other American writers have conceived of humanity and nature holistically, of course, from at least the time of William Bartram; the distinctiveness of Snyder's contribution may be his finding the wild health of the world to be specifically instructive, indeed revolutionary, and with that his apparent, cheerful belief that we are in fact capable of reading nature right and doing right. Comparing Snyder with Robinson Jeffers, for example, seems instructive on this point. The two California poets share the organic and holistic perspective. But Jeffers could not—did not, at least, in verse—draw a social prescription from science's insights, nor did he consider, in another significant difference from Snyder, that what we call primitive ways were in any degree revivable. Where Snyder cites anthropological data as proof that cultures are arbitrary (thus able to be changed), Jeffers appears to equate Western culture with humanity in general, effectively closing down comparative insights and conscious change. Despite personal experiences of what might be called communion with wild nature, Jeffers most often wrote in a tone that is rueful, tragic, and final. Snyder's tone is characteristically exploratory, interested, discovering. Connections (analogous to the routes energy may take in climax ecosystems) appear to interest him profoundly, perhaps above all else, and the sense in his poetry and essays is that these "detritus pathways" are to be trusted. In the end, the most complex, wildest systems in nature are also the healthiest. One may with confidence "send heart boldly travelling."

Another reason for Snyder's durability is that he has always seemed to be not just a poet. We know that Williams was a doctor, Stevens an insurance executive, and Eliot a banker and publisher, but what I suggest here is something more than career-doubling. Snyder projects an integration of ideas, art, and actual way of living that perhaps few writers, in our industrial-consumerist, fragmented society, have attained to. Living as divided creatures in a world of economism, we respond to lives that seem to be of a piece, and honor attempts to achieve natural probity. It seemed germane to Thomas Parkinson, early on, that Gary Snyder was a competent back-country traveler, and it is important, I think, that Snyder has tried for a level of ecological responsibility at his rural California home. When items from daily life surface in his work, for example the thought process revolving around the selection of fence posts in the poem by that name,[6] what is being projected is recognizable as a quest for right living.

With academic ecology now generally conducted as a specialist pursuit, a mere department among departments,[7] and poetry seemingly having retreated to a kind of literary log-rolling society, a poet aspiring to ecological vision would be a revolutionary twice over. He would speak to a constituency impatient with closed systems of any kind. Perhaps Snyder has something, after all, with his idea of poetry as "a binding force in the fabric of community life." But the community would be the wild, whole world: grass, rocks, racing clouds, rain, the other animals, and the human mind in an inquiring, outward-looking mood.

## Notes

1. Gary Snyder, *The Real Work: Interviews and Talks, 1964–1979*, ed. William Scott McLean (New York: New Directions, 1980), xi.

2. "Left Out in the Rain," *Fessenden Review* 12, no. 1 (1987): 5–6.

3. Snyder, *The Real Work*, 116.

4. Snyder, *The Real Work*, 117.

5. Gary Snyder, *Turtle Island* (New York: New Directions, 1974), 84.

6. Gary Snyder, *Axe Handles* (San Francisco: North Point Press, 1983), 24–25.

7. See Edward Goldsmith, "Gaia: Some Implications for Theoretical Ecology," *The Ecologist* 18 (1980): 64–74.

# Gary Snyder's Lyric Poetry: Dialectic as Ecology

Charles Altieri°

"Snyder's commitments, while very likely sincere, are grossly superficial, and his evocations of them at best programmistic and facile."[1] This comment from a recent review by Robert Boyers summarizes the two basic charges he levels against Gary Snyder, charges that must be answered by anyone who wishes to defend Snyder's achievement as a poet. The first charge, the puerility and superficiality of Snyder's themes, can be answered directly only by lengthy and probably fruitless philosophical argument, but one can respond to the second, the attack on the texture of the poems themselves, in practical concrete terms by responding to the challenge Boyers offers to Thomas Parkinson's important article on Snyder: "Why not provide . . . some one or two samples of the poet's achieved work."[2] Providing these examples, in fact, will also provide at least a partial answer to the first charge. For any decent analysis of poetic style must lead into the philosophical perspective embodied in that style. In Snyder's particular case, the perspective may share some surface similarities with the Marlboro man's (as Boyers suggests), but on its deeper levels it has much more in common with the concern for ecology shared by so many scientists and literary figures in our time.[3]

One might even claim that Snyder is preeminent among the literary figures concerned with ecology because he has developed a lyric style which itself embodies a mode of consciousness leading to a state of balance and symbiotic interrelation between man and his environment. The characteristic poem in this style is thoroughly concrete and dramatic, but its drama does not involve the usual process of creating and intensifying conflicts that are eventually resolved. Rather the poem develops casually and depends not on tension between elements but on the mutual support they give one another, on the way they draw out one another's full significance for the processes of living. Snyder describes the essence of that style in the conclusion of an essay subtitled "Notes on Poetry as an Ecological Survival Technique":

° Reprinted from *Far Point* 4 (1970): 55–65, by permission of the University of Manitoba Press.

The Australian aborigines live in a world of ongoing recurrence—comradeship with the landscape and continual exchanges of being and form and position; every person, animals, forces, all are related via a web of reincarnation—or rather, they are 'interborn'. It may well be that rebirth (or interbirth, for we are actually mutually creating each other and all things while living) is the objective fact of existence which we have not yet brought into conscious knowledge and practice.

It is clear that the empirically observable interconnectedness of nature is but a corner of the vast 'jewelled net' which moves from without to within.[4]

Several of the opening poems of *The Back Country* illustrate the way in which a poem creates this "interbirth" and brings this "vast 'jewelled net' " to "conscious knowledge and practice." Snyder's conscious use of "interbirth" is most obvious in "A Walk" (BC, 19):

A WALK

Sunday the only day we don't work:
Mules farting around the meadow,
      Murphy fishing,
The tent flaps in the warm
Early sun: I've eaten breakfast and I'll
      take a walk
To Benson Lake. Packed a lunch,
Goodbye. Hopping on creekbed boulders
Up the rock throat three miles
      Piute Creek—
In steep gorge glacier-slick rattlesnake country
Jump, land by a pool, trout skitter,
The clear sky. Deer tracks.
Bad place by a falls, boulders big as houses,
Lunch tied to belt,
I stemmed up a crack and almost fell
But rolled out safe on a ledge
      and ambled on.
Quail chicks freeze underfoot, color of stone
Then run cheep! away, hen quail fussing.
Craggy west end of Benson Lake—after edging
Past dark creek pools on a long white slope—
Lookt down in the ice-black lake
      lined with cliff
From far above: deep shimmering trout.
A lone duck in a gunsightpass
      steep side hill
Through slide-aspen and talus, to the east end,
Down to grass, wading a wide smooth stream
Into camp. At last.

By the rusty three-year-
Ago left-behind cookstove
Of the old trail crew,
Stoppt and swam and ate my lunch.

The poem at first seems flat until the reader perceives a dynamic process at work. The key to the poem's significance is the exclamation, "at last," when the speaker reaches his destination. The phrase demands that we see some kind of completion in the concluding details. As we think about these details we come to realize that the whole poem is a balancing: it holds in solution the speaker's difficult journey over an expanse of space in the mountains and the comfort and security of the secluded rest, the swim and the lunch which cap off the hike. The phrase "at last" points to the emotional importance of these last details, an importance created only by the exertions of the journey. In other words, the balanced elements each achieve their full significance, obtain their fullest life, only when seen as a dialectic unity: the lunch and swim are only fully appreciated because of the exertions of the hike and the hike is only truly appreciated through the conclusion it makes possible. Snyder's habit of loading his poem with detail is neither frivolous nor without artistic consideration, for the paradox of relationship is that it returns us to the particulars with a greater appreciation of them ("the other becomes the lover through whom the various links in the net can be perceived"). This is especially true for the concluding detail in the poem, the lunch, which is redeemed from its quotidian triviality and reconstituted as one of the most fulfilling aspects of one's normal life. Snyder restores some of the sacramental significance of a meal—a significance not the result of a unique transcendental act but implicit in the normal secular event. And, like the Christian sacrament, the event is both particular and universal, both a unique meal eaten by Snyder and, because of the suggestive power in the detail of the cook-stove, his participation in a universal process by which man interacts with nature. The stove, then, assumes a symbolic significance: it stands as a memorial to Snyder of his connection with the history of human presence in the mountains and it illustrates the way nature itself is partially shaped by and preserves the traces of its interactions with man.

Three other aspects of the poem support its ecological intention of making us appreciate the balances in our lives. First of all there is the tone which by its quiet casualness denies the traditional assumption (taken to extremes in confessional poetry) that lyric poetry is the expression of unique moments charged with extraordinary intensity. Second, the syntax of the poem supports its ecological intent for as the speaker becomes more involved in his actions he

forgoes any explicit references to himself as subject. We get instead
a series of verbs and almost dangling participles that tend to blend
actor and action, man and world. Finally the preponderance of concrete details has two effects. So much pointing asserts the referential
power of language and denies the self-reflexive implications that
accompany more metaphoric styles. It is not words but things that
are being related to one another. And these concrete relations enable
Snyder to communicate a non–Western frame of mind without references to occult philosophy or a series of abstractions. Ecology deals
not with ideas but with modes of action and with the unity of
interrelationships in nature, and its verification is the fullness of the
environment it creates. In a poem that realizes Snyder's ecological
perspective, myth and text no longer require separate statement; they
are unified in one's quiet reverence at the depth of connection
suggested by the poem.[5]

"Trail Crew Camp At Bear Valley, 9000 Feet Northern Sierra-
White Bone and Threads of Snowmelt Water" (BC, 20) and "Six-
Month Song in the Foothills" (BC, 17) are more profound versions
of the same processes found in "A Walk." "Trail Crew Camp" derives
its significance from the dialectic balance it creates between a sense
of expansive space or distance and a sense of humanized and controlled
space. As in "A Walk," the opening two stanzas present a series of
perceptions of the natural scene, here while Snyder is engaged in
one of his jobs as a logger:

> Cut branches back for a day—
> trail a thin line through willow
>     up buckbrush meadows,
>         creekbed for twenty yards
> winding in boulders
>     zigzags the hill
> into timber, white pine.
>
> gooseberry bush on the turns.
> hooves clang on the riprap
>     dust, brush, branches.
>     a stone
>   cairn at the pass—
> strippt mountains hundreds of miles.

The objects here are presented paratactically, and for the most part
generically ("stone," "dust," "creekbed,") so that we get a sense of
the independence of the objects and their distance from human
concerns. This vague impression of distance is complemented by the
poem's progression out into expanding space—not only because of
the concluding vista, but also from the multiplication of details that

precedes it. The third stanza, then, provides the poem's basic contrast by returning to camp and to specific and quite small details:

>           sundown went back
>             the clean switchbacks to camp.
>           bell on the gelding,
>           stew in the cook tent,
>           black coffee in a big tin can.

The balance here is similar to the one achieved by "A Walk," as are the poem's spiritual implications. "Trail Crew Camp," however, provides a complicating element that gives it a curious depth. For amid the small objects of the camp, Snyder focuses on the *big* tin can that holds the coffee. This emphasis on the size of the can is of course a reflection of his own hunger, but it is also a comment on it. Two kinds of containers (the mountains and the can) are thrust into a relationship that evokes a rich sense of the similarities and differences between human hungers and the kinds of objects which appeal to them. This relationship between the mountains and the coffee can also once again asserts the importance that even the simplest aspects of our lives can assume when seen in their proper settings.

"Sixth-Month Song in the Foothills" (BC, 17) is the richest evocation of the significance of small details and it is the most explicitly ecological of the three poems:

>           In the cold shed sharpening saws.
>             a swallow's nest hangs by the door
>           setting rakers in sunlight
>           falling from meadow through doorframe
>             swallows flit under the eaves.
>
>           Grinding the falling axe
>           sharp for the summer
>             a swallow shooting out over.
>           over the river, snow on low hills
>           sharpening wedges for splitting.
>
>           Beyond the low hills, white mountains
>           and now snow is melting. sharpening tools;
>             pack horses grazing new grass
>           bright axes—and swallows
>             fly in to my shed.

Again the poem is constructed around balanced spatial elements whose interactions suggest the meaning of spring. This time there are basic elements—Snyder's own space objectified as his shed, the space of the natural world about the shed, and the expanse of the natural world introduced in the third stanza to suggest the curious combination of smallness and infinity the shed takes on once life is awakened. Spring in the poem is the bringer of vitality: it sets the birds flying, the horses grazing, the snow melting and Snyder to the spring ritual of sharpening his tools. This sharpening becomes metaphoric, or better analogous, to both the general quickening of life produced by spring and to Snyder's awakening mind. Spring sharpens the "razoredge," where man's attention meets the world (EHH, 41; see also EHH, 34). The shed then, as it encloses the swallows without impeding their actions objectifies the new state of mind, which Snyder calls "*That* level of mind—the cool water—not intellect and not—(as Romantics and after have confusingly thought) fantasy—dream world or unconscious. This is just the clear spring—it reflects all things and feeds all things but is of itself transparent" (EHH, 57). The syntax of the last stanza and the emphatic position of "fly in to my shed" in the last line go on to produce complex spatial relationships. Grammatically each of the last three nouns in the poem might fly into the mind, and without the punctuation (i.e. in the rush of oral presentation) all the objects in the stanza can enter the mind. The shed remains a limited place, but at the same time becomes capable of entertaining even the mountains with the same freedom that it entertains the swallows.

The free interchange of awakening mind and nature is beautifully sustained by Snyder's use of participles in the poem. The participle is a verbal noun representing both a state of action and a state of being. Its repeated use evokes the metaphysical state described by Whitehead where what we tend to see as entities are in fact states of action. In the poem, Snyder is careful to describe both his own actions and the actions of nature in participial terms so that he captures this sense of dynamic being. The sense of movement in the participles also captures the renewed vitality we feel in spring. In addition Snyder reinforces the state of action he shares with the world around him by employing the same device he uses in "A Walk." He refuses to supply explicit referents to the participles modifying his own actions, so that they appear as if freed from the limits of subjectivity. The first explicitly subjective reference comes only in the last line and there it serves primarily to stress the blend of subject and object in the free space of the shed. The whole poem serves to set off Snyder's subjectivity, to preserve it while showing that it achieves its fullness only when in total harmony with the processes of the world in which it dwells.[6]

The shed here can serve as a perfect metaphor for this kind of Snyder lyric: the shed is a small enclosure and yet it contains an infinite depth created by the relationships it contains and forms. The poem then becomes an enclosed space that is not a limiting space; relationships are manifest without being forced and without reduction of or tension between any of the elements. This lack of tension is important because it distinguishes Snyder's lyrics from the modernist tradition with which we are familiar. In so much as his poems are based on dialectic and juxtaposition Snyder remains traditional, but the lack of tension leads to radically different emotional and philosophical implications. Yeats's gyres are a perfect emblem of the traditional dialectic. The elements held in relation by the typical Yeats poem are in violent, often unresolvable conflict. Only superhuman heroic enterprise can make a sphere of the gyres and reconcile or resolve such tensions—thus Yeats's stress on the power of the artist and later on the tragic hero. Similar senses of the heroic enterprise entailed in reconciling opposites lead Pound and early Eliot to their belief in the importance of traditional cultures and Eliot to his ultimate reliance on a transcendent still point. For Snyder, on the other hand, the purpose of the poem as dialectic is to reduce tension by affirming the opposites' need for one another. Snyder, then, does not require heroic enterprise; reconciliation of the opposites is possible for all because the reconciliation need not be imposed; it exists in fact. Man does not have to transcend nature; he has only to recognize how that flux itself generates meaning. He need only regain for himself what the primitive has, "this knowledge of connection and responsibility" (EHH, 121).

The still point for Snyder is immanent and in flux, not transcendent and permanent. It is the realization of this still point and its implications that forms the bridge from a knowledge of connection to an acceptance of responsibility. Responsibility comes when one sees the sacramental unity or "divine ecology" (EHH, 112, 124), the unity of all being that informs and transcends the particular balances that come into momentary existence: " 'Beyond' there lies, inwardly, the unconscious. Outwardly the equivalent of the unconscious is the wilderness: both of these terms meet, one step even further on, as *one*" (EHH, 122). The realization of this oneness forms the bridge between connection and responsibility. Once one accepts a unity between himself and the world, Snyder assumes that he must begin to treat the world as he treats his own body.

"Burning the Small Dead" (BC, 22) provides an excellent example of the way Snyder can push the dialectic of spatial relationships one step farther to suggest the unity that lies beyond in the back country of the mind:

> Burning the small dead
>      branches
>  broke from beneath
>   thick spreading
>        whitebark pine.

            a hundred summers
snowmelt        rock      and air

hiss in a twisted bough.

    sierra granite;
        mt. Ritter—
        black rock twice as old.

    Deneb, Altair

    windy fire

The process of the poem up to the last line is a continual pushing
outward in time and space until the contemplative mind reaches the
stars Deneb and Altair which combine age, the coldness of stone, an
immensely large body of fire and the appearance of mere points of
light. The last line then creates a fusion of two forces: it is a return
to the limited space of the burning branches, but it is also a continuation beyond the stars to a kind of essence of fire. We are present
in a particular locale, still contemplating the physical distance of the
stars, and gradually moving into a third windy fire that unites the
two spaces in the recesses of the mind.

    This movement at once both outward into the vast cosmos of
space and time and inward to the perception of a kind of unity with
all being is a typical one for Snyder, especially in his way of structuring
his books. *Earth House Hold*, for example, begins in the American
West with Snyder using the conventional dating systems of Western
man. The record of Snyder's exploration of several cultures concludes
with an essay discussing his marriage on a primitive Japanese island
and the last words in the book, "Eighth Moon, 40067 (reckoning
roughly from the earliest cave painting)," unite Snyder with the
whole human family. In *Myths & Texts*, after a similar excursion
through several cultures, the marriage between Western man and
Eastern woman becomes the marriage of myth and text in a final
vision that enters deep into the mind ("the mountains are your mind")
to suggest the comprehension of the entire universe. Snyder first
gives a physical description of the fire, then moves to a mythic view
of the scene:

            The black snag glistens in the rain
            the last wisp of smoke floats up
            Into the absolute cold
            Into the spiral whorls of fire
            The storms of the Milky Way
            "Buddha incense in an empty world"
            Black pit cold and light-year

> Flame tongue of the dragon
> Licks the sun

> The sun is but a morning star.[7]

*The Back Country* has an even tighter progression through various cultures. Like the poem "Six Years" it follows a cyclic structure (from America, through Japan and India, and back to America) that also presents a progress transcending the merely cyclic existence Snyder condemns in "after Ramprasad Sen" and "Go Round." In both "Six Years" and the volume as a whole Snyder plays off the cycle of time with the gradual emergence of enlightenment.[8] By the end of the volume he takes on the role of advisor to both Eastern and Western cultures ("To the Chinese Comrades" and "For the West").

The full spiritual meaning of *The Back Country*, however, comes not through statement but through return to the dialectical method of the opening in "Oysters" (BC, 112):

> First Samish Bay.
>     then all morning, hunting oysters
> A huge feed on white
> wood State Park slab-plank bench—
>     and table
>         at Birch Bay
>     where we picked up rocks
> for presents.

> And ate oysters, fried—raw—cookt in milk
>     rolld in crumbs—
> all we wanted.

> ALL WE WANTED

> & got back in our wagon,
> drove away.

Snyder is dealing here in concrete terms with the perennial philosophical and theological problems of reconciling the achievement of plenitude with an acceptance of change.[9] Christianity tends to promise plenitude at the cost of renouncing flux, while Eastern religions often come to terms with flux by an ascetic rejection of all desire for plenitude (hence there can be no Eastern *Divine Comedy*). In this poem, though, Snyder's dialectical method shows how one can have both plenitude and change. In fact the two conditions are necessary if we are to appreciate either. Full satisfaction with the feast is possible only because the act can be enjoyed directly on its own terms, as an absolute present unspoiled by desires to prolong or transcend it. The plenitude cannot be imprisoning, cannot "hook" the actors so that they become unwilling to move on (see "Oil," BC, 26). At the same time, when the present is completely accepted, there is nothing to fear from change. The actors can move on without anxiety and open to future moments of fullness.

Snyder reinforces the affirmative dialectic here by picking up and reversing in the last line one of the symptoms of cultural *malaise* he had presented earlier in the volume. In the book's second poem, he records watching "thousands of cars / driving men to work" (BC, 16). Totally liberated now, he overcomes the passivity of Western man trapped by his possessions and the culture which supports them. He moves on, content and in control of his own destiny.

To have all one wants is the American dream, and Snyder with his innocence, pragmatism, vitality and perpetual wandering Eastward or into the wilderness belongs in the tradition of American romanticism. But the contrast created by the last line and, more important, the tone of the poem suggest an entirely new way of realizing that dream. "Oysters" is both the thematic summary of the volume and perhaps the most casual poem in it. The coincidence is not fortuitous. The casual tone reminds us that the realizable American dream lies not in the perpetual quest for self-transcendence but in the inner peace that derives from comprehending the sacramental ecology which lies all around us and in which we play a small but important part.

## Notes

1. Robert Boyers, "Mixed Bag," *Partisan Review* 36 (1969), 313.

2. Boyers, p. 312. Parkinson's article is "The Poetry of Gary Snyder," *Southern Review* 4 (1968), 616–632. I am indebted to this article for the concept of the lack of tension in Snyder's poetry, a concept I take several steps further than did Professor Parkinson.

3. Among literary figures we have for example Robert Creeley's concern for "place" and Charles Olson's interest in both scientific ecology and in history and locality as ecological elements. In recent interviews Allen Ginsberg *(Playboy)* and Kenneth Rexroth *(Contemporary Literature)* have discussed relationships between poetry and ecology, and we have even a critic, Harry Berger, who has contributed an important series of articles on the ecology of mind (mostly in *Centennial Review).*

4. *Earth House Hold* (New York, 1969), p. 129. I have used the following symbols for works by Snyder that are cited in the text: *Earth House Hold*—EHH; *Myths & Texts* (New York, 1960)—MT; *The Back Country* (New York, 1968)—BC.

5. When I use the terms "myth" and "text," I am interpreting Snyder's own use of the terms. "Text" represents pure natural process and "myth" is nature seen in terms of imaginative value. "Text" is analogous to the profane, "myth" to the sacred. Snyder's use of these terms is clarified by Claude Lévi-Strauss's definition of "myth" as a way of blending nature and culture. See *The Savage Mind* (Chicago, 1966), pp. 91 ff. Later in this essay I cite the way Snyder brings myths and texts together in the earlier volume *Myths & Texts.*

6. The sense at the end of the poem that one is now in touch with a new life and is beginning to participate fully in it is supported by the connotations of pregnancy and of the beginnings of a journey in the title.

7. The allusion to Thoreau in the last line does more than put Snyder in the American tradition; it thrusts the whole American Romantic tradition epitomized in this line into the cosmic perspective of the entire closing passage. The sun and Thoreau are only the foothills of the back country.

8. In the concluding section of "Six Years," "December" (BC, 62–63), Snyder relates the cycle of years and months to the cyclic process of a day in a monastery. The gradual movement to enlightenment is suggested by the way the poem returns to the first line. The last line echoes the first, but presents the image in a single line that evokes a new unity of perception. This last line, "a far bell coming closer," is another blend of physical and mental space.

9. Robert Creeley has several poems on this same theme, especially "For WCW" (*Words*, p. 27), but in Creeley these poems lack the concrete details which exemplify the mode of life made possible by Snyder's vision and with Creeley (at least before *Pieces*) the emphasis tends to be much more on the desire than on the fulfillment.

# From Lookout to Ashram: The Way of Gary Snyder

Sherman Paul°

I know of no one since Thoreau who has so thoroughly espoused the wild as Gary Snyder—and no one who is so much its poet. His root metaphor, the "back country," covers all that Thoreau, explicitly or implicitly, meant by the "wild." "Poetry and the Primitive," one of the recent essays collected in *Earth House Hold* (1969), is his most important statement and the resolution of much of his work, an essay comparable in import, though not in distinction of style, to Thoreau's "Walking." Thoreau's essay, originally a lecture called "The Wild," is testamentary, and so is Snyder's, though his is not terminal. It does not conclude a life but draws a phase of life to conclusion and, in this way and by the affirmation of writing, announces a new departure at a deeper depth of realization. The two essays that follow it, "Dharma Queries" and "Suwa-no-se Island and the Banyan Ashram," record his vows and practice, and the latter begins his life anew with his marriage to Masa Uehara, whom he celebrates in *Regarding Wave* (1969), his latest book of poems.

*Earth House Hold,* spanning the years 1952 to 1967, provides an excellent introduction to a poet whose poetry, because of its autobiographical nature and allusions to Oriental and American Indian lore, is not always readily available. Its title feelingly translates "ecology," a science that Paul Shepard and Daniel McKinley consider

° Reprinted from *Iowa Review* 1.3 (1970): 76–77, 79–89, and 1.4 (1970): 70–73, 78–85, by permission of the author.

subversive—subversive, and urgent, in respect to the attitudes and ends of overly technological civilization.[1] Its subtitle, "Technical Notes & Queries to Fellow Dharma Revolutionaries," suggests this revolutionary character, and as a manual for revolution, it offers a way (of thought and action) and indicates the studies and disciplines that, in the author's experience, lead us back to the back country where we may enjoy "Housekeeping on Earth." As "Dharma" implies, this revolution turns on truth; it is what Emerson called a silent revolution of thought, and the thought, much of it, is Oriental, the "primal thought" spoken of in Whitman's "Passage to India." The revolutionaries are spiritual seekers whom Snyder, not without humor, now addresses as guerrillas. He once called them "Dharma-hobos" (in 1956) and Jack Kerouac, in the title of a novel relating his meeting and experience with Snyder, called them "Dharma-bums" (in 1958). Kerouac even prophesied a "rucksack revolution" and in his novel Japhy Ryder (Gary Snyder) says: "Think what a great world revolution will take place when East meets West finally, and it'll be guys like us that start the thing. Think of millions of guys all over the world with rucksacks on their backs tramping around the back country and hitchhiking and bringing the word down to everybody." The revolutionary here—in the 1950's—is one who withdraws from society; he "signs off," as Thoreau would say, and becomes a saunterer, a holy-lander. Bum, for Kerouac, translates *bhikkhu*, monk; hopping freights and hitch-hiking are in keeping with a free life of voluntary poverty. Or, in the phrase Snyder uses to characterize his friend Nanao Sakaki—a phrase that also characterizes him and reminds one of Bashō—the revolutionary may be a "wanderer and poet," whose only moral imperative "in this yuga," as Snyder declares for himself in the first journal, is to communicate. Now, at the end of the 1960's, as the subtitle indicates, this social passivity, so much in the grain of Eastern thought, is disclaimed; "revolutionary" has the meaning of the 1960's and the goal of revolution is represented for Snyder in the I. W. W., slogan, "Forming a new society within the shell of the old." Snyder's book begins where Kerouac's *The Dharma Bums*, a book about individual salvation, ends. It reflects the changing lifestyle, the increasing activism and communitarianism, of the past decade, and its quiet confidence and sense of vast tributary support (mostly out of the past—Snyder dates some essays and poems from the time of the earliest cave paintings) are noteworthy. It may be described briefly as a development from lookout to ashram.

o   o   o

*Earth House Hold* begins in the back country which was also Snyder's boyhood world. Though he was born in San Francisco (in 1930), his formative years were spent in the Pacific Northwest. During the depression, his family tried dairy-farming in Washington, and, after 1942, lived in Portland, Oregon, where he attended Reed College. The Northwest is his personal geography: the low country of "Nooksack Valley," where, sitting in "a berry-pickers cabin / At the edge of a wide muddy field / Stretching to the woods and cloudy mountains," the smell of cedar reminds him of "our farm-house, half built in '35"; and the high country of the mountain wilderness of the North Cascades which he first entered in his youth. This landscape, especially the mountain wilderness, is aboriginal, like the "Fur Countries" that had early rejoiced Thoreau and the *"great west* and *northwest* stretching on infinitely far and grand and wild" that he later said qualified all of his thoughts—"That is the only America I know . . . That is the road to new life and freedom . . . That great northwest where several of our shrubs, fruitless here, retain and mature their fruits properly." Wilderness of this kind, Snyder reminds us, as much from personal experience as from historical report, is what Americans confronted on the frontier. Here was "a vast wild ecology" that was "mind-shaking." For Americans, nature, he says, meant wilderness, an "untamed realm of total freedom—not brutish and nasty, but beautiful and terrible." And it meant the Indian, whose ways Snyder, like Thoreau, seriously studied (his bachelor's thesis, "The Dimensions of a Myth," treats the Haida)[2] and whose ghost, he says in the portentous manner of Lawrence, "will claim the next generation as its own."

Snyder possessed this primitive landscape in many ways, among them by learning woodcraft as a boy, mountain climbing as a youth, and working in the forest as a trail-maker, logger, and lookout in his early manhood. And while he was possessing it, he was, as a student of folklore, mythology, religion, and Oriental languages, extending and deepening its meanings, transforming the back country into a spiritual domain. By the time he goes to Crater Mountain Lookout in 1952, the back country has become the "Buddha land," a place of spiritual enlightenment to which one ascends by means of the disciplines he practices there. Crater Mountain becomes "Crater Shan," another Cold Mountain, whose namesake Han-shan wrote the "Cold Mountain" poems that Snyder later translated, poems defining the back country as a condition of being: "Freely drifting, I prowl the woods and streams / And linger watching things themselves. / Men don't get this far into the mountains."[3] All high places become one and have this significance, as later, when climbing in the Glacier Peak Wilderness Area, Snyder recalls Cold Mountain and imagines himself a Tibetan mountaineer, a Japanese woodcutter, and an exiled Chinese traveler. The nature he enters is universal, like that Thoreau said he entered on his daily walk: "I walk out into a nature such as the old prophets and poets, Menu, Moses, Homer, Chaucer, walked in. You may name it America, but it is not America . . . There is a truer account of it in mythology than in any history of America . . . ."

For the back country is *back*. It is reached by going back to what Peter Levi, in a recent review of Snyder's poetry, called the "sources" ("Snyder's work is a restoration of the sources, a defence of the springs," awakening in us a sense of a "lost dimension of life"). And back is *down*, a descent, as William Carlos Williams spoke of it, to the fertile chaos, the very "mother stuff" of our being, to the unconscious from which, Snyder believes, we can reconstruct, by means of meditation, whatever aspects of previous cultures we desire. Like the primitive wilderness—the "naked" world where both Thoreau and Snyder believe we are most alive—the sources are still there, a deeper down where love is rooted and creative forces play, the *nature* that is always woman ("no human man can belong to mountains except as they are nature, and nature is woman"). Here the mind is untamed and the "seeds of instinct," to use Thoreau's phrase, are nurtured (for a true culture, Thoreau remarked, does not "tame tigers"). It is a darkness, too, perhaps like the "back" where Coyote lives ("His house was back in the back of the hills") or the "Deep North" of Bashō's last journey, the "other shore," or the world after death, the back country of Snyder's "Journeys" that one enters only by dying. Finally, as wilderness and unconscious, outer and inner equivalents, the back country is *beyond*—beyond society, civilization and its discontents ("I did not mean to come this far," Snyder writes in "Twelve Hours out of New York,"—"baseball games on the radio / commercials that turn your hair—"). It is the "old, dirty countries," the backward countries he has wandered in, places where the old traditions are still living, and places like Suwa-no-se Island where the primitive communal life he now advocates can be lived.

*Earth House Hold*—the very title declares it—records this deepening awareness of the significance of the back country. In it, one follows the random course of (a) life, sees it nurturing a poet, focusing and concentrating itself. The concluding essays, the most recent, comprise a platform or program, and are ardently didactic. But the early journals are exercises in recording one's life, part of a discipline of being. In this, they remind one of the journals of Emerson and Thoreau. The young man to whom they introduce us—they give us our first and earliest glimpse of Snyder—is already pursuing the way and is wholly intent on overseeing and shaping his perceptions; this, perhaps, accounts for the impersonal quality of the personal in Snyder's work and distinguishes him from the other autobiographical (confessional) poets of his generation. The journals are the work of a Zennist and a poet, a poet who has learned much about form from Pound but more, I think, from Chinese and Japanese poetry.

The first part of "Lookout's Journal," that covering the summer of 1952 on Crater Mountain, is the best of all the journals in *Earth House Hold*. In none of the others is the experiment in form and the experience so fully realized. It is, I think, a more daring work than any of the early poems collected in *Riprap* (1959)—larger, more open, able to contain, substantively and formally, more experience. The trajectory of experience it presents passes through *the* experience which, unrecorded, is of the kind given in the carefully wrought Poundian-cadenced poem of purification, clarity, and serenity commemorating the following summer's lookout, "Mid-August at Sourdough Mountain Lookout," the initial poem of *Riprap:*

> Down valley a smoke haze
> Three days heat, after five days rain
> Pitch glows on the fir-cones
> Across rocks and meadows
> Swarms of new flies.
>
> I cannot remember things I once read
> A few friends, but they are in cities
> Drinking cold snow-water from a tin cup
> Looking down for miles
> Through high still air.

This might be called a satori poem. It fulfills the need recorded in the first journal: "to look within and adjust the mechanism of perception." And it reminds one of Thoreau's realization at Walden ("Both place and time were changed, and I dwelt nearer to those parts of the universe and to those eras in history which had most attracted me") and of Emerson's reliance on the power of prospects.

The journal gives the essential particulars of experience that contributed to such attainment. It begins in late June, at the Ranger Station, with the following brief entry:

> Hitchhiked here, long valley of the Skagit. Old cars parked in weeds, little houses in fields of braken. A few cows, in stumpland.
>
> > Ate at the "parkway cafe" real lemon in the pie
> > "—why don't you get a jukebox in here"
> > "—the man said we weren't important enough"

One probably notices first the abbreviated syntax—an expression of economy, one that tells us that the traditional syntax isn't essential enough and telegraphs a quick grasp of things, like sumi painting. We are given objective fragments, but even in this simplest entry they are arranged and placed on the empty space of the page. Like a haiku poem, they work by means of the art of omission, by what they suggest. They tell of arrival but indicate the journey (compare this entry with Kerouac's account in *The Dharma Bums*) and give the sense of increasing sparseness and emptiness. We are in the back country now, old cars in the weeds, little houses, a few cows in the stumpland, a place not important enough—frequented and commercial enough—for a jukebox but still backward enough, in its values, as Hemingway would have noted, to serve unadulterated lemon pie. As Snyder pointed out in reviewing a book of prose translations of Chinese poems, "any irregular line arrangement creates a manner of reading and a rhythm, which is poetical." So here. The entry is a poem. The balanced cadence of "Old cars parked in weeds, little houses in fields of braken" is artful.

Each entry is a formal design, a field of experience, in which the poet intends the fragments (thoughts, perceptions, notations of objects) to relate, become whole. The unity of the entry is often the unspoken ground to which all refer, as in the following:

> Granite creek Guard station      9 July
> the boulder in the creek never moves
> the water is always falling
> together!

> A ramshackle little cabin built by Frank Beebe the miner.
> Two days walk to here from roadhead.
> arts of the Japanese: moon-watching
> insect-hearing

> Reading the sutra of Hui Něng.

> one does not need universities and libraries
> one need be alive to what is about

> saying "I don't care"

The ground, here, is the resolve to pursue the way; the entry is really very intense and builds to the attitude of not caring about the "world" below. The poet is still struggling with—perhaps rehearsing—the "complete and total choice" he made about this time to relinquish a "professional scholar's career in anthropology" and set himself loose "to sink or swim as a poet." The entry begins with the poet's play (the rhythmic capitalization of the location) and with a haiku poem appropriate to resolute thought, and it moves associatively from the isolated little cabin of a miner to the meditative arts practiced in seclusion by the Japanese, to his own discipline (reading the sutra) and thoughts (the recognition of a Zen truth about learning), and determined statement of choice.

This principle of form applies to the journal as a whole and to many of the poems. Snyder observes in this journal that form is "leaving things out at the right spot / ellipse, is emptiness." This emptiness is not empty; it is the ultimate, the fullness of life of which a few carefully selected and carefully placed things may make us aware. The journal is not a diary or daybook: There are only sixteen dated entries for a period of two and a half months. While suggesting the distance between events, in an isolated place, these point to a fertile emptiness and not, as do the equally infrequent entries of the Sourdough Journal, to slackness and boredom. They also chart a complete event, the actual ascent and descent of "Crater Shan"—a pattern of experience that repetition, it seems, does not always recover in its original freshness and exhilaration.

On all accounts (we hear of it in *The Dharma Bums*), Snyder was an exemplary lookout. But this is not the primary work recorded in the journal. His work, he notes, is "*Zazen* non-life. An art: mountain-watching." It begins with his arrival—with his openness and attentiveness to persons, places, and things. The second entry, for example, is a characterization by speech of Blackie Burns, a forester, one of the roughs, to use Whitman's term, to whom Snyder dedicated *Riprap*. His speech, though strong, is not coarse, like some of the woodsmen's anecdotes of the Sourdough Journal, and its theme is significant. Burns announces the ecological concern of Snyder's work: "GREEDY & SELFISH NO RESPECT FOR THE LAND." The capitalization, part of Snyder's design of Burns' speech, also serves to emphasize what is most important, an attitude of mind fostered by the Western Tradition (the Judeo-Christian tradition, according to Paul Shepard, which contributed to "the hatred for this world carried by our whole culture"). Greed and selfishness, Buddha said, were the principal causes of dissatisfaction and suffering and were to be overcome by disciplining the mind, by changing one's point of view. Changing one's point of view (adjusting the mechanism of perception) is the revolutionary issue; only a discipline as radical as that undertaken by Snyder will, he believes, create an ecological conscience, prepare us to respect the land, the very ground of our being. The ecological issue, therefore, is at the center of his spiritual undertaking, as is poetry. A few entries later, he writes: "—If one wished to write poetry of nature, where an audience? Must come from the very conflict of an attempt to articulate the vision poetry & nature in our time." Snyder is pre-eminently a poet of nature. And at the beginning of his career he knows, as he says in the subtitle of a recent essay, that poetry (requiring the highest discipline of the poet, and communicating the "vision") is an "ecological survival technique."

The entries that follow his resolution on Zen enlightenment record the strenuous and wayward pursuit. The entry of July 11, somewhat in the nature of a Whitman catalog, conveys by its randomness an eager readiness for new experiences other than those recorded. The first entry from the mountain lookout gives the elevation, which, honestly acknowledged, is only a matter of feet ("8049 feet"). Everything goes wrong, he's dispirited ("Even here, cold foggy rocky place, there's life—4 ptarmigan . . .") and has only energy enough to read science-fiction. But the second half of the entry, with the comparison of the light of the lookout to that of a shoji, reports reviving spirits and resolve; and thereafter, with the entry of July 28 from "Crater Shan," the journal gives an account—happy and contented, I think, when compared to the Sourdough Journal—of his discipline and its fruits.

Unlike the other lookouts whose radio conversations he enters in the journal as necessary fact, as ballast to his own experience, he is intensely occupied ("poor lonely lookouts," he remarks, "radioing back and forth"). He is not lonely, no more than Thoreau at Walden, who explained that "nearest to all things is that power which fashions their being." He has a close schedule of work and study, and, like Thoreau, metaphorically and literally, is transacting business with the "Celestial Empire":

> —first I turn on the radio
> —then make tea & eat breakfast
> —study Chinese until eleven
>
> —make lunch, go chop snow to melt water,
> read Chaucer in the early afternoon.

On August 10, he reports, "First wrote a haiku and painted a haiga for it; then repaired the Om Mani Padme Hum prayer flag, then constructed a stone platform, then shaved down a shake and painted a zenga on it, then studied the lesson." Transcriptions from the texts he is reading or recalls indicate his progress—most are from Oriental scripture, but Chaucer's line on "drasty ryming" is cited (perhaps he is reading *Paterson IV)* and an American Indian song is used to express his own feeling ("Is this real / Is this real / This life I am living?"). Sometimes a haiku poem marks his contentment—and the loneliness: "sitting in the sun in the doorway / picking my teeth with a broomstraw / listenin to the buzz of the flies." By exposure, he comes to know his environment: "The rock alive,    not barren. / flowers    lichen    pinus    albicaulis    chipmunks / mice    even grass." He meditates on the vastness of time, and the sufficiency of time, for change in the lithosphere, and, as the syntax tells us ("When a storm blows in, covering the south wall with rain and blotting out the mountains.") he himself is caught up in the tremendous elemental action, the finality of it. And then, toward the end of his stay, he makes the crucial entry: "Almost had it last night: *no identity*. One thinks, 'I emerged from some general, non-differentiated thing, I return to it.' One has in reality never left it; there is no return / my language fades. Images of erosion." Whether he ever has it is left in doubt, but the concluding entry shows that whatever good to senses and spirit he has had has not been lost on his return to San Francisco: "Boys on bicycles in the asphalt playground wheeling and circling aimlessly like playful gulls or swallows. Smell of a fresh-parked car."

This exceptional journal—a brief *Walden*—was the work of an exceptional young man, only 22, who already knew the imperatives of art set forth in the poetic directive of "Riprap." Like Roy March-banks, another of the roughs by whom he was taught as a member of a trail crew in Yosemite National Park in 1955, he respects workmanship, in this instance the perfect selection and placing of granite rocks in "tight cobble patterns on hard slab." So he instructs himself in a poem that exemplifies his skill and remains his test of art:

> Lay down these words
> Before your mind like rocks.
>      placed solid, by hands
> In choice of place, set
> Before the body of the mind
>      in space and time:
> Solidity of bark, leaf, or wall
>      riprap of things:
> Cobble of milky way,
>      straying planets,
> These poems, people
>      lost ponies with
> Dragging saddles—
>      and rocky sure-foot trails.
> The worlds like an endless
>      four-dimensional
> Game of *Go*.
>      ants and pebbles
> In the thin loam, each rock a word
>      a creek-washed stone
> Granite: ingrained
>      with torment of fire and weight
> Crystal and sediment linked hot
>      all change, in thoughts,
> As well as things.

The imperatives of composition are modernist: the unit of composition is the single word, like rock, a solid particular thing of weight and texture that exists in place and time and appeals to the senses ("body

of the mind"); and the act of composition is architectural, a building
by words, a deliberate handwork—the kind of labor with things that
Thoreau said removed the palaver from the scholar's style and that,
for Snyder, identifies him with workingmen. Poetry is his craft: "a
riprap on the slick rock of metaphysics," as he says later in *Myths
& Texts*. The "riprap of things" includes all things, the "cobble of
milky way"—the phrase is wonderfully extravagant in Thoreau's
sense, like his own metaphor of fishing in the upper air—and "ants
and pebbles," the diminutive things that, one recalls in "Song of
Myself," were the objects of Whitman's altered perception, the proofs
of love. The substance of the *poetry*, what the art of poetry, the
riprap of words, achieves is universal: a footing in the existential
world, the granitic result of experience under pressure in a world of
time and change that, carefully used, is the foundation of the way.

✺   ✺   ✺

All of [the other] journals lack the continuous intensity of the
first, but all are significant landmarks in Snyder's development and
valuable glosses on the poetry that accompanies it. The Sourdough
Journal conveys the sense of some burden of crisis, of waiting-out
experience—"Chinese [*Hsiao-ching*]; plus Blake's collected, *Walden*
and sumi painting, pass the time." The only entry approaching those
of the first journal is a long meditation on desire and discipline that
ends with the following example of awareness of relationship: "the
desk is under the pencil." As the poem on Dick Brewer's visit tells
us, he is lonely and determined to go to Japan ("Me back to my
mountain and far, far west"). The journal ends with an entry from
Berkeley where he has gone to prepare himself for Zen study there.
    The period at Berkeley (1953–1956) was long and solitary. "I
was living in a little cottage," he recalls, "and studying Chinese and
Japanese . . . and going up to the woods and mountains in the
summer, writing and reading. Intellectually, and in every way, that
was a period of great excitement for me . . ." (The last months of
this period are recorded in *The Dharma Bums*.) This intellectual
quickening and growth is apparent, I think, in the journal of his first
stay in Japan, for in this journal his thoughts are coalescing and
acquiring their subsequent direction. As in the earlier journals, he is
aware of the vastness and complex processes of geological time; he
meditates, he says, on "ecology, food-chains and sex." The relation
of sex to food-chains and ecology is indicated in this entry: "Depth
is the body. How does one perceive internal physical states—yoga
systems I guess—well well. soil conservation / reforestation / birth
control / spelling reform: 'love the body.' " Sex has become a prominent element in his thought, and he is working out a love ethic. He
approvingly cites Lawrence; he sees that "the Goddess is mother,

daughter, and wife at the same time" ("Looking at girls as mothers or daughters or sisters for a change of view. Curious switch"); and he begins to chart the connections between Zen, Avatamsaka and Tantra: "The giving of a love relationship is a Bodhisattva relaxation of personal fearful defenses and self-interest strivings—which communicates unverbal to the other and leaves *them* do the same. 'Enlightenment' is this interior ease and freedom carried not only to persons but to all the universe . . . So Zen, being founded on Avatamsaka, and the net-network of things; and Tantra being the application of the 'interaction with no obstacles' vision on a personal-human level—the 'other' becomes the lover, through whom the various links in the net can be perceived. . . ." Poetry, too, is now defined as an act of love, and the poet of nature is a poet of love: "POETRY is to give access to persons—cutting away the fear and reserve and cramping of social life: thus for Chinese poetry. Nature poetry too: this is what I've seen."

This ethic is central, of revolutionary consequence. It contributes to ecological survival: "the organism alters itself rather than continue fruitless competition." And it contributes to a social vision which is set forth in two dreams:

> —dreamed of a new industrial-age dark ages: filthy narrow streets and dirty buildings with rickety walks over the streets from building to building—unwashed illiterate brutal cops—a motorcycle cop and sidecar drove up and over a fat workingman who got knocked down in a fight—tin cans and garbage and drooping electric wires everywhere—

> One night I dreamt I was with Miura Rōshi, or maybe an unheard of Polish revolutionary poet with a bald head—looking at Berkeley. But a new Berkeley—of the future—the Bay beach clean and white, the bay blue and pure; white buildings and a lovely boulevard of tall Monterey pines that stretched way back to the hills. We saw a girl from some ways off walking toward us, long-legged, her hair bound loosely in back.

The latter dream, one of the testimonies of intensive meditation, is a Joycean epiphany calling the poet to his work. It answers the choice he puts himself earlier: ". . . the poet must choose: either to step deep in the stream of his people, history, tradition, folding and folding himself in wealth of persons and pasts; philosophy, humanity, to become richly foundationed and great and sane and ordered. Or, to step beyond the bound onto the way out, into horrors and angels, possible madness or silly Faustian doom, possible utter transcendence, possible enlightened return, possible ignominious wormish perishing."

He has found a way-in, not a way-out, not Rimbaud's way; and when he goes to the back country it is not to trade but, in the phrase from this journal that defines the work of the later essays, to "knit old dharma-trails." And, he says in "Tanker Notes," he will rely as a poet on neither contrivance nor visionary derangement but only on the Muse, on reverential love, on the cool water of inspiration, the "clear spring" of the mind, deeper than the intellect and the unconscious, that "reflects all things and feeds all things but is of itself transparent."

*Riprap* (1959), Snyder's first book of poems, already fulfills some of these ends. The title declares a humble yet exacting art in the service of the things of experience; it names a back country book that will be the foundation for others. The initial poem, "Mid-August at Sourdough Mountain Lookout," establishes the elevation he seeks, the "clear, attentive mind," spoken of in "Piute Creek," that "Has no meaning but that / Which sees is truly seen." Except for "T-2 Tanker Blues," none of the poems is Beat, and this is Beat only by virtue of loosening an otherwise tight form and adopting an explicitly oral instead of an inner, meditatively spoken mode. Robert Sward's impression of the poems as "restrained and relatively formal," quiet and "apart" in tone, is just—these poems possess much stillness. All of them are autobiographical or confessional in the Whitmanian sense defined by Robert Bly: they embody "the pervading presence of the poet who simultaneously shares in the processes of life and reveals some of its meaning through his actions." They are arranged chronologically, and so follow the development recorded in the journals, and, like the journals, only with more concentration, they treat the first excursions into the back country and the attempt to truly inhabit it.

Nothing antedating the lookout period is included; only later will the poet remember the immediate past which these poems, especially the first, put behind him. There must have been earlier poems worthy of inclusion, for the poet of these poems is well-practiced in his art. But none is included because *Riprap*, like the journals, represents a decisive beginning. He is into the back country: beyond abstraction into sensation, as in "Water" and "Thin Ice"; beyond the timebound present into timeless primordial reaches of time, as in "Milton by Firelight" and "Above Pate Valley"; beyond Western romance into the mysteries of the Goddess, as in "Praise for Sick Women" and "For a Far-Out Friend." Beyond society, his poems are of the wilderness, the sea, the old countries. Beyond self, they need no reticence.

Some of the poems already mentioned are notable, especially "For a Far-Out Friend" and "Piute Creek," even though the former is marred by a weak ending and the latter by the phrase, "bubble of the heart." The central poem, and one of the best, along with the opening and closing poems, is "Nooksack Valley." Placed mid-way, it represents a turning-point toward the world of "A Stone Garden," a longer poem that may be said to answer it.

"Nooksack Valley" is a meditative poem that moves with the poet's thought and has the free form that typifies his work. The indented uncapitalized sentences are not unusual; they suggest the way thoughts, already in flow, enter the mind. Sentences, as Charles Olson reminds us in defending non-sentences, represent completed thought. But the completed thought of this poem is the poem, all that happens in the mind during the short time it takes to heat the coffee.

> At the far end of a trip north
> In a berry-pickers cabin
> At the edge of a wide muddy field
> Stretching to the woods and cloudy mountains,
> Feeding the stove all afternoon with cedar,
> Watching the dark sky darken, a heron flap by,
> A huge setter pup nap on the dusty cot.
> High rotten stumps in the second-growth woods
> Flat scattered farms in the bends of the Nooksack
> River. Steelhead run now
>         a week and I go back
> Down 99, through towns, to San Francisco
> and Japan.
> All America south and east,
> Twenty-five years in it brought to a trip-stop
> Mind-point, where I turn
> Caught more on this land—rock tree and man,
> Awake, than ever before, yet ready to leave.
>         damned memories,
> Whole wasted theories, failures and worse success,
> Schools, girls, deals, try to get in
> To make this poem a froth, a pity.
> A dead fiddle for lost good jobs.
>         the cedar walls
> Smell of our farm-house, half built in '35.
> Clouds sink down the hills
> Coffee is hot again. The dog
> Turns and turns about, stops and sleeps.

Having gone back to say goodbye to the north country, the poet finds himself in a landscape that confronts him with the experience and loyalties of his lifetime. Yet, as the form of the poem indicates, the very setting that awakens his agitation calms it. It does so—and this, I think, accounts for the poem's achievement—because the more deeply he enters it the more deeply it interpenetrates him. The trip north, presumably to fish for steelhead, has reached a "far end."

(One thinks of Hemingway at Big Two-Hearted River.) The poet is not elated but depressed—passive, indoors, "Watching the dark sky darken . . ." The landscape, so carefully described, corresponds with the poet's feelings of loneliness and heaviness, coldness and darkness; it contains his past and summons it to the turning, to the anguish, at the center of the poem, that is never fully admitted to mind because it remains in abstract terms. But the very land that calls up "damned memories" is the back country he loves ("Caught more on this land"), and knowing it, as he now knows it here, is what has awakened him and made him reject (again) the lures of civilization. What keeps the "Schools, girls, deals" from getting in and destroying the poem is the powerful objectivity of his present situation, the particular realizations he had of it, the smell of cedar at the end, pervasive, penetrant, that revives his earliest memory of home, of the child's unspoiled and sustaining world in which he began and to which, however far away he goes, he can in memory again return. The poem expresses his profound attachment to *this* back country even as he prepares to leave it for another.

The country to which he goes is Japan, "a great stone garden in the sea." And in the poem of that name, a stone garden of his own composed of four large blocks of poetry, he treats his discovery there of love, family, and home. Judged by the few poems on Japan, this is the wonderful reward of his experience. "Toji" tells of unusual acceptance ("Nobody bothers you in Toji") and "Kyoto: March" of the lovers beneath the roofs of frosty houses, who

> part, from tangle warm
> Of gentle bodies under quilt
> And crack the icy water to the face
> And wake and feed the children
> And grandchildren that they love.

Love of this kind, tendered in this way, is at the heart of "A Stone Garden."

In the first stanza the poet has a waking dream of the immemorially gardened land, a dream of past-in-present, while on a train carrying him from the countryside to the city—to Tokyo, where, "like a bear," he tracks "the human future / Of intelligence and despair." His awareness of culture, of form, of a mastered ecology achieved by centuries of care, contrasts with the urban jungle inhabited by "A horde of excess poets and unwed girls . . ." Yet in the city, where he "walked a hundred nights" (this stanza begins with the recollection of "a girl I thought I knew," perhaps the "Robin" of later poems, and, like the first which bespeaks restlessness, bespeaks loneliness) he observes

> The thousand postures of all human fond
> Touches and gestures, glidings, nude,
> The oldest and nakedest women more the sweet,
> And saw there first old withered breasts
> Without an inward wail of sorrow and dismay
> Because impermanence and destructiveness of time
> In truth means only, lovely women age—
> But with the noble glance of I Am Loved
> From children and from crones, time is destroyed.

Such love conquers time—his own rare insight into the beauty of old women convinces us of this. But it does this also because it venerates the fertile mystery upon which, in the poet's view, this culture is built and sustained through all vicissitudes, the mystery he associates with the "glittering smelly ricefields," the permanence of nature. His own invocation to this power—"O Muse, a goddess gone astray"—follows in the third stanza, where, in telling of the difficulties of *the* poem he would write ("one time true"), he confesses failure: "The long-lost hawk of Yakamochi and Thoreau / Flits over yonder hill, the hand is bare, / The noise of living families fills the air." Yet finally he writes that poem in the fourth stanza, which, like the others, follows from something he meditates on—"What became of the child we never had—":

> Delight binds man to birth, to death,
> —Let's gather in the home—for soon we part—
> (The daughter is in school, the son's at work)
> & silver fish-scales coat the hand, the board;
> The charcoal glowing underneath the eaves,
> Squatting and fanning til the rice is steamed,
> All our friends and children come to eat.
> This marriage never dies. Delight
> Crushes it down and builds it all again
> with flesh and wood and stone,
> The woman there—she is not old or young.

The urge to transcend "the noise of living families," to grasp the hawk or turtle-dove of poetry, is what this poem subdues. Sometimes flawed in syntax, cadence, and rhyme, the poem is nevertheless of importance in Snyder's development: he would relinquish even the self-love of poetic ambition and willingly serve the Muse that so deeply inspires him and makes love, fulfilled in community and culture, a way of enlightenment.

o   o   o

The unity of *Riprap* is essentially one of stillness, and that of *Myths & Texts* is thematic. The unity of *The Back Country* depends upon the notion of travel and the metaphoric force of the title, but neither secures it so much as the presence of memory which now begins to fill some of the poems. This is a third volume of poems, and so its ground is familiar to poet and reader and, in a sense, recovered. Now experience is compounded by remembering and deepening of life. Though the book, especially the opening section, "Far West," contains poems that might have been included in *Riprap*, its dominant tone is of another kind. There is agitation in *Riprap*, but it is resolved by a course of action, the journey to Japan. Now, much that the poet has carried with him on his travels is admitted, as in "Looking at Pictures to be Put Away":

> Who was this girl
> In her white night gown
> Clutching a pair of jeans
>
> On a foggy redwood deck.
> She looks up at me tender,
> Calm, surprised,
>
> What will we remember
> Bodies thick with food and lovers
> After twenty years.

And as he continues to travel, still by working aboard ship, he begins to ponder in "7.IV.64," and not with the levity the poem intends, his place in life:

> all my friends have children
> & I'm getting old.    at least enough to be
> a First Mate or an Engineer.
> now I know I'll never be a Ph.D.

What is now admitted in the poems, and we realize was hitherto almost wholly excluded, is the poet's experience of love. The more he travels the more he is possessed by thoughts of love and friendship, and by a sense of loss, by the memory of innocent desire with which he first knew them. Back, mirror-imaged, may be a reflection of this.

Friendship is a minor strain, best represented in "August on Sourdough, A Visit from Dick Brewer" and "Rolling in at Twilight." The gesture of the poem itself, which names the friend and fixes forever an exemplary act, testifies to Snyder's feelings for the deep and open relationship of youth. In the first poem Dick Brewer "hitched a thousand miles" to see the poet, who, in turn, loaned him his poncho; in the second, Phil Whalen has laid in some groceries against the poet's probable arrival.

Love is the major strain and is first presented here in "After Work":

The shack and a few trees
float in the blowing fog

I pull out your blouse,
warm my cold hands
        on your breasts.
you laugh and shudder
peeling garlic by the
        hot iron stove.
bring in the axe, the rake,
the wood

we'll lean on the wall
against each other
stew simmering on the fire
as it grows dark
        drinking wine.

Love here is a prized part of a steady continuum of living whose
sensations the poet fully savors and deeply appreciates. It is depicted
as a homecoming. And it is as simple and directly physical and without
haste as the poem, for the poet who transfers the rhythm of his
experience to the poem knows the values of relation and contrast,
the care of the husbandman, and is as confident of the pleasures of
love as of other goods of life, the food to come, the wine, the
enveloping warmth and darkness.

This poem is among the new poems in the latest edition of *The
Back Country*. Along with the concluding poem of section one, "For
the Boy Who Was Dodger Point Lookout Fifteen Years Ago," it
introduces the theme of loss and longing that before was not broached
until the poems for Robin in section two. This concluding poem is
explicitly retrospective. A head note tells us that the poet, now hiking
alone in the Olympic mountains, remembers a trip in the same area
many years before with his first wife (an experience treated in another
poem, "Alysoun," which begins section three). The poem is for the
boy-lookout and for the boy the poet had been. It describes the
mountain meadows and from the vantage of the lookout, to which
the poet has climbed to talk with the lonely boy, the tableau of
Alison (Robin) bathing naked in a pond. From this distance she is
"Swan Maiden," merely a lovely icon as well as significant myth-
motif. For what is important is the meeting of poet and lookout "in
our / world of snow and flowers"—the representation of friendship
as perhaps higher and purer than love. The concluding stanza, not
without Hemingwayesque sentimentality, contrasts the pristine relations of love and friendship with the present desperate confusion of
the poet:

> I don't know where she is now;
> I never asked your name.
> In this burning, muddy, lying,
> blood-drenched world
> that quiet meeting in the mountains
> cool and gentle as the muzzles of
> three elk, helps keep me sane.

In section two, "Four Poems for Robin" carry this theme. They tell of the lonely poet who remembers in his body ("I remember your cool body / Naked under a summer cotton dress") and now knows that in the "pointless wars of the heart" he lost the "grave, awed intensity" of young love: ". . . what the others All crave and seek for; We left it behind at nineteen." "December at Yase" tells of the wars of the will ("I was obsessed with a plan"; "I thought I must make it alone. I / Have done that")[4] but also acknowledges that he might have had another karma—something which his body also hints in "Siwashing it out once in Siuslaw National Forest" where he writes:

> I don't mind      living this way
>
> Green hills      the long blue beach
>
> But sometimes      sleeping in the open
> I think back      when I had you.

With section three, "Kali," the theme of love becomes more prominent. As a way of designating his travels, "Kali" stands for India; the section includes the poems on India that are counterparts of "A Journey to Rishikesh & Hardwar" in *Earth House Hold.* But Kali is the Mother Goddess, and many poems, variously, praise her. The opening poem to Alison acknowledges her as the first of many Kalis in the poet's experience. There are poems of the whorehouse and of erotic adventure and of marital celebration (Snyder married Joanne Kyger in 1960). But all—and this is invariably true of Snyder's treatment of love—are tender and reverential. Love for him, as other poems here on darkness and drunkenness suggest, is a dark ecstatic mystery. It is so in "The Manichaeans," where love is presented as a cosmic power, creating light, warmth, and life. This ambitious poem tries to assimilate myth to present experience and is less successful in doing this than "August Was Foggy," a simple poem of the last section that, in the concluding stanzas, achieves it:

> The first green shoots of grass.
>      you
> like some slender
> fresh young plant

> turn smooth and cool across me
> in the night
>
> touch, and taste, and interlace
> deep in the ground.
> new rain.
> as we begin our life.

This poem also conveys those aspects of Tantra, so important to the poet's love ethic, considered in "Nanao Knows" ("Each girl is real") and "How Many Times" ("open, / were I　　as open"). The poet's travels are a journey to love, a pursuit of the way.[5]

And as the other love poems of the last section show he has learned much on the way. "Across Lamarck Col" not only confesses his fault ("your black block mine") but the fact that all subsequent love affairs assert his loss, his fidelity to original feeling. And another fine poem, as good in its complexity as "August Was Foggy" is in its simplicity, realizes the equation of mountain=nature=woman. "Beneath My Hand and Eye the Distant Hills, Your Body" is a geography, geology, aesthetics, and metaphysics of love in which abstractions are used to deny themselves and yield the solvent feeling of experience. In this poem, Snyder shows as well as anywhere what it is that he has gone in search of and brought back from the East.

His most recent work, *Regarding Wave*, celebrates the world-as-woman and love as its ever-generative force, the spirit that moves him to poetry and now to marriage and fatherhood. The title and essential ideas of the book are glossed in "The Voice as a Girl," a part of the essay, "Poetry and the Primitive." He explains here what he tries to convey in the poems: that, for him, the universe is alive and enters his body as breath, thereby enabling him to sing out "the inner song of the self"; that poetry is such inspired speaking, a response of the self that is deeper than ego to the touch of the world. The attitude he wishes to present is not that of the Western tradition of the Muse and Romantic Love, though its notion of "woman as nature the field for experiencing the universe as sacramental" is all of the primitive tradition that is left to us. Not woman as nature but nature as woman is what he sings—not a particular woman divinized, as in the cult of Romantic Love, but the Goddess herself. The Goddess Vak. "Poetry is voice, and according to Indian tradition, voice, vak (vox)—is a Goddess. Vak is also called Sarasvati, she is the lover of Brahma and his actual creative energy . . ." Sarasvati means "the flowing one"; and "as Vak is wife to Brahma ('wife' means 'wave' means 'vibrator' in Indo-European etymology) so the voice, in everyone, is a mirror of his own deepest self." Such is the meaning of *Regarding Wave*, the poet's reverential praise of the continual creation in which he humbly and gratefully participates.

It is always difficult to write a poetry of praise. None of the poems in this book is especially epiphanic. Snyder's achievement is not in single poems but in the sustained feeling and quality of the book as a whole. The book is well unified by a three-part structure that may be considered wave-like, by a wave-like line and stanza, by the breath-phrasing of the line, not unusual with Snyder, but emphasized here, and by its singleness of theme. The wave is to Snyder's apprehension of nature what the leaf is to Goethe's—it is the ur-phenomenon. He celebrates it variously: in ocean, river, sands, pebbles, clouds; in flow and process and growth; in ecology and food chains. And against this celebration of organic creation, he sets a counter-theme of spoliation and violation of the female. The book begins with an invocation to the wave.

> Ah, trembling spreading radiating wyf
>     racing zebra
> catch me and fling me wide
> To the dancing grain of things of my mind!

and ends with the prayerful awareness of the still flowing wave in all things:

> The Voice
> is a wife
>     to
>
> him still.[6]

And the book is especially well unified by its occasion, the fullness of the new life, a primitive, "archaic" life, he has found with Masa Uehara at the ashram on Suwa-no-se Island, their marriage there (with which account the superb last essay of *Earth House Hold* ends), and the birth of their child out of the sea of the womb. In "It Was When," a catalog (or Whitmanian litany) of sexual consummations, he tells how "we caught"—and

> Waves
>     and the
>         prevalent easterly
>           breeze
>       whispering into you
>         through us,
>            the grace.

In "The Bed in the Sky," he turns from the cold outdoors, where he feels he ought to stay to watch the moon, to the indoor warmth of bed and wife and the stirring child in her belly. "Kai, Today" announces the sea-birth of his son, and "Not Leaving the House," tells of the change this advent has brought: "From dawn til late at night / making a new world of ourselves / around this life."

This is not a book of travel nor of place, though the third section is largely devoted to the "burning island." Place is important but finally indifferent. What matters in this account of working in the elements of sea and land, of planting seeds and caring for new life, is that the current of the universal being has flowed through him and he has become, more selflessly, a servant of life. And something hitherto unattained has at last been attained: the wish of the lookout who long ago noted in his first journal, "Or having a wife and child, living close to the ocean, with skills for gathering food." This book commemorates the taking up housekeeping on earth.

From lookout to ashram. From Walden, we might say, to Fruit-lands. The imperative throughout is Thoreau's: "Every man is tasked to make his life, even in its details, worthy of the contemplation of his most elevated and critical hour." But the direction is Alcott's: from solitude to society, from the individual to the family. Meditation is a seeing into the self that entails its acting out, and this action, Snyder says, in "Buddhism and the Coming Revolution," is "ultimately toward the true community (sangha) of 'all beings.' " The revolution— or transformation—he calls for is to be made in family life, for its agency is love and "love begins with the family and its network of erotic and responsible relationships." To change the form of family life is to alter society radically, at its root. And Snyder's Edenic vision of "ecological balance, classless society, social and economic freedom" is as radical for our society as the matrilineal communal family that he believes enables it—the "family as part of the divine ecology."

The feelings to which this familial-social vision answers are neither unfamiliar nor radical. Literature, and the literature of youth, has always reported them. Snyder, whose writing tells nothing of his past family life, tells in "Passage to More Than India" of his own discovery, at 18, in a community house, of "harmony and community with fellow beings." This too, much later, is what he found ideally at the Banyan Ashram on Suwa-no-se Island. Such feelings, like so much that is considered radical, are conservative—conserving essential and full humanity—and Snyder is right to connect them with occult traditions and a persistent Great Subculture. What is radical now is not merely the repudiation of present social forms ("the modern family is the smallest and most barren that has ever existed"; "the traditional cultures are in any case doomed") but the search for social solutions in the past, the distance back being, perhaps, the measure of this. Snyder is radical because he holds, as he says, "the most archaic values on earth" and because he tries to advance them by realizing them anew in his life and his work. Yet there is nothing archaic in his appropriation of them: they are his (and ours) by right of modern psychology and anthropology as well as meditation. No more than Thoreau, can he be put down as a primitive: "I try to hold both history and wilderness in my mind," he says, "that my poems may approach the true measure of things and stand against the unbalance and ignorance of our times."

This declaration addresses our fearful centralizing technology and the sovereignty of the present that speeds it on; and it is noteworthy because it announces again, for still another generation, the great theme and major work of our time, the restoration of culture in its true measure. Like Lawrence and Williams before him, to cite only two of the pioneer modern writers with whom he stands, Snyder would redress our culture by restoring the vital and the feminine, by voyaging historically and psychically to Pagany, and by charting for us new contours of feeling.

We should not expect him by himself to work this great change. This is the mistake of those who confuse poetry with politics, critics like Peter Levi, who says that we need Snyder's poetry but adds that "his medicine is not going to cure anything. . . ." His work is political because it bears witness; on this account one respects the ways it combines autobiography and utopia. We should accept his optimism— can an ecological conscience be created in time to save a devastated universe?—as a condition of the work, as an act of faith founded on profound basic trust. It is not the register of social naivete. The distance from lookout to ashram is long and difficult; it is not easy for us to enter the back country nor find the archaic springs. We cannot expect literature to cure us, only to hearten us by showing us new and true possibilities and how much may be achieved in life and art by conscious endeavor. Snyder's work, already a substantial achievement, does this. And it may be especially heartening to us because in it an American poet has finally turned to the Orient and shown how much of America might yet be discovered in a passage to India.

## Notes

1. *The Subversive Science: Essays toward an Ecology of Man*, Houghton Mifflin Co., New York, 1969.

2. The range of inquiry of this important work in Snyder's development is suggested by his conclusion: "In its totality the study of a myth is the study of 'man and his works.'" In the course of considering the anthropological, folklorist, psychological, literary, and social aspects of myth, Snyder surveys much that is of consequence to his later writing and seems to be making a statement about his vocation as poet.

3. *The Dharma Bums*, much of it about mountain climbing, is dedicated to Hanshan.

4. Snyder was married to Alison Gass from 1950 to 1952. *Riprap* begins almost immediately afterward.

5. It should be noted that Snyder honestly acknowledges the correlative emotions in "To Hell with Your Fertility Cult" and "Tasting the Snow."

6. Snyder uses as space divider in this poem and "Rainbow Body," the *Vajra* device ( ) also used in "Dharma Queries." It is, he says, "an ancient wisdom / thunderbolt symbol."

# Buddhism and Energy in the Recent Poetry of Gary Snyder      Bert Almon°

For all its attention to the physical world, the poetry of Gary Snyder has always had a metaphysical dimension. He once called poetry "a riprap (cobbled trail) over the slick rock of metaphysics," but metaphysics can also provide a trail over the slick rock of the poetry, providing a path where we might see only a difficult physical terrain. I will put aside the important matter of the influence of American Indian spirituality on Snyder's work and investigate the Buddhist context. Snyder's interest in Zen Buddhism is well-known: he is the poet who spent years in Japan studying it. While much of the material in recent works, such as *Regarding Wave* (1970) and *Turtle Island* (1974),[1] may certainly be clear without a knowledge of Buddhism, some is not, and Snyder's fundamental opposition to industrial civilization can be clarified by understanding the Buddhist influence.

Zen is one of the schools of the Mahayana branch of Buddhism prevalent in Buddhist countries outside of Southeast Asia. It is a very special school, one minimizing philosophy and emphasizing direct experience. Western readers familiar only with the Zen tradition— the Zen master stories, the *koan* exercises—may not be aware of certain basic Mahayana concepts. The Mahayana schools have an ideal of active compassion that extends to all living beings: even the grass should be led to enlightenment by the Bodhisattva, the "enlightenment being" who vows to deliver the whole universe.[2] The Bodhisattva practices *upaya*, "skillful means," strategems and teachings fitted to the various beings he wishes to deliver. For the enlightened mind, the world is a state of being beyond all conflicts and oppositions. As Snyder puts it in "Four Changes," an important essay in *Turtle Island:* ". . . at the heart of things is some kind of serene and ecstatic process which is beyond qualities and beyond birth-and-death." This state of nirvana is not accessible to most of us, and we experience *samsara*, the world of birth-and-death. On this relative level of being,

° Reprinted by permission from *Mosaic* 11.1 (1977): 117–125.

the universe is conceived of as a dynamic realm of interdependent and transient phenomena.[3] Living beings are temporary groupings of elements of this flux, a conception that Snyder translates into the terms of Western physics: ". . . we are interdependent energy-fields of great potential wisdom and compassion . . ." he says in "Four Changes." He puts it this way in the "Introductory Note" of the same collection: "The poems speak of place, and the energy-pathways that sustain life. Each living being is a swirl in the flow, a formal turbulence, a 'song.' " In Snyder's work, the concept of interdependence is translated into ecological terms, and the conception of the world as flux is rendered in terms of physics: the world is a dynamic field of energy.[4] Modern physics shows no interest in the potential wisdom and compassion of energy fields certainly. Science is an instrument of understanding and altering the world. Archimedes is with us yet, even if he may soon have no world to move. Ecology, on the other hand, is one science that does concern itself with wisdom. The ecologist knows how serious the consequences of acting without foresight and compassion can be. Ecological compassion is not a matter of sentimental humanitarianism, just as Snyder's notion of compassion does not rule out taking life to sustain life.

But the poems in *Riprap*, and many in *Myths & Texts*, do not convey a world of flux. The poems are often contemplative: meditations set in stable landscapes, even if the poet laments transience and notes the passage of birds. Sherman Paul has said that "The unity of *Riprap* is essentially one of stillness . . ."[5] and I must agree with that insight. Zen awareness and Zen detachment permeate the early poems. Often they evoke quiet landscapes and sweeps of geological time. The scenes are *composed*, and composed very skillfully. The art of *sumi* painting comes to mind: vistas of clouds and mountains, a human figure or two almost lost in the mist, birds flying off into limitless space, all done in a few strokes. Not the intricate hum of transient elements in the void. And even the poems in *Myths & Texts*, though they describe logging and hunting, more often deal with contemplation than action.

There are transitional poems in *The Back Country*, but the striking change comes with *Regarding Wave*. Instead of a panoramic view of mountains or valleys, the poems frequently offer a world placed under the microscope. And rather than contemplation, the attitude is involvement. The proper analogy with painting would be the *tanka* art of Tibet, which arouses and transforms psychological energies through a blaze of color: processes instead of scenes. Consider the opening of the first poem ("Wave") in the book:

> Grooving clam shell,
>     streakt through marble,

sweeping down ponderosa pine bark-scale
rip-cut tree grain
sand-dunes, lava
flow

The dynamism of wave-forms is traced even in static objects. Physics and Mahayana Buddhism would agree that there are no stable objects, merely the illusion of stability. One of the objects of Buddhist meditation is to achieve awareness of impermanence in all aspects of reality, external and internal. The poetry of *Regarding Wave* often deals with what "Wave" calls ". . . the dancing grain of things / of my mind!" The "dancing grain" is a fine metaphor, and the activity of dancing is one of Snyder's favored means of conveying a dynamic world. Running water is another recurrent image used in the book. And the poet adopts the standard meditation strategy of imagining the physical world permeated with the sounds of the *Dharma* (Buddhist teachings) in several poems. In "Regarding Wave," the *Dharma* is "A shimmering bell / through all," and the slopes of the hills are said to flow. "All the Spirit Powers Went to Their Dancing Place" turns the very landscape into sound: "Hills rising and falling as music, long plains and deserts / as slow quiet chanting."

The style of *Regarding Wave* tends toward the break-up of straightforward description and narration. The lines frequently take the form of image clusters: phrases and single words replacing the extended utterance as the unit of expression. (I say "extended utterance" because Snyder's terseness sometimes led him to avoid the complete sentence in the early poems.) The images themselves often evoke minute particulars, such as seeds, sand grain, thorns, or bark-scales. The world is examined with a close-up lens. Not that the images are always visual. Tactile, auditory, gustatory, olfactory and kinesthetic impressions are prominent and heighten the impression of involvement.

I will return to the matter of involvement in a moment, but I should mention that *Turtle Island* reverses these stylistic trends. We still come upon lines like "Snow-trickle, feldspar, dirt." But the poet is more concerned with narrative, even exposition, and the style is therefore more conventional, less concerned with rendering the flow of process. Social criticism and the desire to come to terms with Western America take precedence over the dancing grain of things. There are poems like "On San Gabriel Ridges" which would easily fit into *Regarding Wave,* but in the later volume Snyder is engrossed with the anecdotal and didactic, and the writing reflects those intentions. The sweep of evolution (300,000,000 years go by in one poem) and the workings of the American political system get more attention than the intricate dynamics of sand grains.

Snyder's Buddhist training has been in the Zen school, but his philosophical position is now influenced by the Vajrayana sect, whose outlook he discusses in *Earth House Hold.* Vajrayana (literally, "The Diamond Vehicle") is a Tantric school, predominant in Tibet before the Chinese invasion of 1959, and still widely practiced in the Himalayan region. Tantra is an approach found in Hinduism as well as Buddhism.[6] The Tantric method is to involve the practitioner with the very reality that most Hindu and Buddhist sects seek detachment from: the world of birth-and-death, the realm of the passions. The key is to transform this reality rather than to escape from it. The attitude toward the emotions in Vajrayana Buddhism is particularly important: passions are aroused and transmuted, not repressed. Anger and desire, for example, can be made instruments of enlightenment. They are changed from poisons into wisdom. Readers who assume that Buddhism is a religion of passivity and kindness may be puzzled by Snyder's ferocity in some of the *Turtle Island* poems. Anger can be a teaching method (consider the Zen master and his stick), and it can also be transmuted into compassion. Better, it is one of the possible forms of compassion, as in the polemics of the ecology movement.

Snyder's "Spel against Demons" is a good example of the role of wrath in his poetry. The poem originally appeared with "Smokey the Bear Sutra" and "The California Water Plan" in a limited edition entitled *The Fudo Trilogy.*[7] It alone was reprinted in *Turtle Island.* "Fudo" is the Japanese name for a Mahayana deity called "Achala" or "Acala" in Sanskrit. His iconography and the *sadhana* (ritual of worship, visualization and invocation) devoted to him are described in "The California Water Plan." The deity represents the struggle against evil and is sometimes called the Lord of Heat. His imagery is summed up in Alice Getty's *The Gods of Northern Buddhism:* "His appearance is fierce and angry. The sword in his right hand is to smite the guilty and the lasso in his left to catch and bind the wicked." He is associated with fire: "Behind him is a glory of flames, symbolizing the destruction of Evil . . . ."[8] Snyder's Smokey the Bear is fancifully presented as a form of Achala, or Fudo, and the "Smokey the Bear Sutra" is a droll parody of Buddhist scriptures. "Spel against Demons" is also modeled on a Buddhist literary form, the *dharani.*

A *dharani* is a charm or spell, usually invoking a Buddha or Bodhisattva. Although D. T. Suzuki gives examples of the form in his well-known *Manual of Zen Buddhism*, the *dharani* represents a magical dimension of Buddhism which has received little attention in the West.[9] "Spel against Demons" attacks "The release of Demonic Energies in the name of / the People" and "The stifling self-indulgence in anger in the name of / Freedom." Mindless terrorism is denounced as ". . . death to clarity / death to compassion." The poem represents anger without rancor: [it] calls upon Achala to bind "demonic killers" with his diamond noose and describes this deity ". . . who turns Wrath to Purified Accomplishment." The poem ends with a Sanskrit *mantra*, a power-formula—the "spel" of Achala.

It is not, then, contradictory for Snyder to include poems of anger and denunciation ("The Call of the Wild," "Steak," "Control Burn") in the same section of *Turtle Island* that contains the warm family scenes of "The Bath" and the compassionate descriptions of "The Dead by the Side of the Road." The Vajrayana tradition embraces a life-giving exploitation of anger: some of the meditation masters of the Vajarayana were willing to use wrath and even force as teaching tools.[10] The sensuous delight in the flesh that Snyder conveys in "The Bath" is equally respectable. The body is not the "running sore" for Vajrayana that it is for the Southern branch of Buddhism, the Theravada. Mindless craving is condemned, but the power of the senses is power that the spiritual life can harness.

The anger usually has a compassionate thrust. And the outrage Snyder feels often grows out of the abuse of living creatures that many religions ignore: animals and trees. The theoretical scope of Buddhist compassion is unlimited. The object of compassion is any living being, not just human beings. The Buddhist, like the North American Indian, gives a kind of equality to ". . . the other people— what the Sioux Indians called the creeping people, and the standing people, and the swimming people . . ." (*Turtle Island*, "The Wilderness"). Many of Snyder's "people" are birds, coyotes, whales, insects or even plants. It is easy to dismiss this sympathy as sentimental pantheism but Snyder knows that the ecological crisis grows out of such attitudes. His problem as a poet of the whole range of living beings is to create poems in which animals and plants appear as autonomous presences, not as mere symbols for human feelings or concepts. Naturally, the terms used are anthropomorphic, but anthropomorphism is a problem only for a world view that assumes an absolute gulf between man and other beings. Buddhism provides what Robinson Jeffers would call a transhuman perspective. The aim is not to raise the supposedly lower orders to a human level, but to see all beings as co-citizens in a community of life. Snyder assumes that the artist can imaginatively enter into the lives of other organisms and speak for them. In "The Wilderness," he says: "I wish to be a spokesman for a realm that is not usually represented in intellectual chambers or in the chambers of government." According to Snyder, the way to be such a spokesman is to create paintings, dances or songs to express an interpretation of other beings.

Snyder is perhaps most skilled at interpreting birds: *Myths & Texts* contains some fine descriptions of them, and poems such as "The Wide Mouth" in *Regarding Wave* (depicting a sparrow) and

"The Hudsonian Curlew" in *Turtle Island* are high points in the books. Deer, bears and coyotes get attention also. Plants present the biggest challenge: they are the basis of any ecological system, the "proletariat" on which other living beings feed, directly or indirectly, but they are very static characters, clearly. Snyder managed action in his early poems on plant life by describing forest fires and logging, and in *Regarding Wave* he deals with the dissemination of seeds by wind and water and on the fur of mammals. The distribution of seeds reminds us that plants have an active role in the shifting pattern of life.

Plants form the base of what in "Four Changes" Snyder calls ". . . a vast and delicate pyramid of energy-transformations." Those transformations usually take the form of eating and being eaten. Food is one of Snyder's favorite themes. Many of the poems in his books deal with eating, and sometimes on an Odyssean scale. For example, *The Back Country* ends, not with the mythical splendors of "Through the Smoke Hole," but with "Oysters," a poem about hunting and eating the shellfish. The implied theme of the poem is the abundance of nature. Poems like "Shark Meat" in *Regarding Wave* create an awareness of the interdependence of all phenomena. The shark traveled far to become part of a feast on Suwa-no-se Island.

> Miles of water, Black current,
> Thousands of days
>     re-crossing his own paths
>     to tangle our net
>         to be part of
>         this loom.

And "The Hudsonian Curlew" in *Turtle Island* evokes the complexity of the physical world in which such birds live, then goes on to present the eating of them as an incorporation of their being into the eater: "dense firm flesh, / dark and rich, / gathered news of skies and seas." Eating becomes a reverential act, rather than a brutal necessity. Snyder is probably more indebted to North American Indian attitudes toward hunting and eating in this poems than he is to the Buddhist tradition. Buddhism teaches gratitude toward food—acknowledgement that it represents a loss of life—and that attitude is common among the American Indians, but Buddhism also encourages vegetarianism in order to minimize suffering. It is mindfulness of the interconnections involved in eating which Snyder draws from Buddhism. On the question of vegetarianism he takes the side of the primitive hunter who believes that humility, gratitude and acts of propitiation expiate the blame for eating meat or taking furs. Snyder does see Buddhism and American Indian attitudes as compatible, and both are influences in the poems. In "One Should Not Talk to a Skilled Hunter about What

Is Forbidden by the Buddha" (which invokes a Zen master's authority in the title), Snyder describes a Buddhist ceremonial in honor of a gray fox which is to be skinned: chanting the *Shingyo*, or *Heart Sutra*,[11] a text often recited to the dying and at funerals. Another poem in *Turtle Island*, "The Dead by the Side of the Road," presents the use of animals killed by accident. The ceremony described, offering corn meal by the dead body, is North American Indian. The Buddhist tradition that meat not killed by or specifically for one can be eaten without blame, and the conclusion of the poem is an act of mindfulness in the Buddhist sense: it emphasizes that some blame does attach to human beings for building highways across animal trails. The Buddhist and North American Indian elements in Snyder's poems are more likely to reinforce than contradict each other.

Both traditions condemn thoughtless murder of any creature. The poems in *Turtle Island* reject such killing. "Steak" condemns those who eat grain-fattened beef without realizing the cost to the land or acknowledging the suffering of the animals. The poem concludes with an image of the live cattle which are being fattened-up:

> Steaming, stamping,
> long-lashed, slowly thinking
> with the rhythm of their
> breathing,
> frosty—breezy—
> early morning prairie sky.

The key word is "thinking." We prefer not to realize that cattle are sentient beings, capable of suffering.

The greatest anger in *Turtle Island* is reserved for wanton killing for mere gain or comfort, a different matter from eating to sustain life. "The Call of the Wild" is particularly effective, with its acid portrait of the man who has coyotes trapped because they make noise, and its terse, disgusted chronicle of the city hippies who move to the country but sell their cedars because someone tells them that "Trees are full of bugs." The anger is tempered with awareness and compassion that reduce the potential for a self-righteous tone. In "I Went into the Maverick Bar" the speaker disguises himself as a middle American ("My long hair was tucked up under a cap / I'd left the earring in the car") and observes the mores of his countrymen with some sympathy. I am reminded of the Bodhisattva named Vimalakirti, who was famed for going into brothels and taverns in order to practice compassion. He always appeared to be one of the revelers, but only as a form of *upaya*, skillful means.[12] One of the most interesting poems in *Turtle Island* is "Dusty Braces," in which the poet acknowledges the influence of his wandering, land-destroying ancestors and gives them "nine bows," a traditional form of homage in Buddhism. But acknowledging his *karma*—the formative influences on him—doesn't mean that he accepts the destructive ways of those ancestors.

The indignation recorded in *Turtle Island* reaches a climax in "Mother Earth: Her Whales," a denunciation of the "robots" who ". . . argue how to parcel out our Mother Earth / To last a little longer." This poem, like "Toward Climax" later in the book, strikes me as a good prose essay mysteriously incarnated as a bad poem. "Mother Earth: Her Whales" has too many discordant elements: a manifesto calling for an uprising of "otters, wolves and elk," lyrical passages describing the lives of the whales themselves, rhetorical denunciations of the "robots" at the Stockholm Conference on the Environment, fragments of ballads, and historical sketches. A reader can share the disgust and yet feel that the poem is not successful. Prose might have been a better vehicle for conveying the sense of outrage.

This particular poem does make it clear that the poet wants to take on all exploitative civilizations:

> how can the head-heavy power-hungry politic scientist
> Government    two world    Capitalist-Imperialist
> Third World    Communist    paper-shuffling male
>     non-farmer    jet-set    bureaucrats
> Speak for the green of the leaf? Speak for the soil?

The technological abuses of Western civilization are envied by the non–Western nations: the instrumental approach—pragmatism and exploitation—is shared by many developing as well as developed nations. The energy crisis has shown that this approach is ultimately self-defeating. It breaks down those "energy-pathways" that sustain life. And energy in the narrow sense, mere fuel, can be exhausted.

Technically advanced societies, and those aspiring to such status, regard energy as a means of controlling, altering and exploiting the natural world. The environment is a mass of raw material to be exploited. For Mahayana Buddhism, the world is a dynamic process to be interpreted through contemplation, or even transmuted (as in Vajrayana)—not cut-down, burned-out, torn-up or strip-mined. In Zen monasteries the ideal is to waste nothing, not even a drop of water. The Buddhist approach is one of gratitude for what one receives, while the industrial approach is to devise ways of getting more. One of Snyder's themes in *Turtle Island* is exploitation and wanton destruction. Much of the wrath can be accounted for by the shameless way in which governments that very slowly awoke to public pressure for environmental protection measures have moved quickly to give up those measures whenever they interfere with the need for energy. A shortage of energy in the limited sense—fuel—justifies further damage to the ". . . vast and delicate pyramid of energy-formations" which makes life possible. The real sources of energy are the sun and the mental energy within the mind. Opposed to these sources is the "Liquid Metal Fast Breeder Reactor," which Snyder sees as "Death himself," a source of contamination likely to heighten the environmental damage already done by conventional approaches to creating industrial energy. The poet insists that "We would live on this Earth / without clothes or tools!" But this is not possible without vast transformations in our way of life, of course, and the prose essays in *Turtle Island* are meant to encourage such changes. His commentary on "As for Poets" declares that ". . . there is another kind of energy, in every living being, close to the sun-source, but in a different way. The power within. Whence? 'Delight.' The delight of being alive while knowing of impermanence and death, acceptance and mastery of this." Such power, he says, ". . . will still be our source when coal and oil are long gone, and atoms are left to spin in peace." He defines "Delight" in terms of Mahayana metaphysics, though he draws the term from William Blake, who said that "Energy is Eternal Delight." It is interesting to note that Herbert V. Guenther, seeking a term for the *Karmamudra* experience of sexual ecstasy in Tantric Buddhism, hit upon Blake's "Eternal Delight" also.[13] For Snyder, Delight grows out of a perception of the world as a luminous, interdependent reality, which can be perceived as serene and joyful when observed without dualistic thinking:

> Delight is the innocent joy arising
> with the perception and realization of
> the wonderful, empty, intricate,
> inter-penetrating,
> mutually-embracing, shining
> single world beyond all discrimination
> or opposites.

In "Charms" *(Turtle Island)*, Snyder follows the Tantric tradition in suggesting that "The beauty of naked or half-naked women" evokes this perception of ". . . the Delight / at the heart of creation." There are other ways of evoking Delight, and the celebration of animals, plants and birds is one means of summoning up a joy in the energy of things. The flux of physical reality need not be perceived as a conflict if there is no desire to conquer or exploit it. And even the passion of anger can be plowed back into "Fearlessness, humor, detachment," genuine forms of power.

Notes

1. Gary Snyder, *Regarding Wave* (New York, 1970); *Turtle Island* (New York, 1974).

2. D. T. Suzuki's *Outlines of Mahayana Buddhism* (1907; rpt. New York, 1963) is a basic source on Mahayana metaphysics and the Bodhisattva ideal.

3. The most comprehensive study of Buddhist conceptions of physical reality available in English is Herbert V. Guenther, *Philosophy and Psychology in the Abhidharma* (1957; rpt. Berkeley, 1974). I am indebted to Ch. IV, "The Interpretation of the World We Live In," pp. 144–190.

4. Ed Zahniser notes Snyder's conception of the world as energy in an untitled review of *Turtle Island* published by *Western American Literature*, 10 (May 1975), 67–72.

5. Sherman Paul, "From Lookout to Ashram: The Way of Gary Snyder," Part Two, *Iowa Review*, 1 (Fall 1970), 78.

6. Chogyam Trungpa, *Cutting Through Spiritual Materialism* (Berkeley, Shambhala, 1973), gives a clear account of the principles of Vajrayana Buddhism, especially the role of the passions.

7. Gary Snyder, *The Fudo Trilogy* (Berkeley, 1973).

8. Alice Getty, *The Gods of Northern Buddhism* (1914; rpt. Rutland, Vermont and Tokyo, 1962), p. 35.

9. D. T. Suzuki, *Manual of Zen Buddhism* (1935; rpt. New York, 1960), pp. 21–25.

10. Marpa's bullying of Milarepa is a fine example. See Chogyam Trungpa, *Cutting Through*, pp. 37–40.

11. Suzuki, *Manual,* pp. 26–27, translation and notes.

12. Charles Luk, trans., *The Vimalakirti Nirdesa Sutra* (Berkeley, 1972), p. 17.

13. Herbert V. Guenther, *The Life and Teaching of Naropa* (London, 1963), pp. 202–221.

# Gary Snyder's "Burning Island"    David Robbins°

## I

Gary Snyder's "Burning Island" (in *Regarding Wave*[1]) is not the type of poem that is likely to receive attention now. Recent criticism has been concerned with Snyder's relation to the "open form" tradition and with the aesthetic problem of "belief" statements in *Turtle Island*.[2] There are good reasons, however, for rereading an older poem displaying considerable structural and textural complexity in the service of Snyder's world view. First, the dichotomy between "open" and "closed" form means more to those who are plotting the map of literary history than it does to Snyder. His openness is radical enough to include anything that will "bring poetry back from our special practice, so to speak, to the open realm of human dialogue where we can address it to anyone."[3] (This is an "international definition

° Reprinted by permission from *A Book of Rereadings in Recent American Poetry* (Lincoln, Neb: Best Cellar Press, 1979). © 1979 Greg Kuzma.

of poetry," Snyder remarked in his interview with the "open field" historian, Ekbert Faas.) Asserting the value of closure devices for memnotic strength and "public clarity," Snyder characteristically adds: "Anything that works, I'll use."[4]

As for belief, Snyder's use of poetry as shamanic utterance "speaking for" the life of non-human nature, is profoundly at odds with prevailing intellectual fashions (e.g., structuralism and the nature-culture split in anthropology, and the contempt for mimetic-referential values in literary theory). Critical deference to his worldview tends to be of the "willing suspension of disbelief" sort more often than serious encounter. The issues Snyder raises are left to the ecology journals, where his work is always at home. Someday Snyder's fusion of Buddhism, primitive religion and ecology will be recognized for what it is: a great, single-handed accomplishment of intelligence and feeling, a turning point in our culture. (Hence too, recognition of Snyder's due status as an "international" writer of the post-industrial era.) The discomfort of the purist literary sensibility surfaces in Charles Altieri's attack on much of *Turtle Island.* Altieri, who has written brilliantly on Snyder's lyric technique, praises Snyder's "disciplined intelligence and refined feelings" only to find them violated by the wildness of his social purposes and cross-cultural concerns.[5] It is the familiar modernist plea for a pure poetry of particulars, but Snyder prefers a term like "utterance" for his work in order to allow everything into "the realm of human dialogue".

In his 1953 journal on Sourdough Mountain, Snyder writes: "Discipline of following desires, *always* doing what you want to do, is hardest."[6] This wilderness version of "disciplined intelligence" makes poetry the vehicle of whatever wants saying, singing or just passing on, from the inner and outer "back country" Snyder inhabits. The poem works when it gives voice to places where people would be if they weren't too scared ("civilized") to go there. "Form" has no *a priori* meaning here, and Snyder himself is never very comfortable with the term. When I speak of Snyder's form, as I do in this essay, it is to point to the strategic necessities of a particular utterance in the world. There are always two aspects to this. Expressively, "form" is whatever holds the poem within the "energy-mind-field-dance," staying wild and distant from the "mass ego" of "class-structured civilized society."[7] (This does not imply the primacy of image over idea—no conventions are privileged.) Rhetorically, "form" means the guerrilla tactics of utterance, whatever enables it to slip through spaces in the social filter and make contact with the unheard voices of desire in others. Snyder's "discipline of following desires" proves to be a social vision because we share them with the poet—desire for physical fulfillment in the world, yes, but also, beneath all skepticism, desire for that freedom of infinite compassion which is the true, ancient motive for "ecology".

It may be misleading to think of Snyder as simply developing "beyond" the poetry of *Regarding Wave*. The ongoing composition of *Mountains and Rivers without End* (begun in 1956) suggests another perspective, from which Snyder's poems not only follow the grain of his life changes but exist as interdependent aspects of a larger picture. "If you are a poet," Snyder said at one reading, "you re-write your own myth."[8] This means not only finding utterance for what Lawrence called the "momentaneous," but intuiting a timeless "form beyond forms," whose secret is the myth-like rightness of the poet's life for its age and society. In fact, Snyder's various styles do keep re-emerging, and his earliest work not only elucidates his latest, it exists in balancing complementarity, as public readings often show. The timeless "wide gaze" of *Myths & Texts* (1960) throws another light upon this totalizing imagination—the poet's life is needed to "fill out the whole picture" of man's relation to the planet.[9] Each of Snyder's key perspectives, in fact, hefts the personal-temporal flow into an impersonal, spatially glimpsed totality: ecological events are judged in the vast context of the "web of Gaia"; primitive life-experience inhabits "a place called noon," "a world of ongoing recurrence" where the individual is perpetually renewed on the plane of cosmic time; and Asian teachings inspire Snyder's view of the "now" as "a marvelous emptiness in all possibilities and directions. Which embraces the game of time and evolution."[10] Thus each poem is uniquely transparent to the world, yet it also stands as a metonym for a lifetime of right utterance. And as Robert Kern has suggested (with sure reference to Snyder's catalogues, "impersonalizing" the personal), each poem is also a metonym for "experience which we all can share."[11]

The sequence of poems in which "Burning Island" appears marks a crucial moment in Snyder's life, when his archaic living situation on Suwa-no-se Island (summer 1967) coincided with his entry into new responsibilities of marriage and fatherhood. A dramatic, richly textured style emerges, steeped in syllabic harmonies that are indebted to Oriental poetics. Instead of the observing poet's "riprap of things" placed "before the mind like rocks," the island world is a slowly exploding cosmic mystery, a spiralling equilibrium ("wave") within which the poet must keep finding his balance through relationships. The phrase "regarding wave" is the title of this section, of its last poem and of the entire volume. It shimmers with a double-seeing playfulness—who is the subject, who the object?—that is characteristic of these poems. It is as though, myth-like, Snyder had to abandon his personal independence before he could speak from that "knowledge of connection and responsibility" which he always praised in primitive cultures.[12] Indeed, the great action behind the island cycle is the ancient ritual of marriage as a cosmogonic event, signifying creation's renewal. (In *Cosmos and History*, Mircea Eliade argues that marriage cannot exist as a purely human event in archaic cultures, that its power lies in imitating the transformation of chaos into cosmos.[13]) Poetically, this is not an occasion for "open form" experiments but for celebrating interconnections with every verbal resource. Thus we find balances and reciprocities everywhere, and dovetailing patterns and iconic clues, and song-like harmonies between realms as between sounds—"closed" features which point our expectations toward the satisfactions of totality.

The body (Snyder's alone or his and Masa's) is the focus of this cosmic integration. "Burning Island" introduces the cycle's controlling figure—the human body as counterpart of the "vast breathing body" that is the universe. We are meant to recall the Hindu myth of Indra's net, in which each jewel reflects all the others and each reflected jewel reflects the others, and so on infinitely. In *Hwa-yen Buddhism*, Francis Cook calls this a "cosmic ecology," implying "a more pervasive and complicated interdependency than we have so far imagined."[14] Snyder calls it "interbirth, for we are actually mutually creating each other and all things while living."[15] The island poems illustrate this profound sense of interconnection with a variety of actions: eating ("Shark Meat"), sex ("It Was When"), birth ("Kai, Today"), emerging patterns in nature ("Rainbow Body"), symbolic impression ("Everybody Lying on Their Stomachs . . ."), and visionary gnosis ("Regarding Wave").

The appearance of a static, reiterated attitude may color our first reading of "Burning Island," since the poem is clearly a series of invocations to gods and powers of the island. Snyder describes this wedding ceremony at dawn in his essay on the island experience: "Standing on the edge of the crater, blowing the conch horn and chanting a mantra; offering shochu to the gods of the volcano, the ocean and the sky."[16] But when we attend to the shiftings of stance, our sense of the poem sharpens and complicates. At the outset, the summoned island powers are independently assertive, overwhelming the poet even as he salutes them. Then they are disclosed as forms and patterns, then as a single mysterious presence in the midst of human activity. The poem's surface is thus a field of shifting tones and references without a governing perspective, a wholly immersed consciousness. Students who have difficulty with this poem, I've found, collide instructively with this feature of it. It is very much to the point that our expectation of meaning is thwarted. The poem "brackets" that expectation, as the phenomenologists say. We learn that we are not given a stance, because that is precisely what the speaker is seeking. We are seduced into the trust Snyder bears toward experience, allowing it to evolve its own form in relation to the attentive mind.

The shifts of subject which impel the poem's spiralling comprehension are controlled by a curious reflex—a constant leaping from limit to limit, in effect a dialectic of place. "Burning Island" thus amplifies its range of reference as it moves, oscillating between antithetical realms which depend on each other for their continuance. Ultimately it reveals consciousness obeying laws which are no different for itself than for everything else in the universe. It enacts "the reciprocities and balances by which man lives on earth," as they unfold in time.[17]

The dramatic handling of time is the other peculiarity of "Burning Island" which it may help to anticipate here. The poem opens recollectively, with the speaker's impressions of being overwhelmed by the island gods. Then the focus shifts to the speaker's actual situation in the moonlight. The sense of an other-than-human presence dramatically interrupts the narrative flow; recollection is suddenly grounded in immediate experiencing. The effect is to dovetail past and present dimensions into a single stream, a dramatic present of heightened vividness. (Barbara Herrnstein Smith calls this "simultaneous composition." The poem "represent(s) the record of a train of thoughts evoked by a series of ongoing events."[18]) This flow of the past into the present of the telling underscores the poem's heuristic intent, for we are wrenched into a sense of meditation in action, provoked into a readiness for new connections and new stances. The same tactic—"folding" the poem where the past becomes the present and recollection becomes behavior—is the structural principle of "Shark Meat," later in the cycle.

## II

From the outset, the powers of Suwa-no-se Island set disadvantageous, even perilous terms for the supplicant as he seeks a decorum of relation with them. We certainly do not feel his active presence in the opening. He is thrown off balance by the sea: "O Wave God who broke through me today." The impact is due to the instant defeat—propitious fate for an invocation!—and to the line's mimetic strength. The "O" of the speaker's address is sucked into the surge of that same vowel through the line, closing in an echo of "wave." Even the space enriches the mimetic atmosphere, suspending the god's name momentarily before his action "breaks". The "me," broken through by the force of this god, is stripped of its agency as doer and as knower. This is why "Sea Bream / massive pink and silver" remains tyrannously elemental, refusing a more specific identity. The fish are at home and unapproachable in their kingdom:

"cool swimming down with me watching / staying away from the spear." It is the Sea Bream, of course, who remain "cool". The delay of the subject teasingly suspends the meaning—"cool swimming down" *might* refer to the speaker—until we are forced to reverse the subject-object relationship. It is the hunter who is coolly handled, who is not permitted to intend anything. On the plane of utterance, too, the invocation has been swept into the purposes of the Wave God's kingdom. The defeat of humanistic expectations occurs on three levels: that of the hunter, that of the speaker, and that of the reader. They are worth distinguishing here because the dynamics of the poem depends on the interplay of the planes they represent—experience prior to the poetic event, the dramatic present of the speaker himself, and the shifting expectations of the reader, forced to abandon meaning for event until the meaning springs out of events by its own natural logic.

With this opening Snyder dramatizes the vulnerabilities of the Paleolithic world he has come to recover. From his essay on the island experience, we may assume that the speaker has yet to learn (through the hunting arts of "identity, intuition, stillness") how to "let the fish choose you."[19] We may also note features of the traditional religious experience of humbling the ego. But how utterly relaxed the expression is! The ease is the true sign of the mastery at work in this opening, lightly hefting the burden of awareness which the poem is going to pay out gradually.

The reversal of roles, inescapable in the first section, is playfully taken for granted in the second. The volcano god is a capricious giant, the island is his playland, and humans, small and vulnerable, are easily delighted and bewildered there.

"Volcano belly Keeper who lifted this island / for our own beaded bodies adornment / and sprinkles us all with his laugh—" The sudden vigor of these onflowing, rhythmically assured lines owes as much to the speaker's delight in the stance struck (it is, momentarily, a *point d'appui*) as to the thought of the island's pleasures proved. "For our own beaded bodies," beyond its playful punning, implies an equality of citizenship with the fish. That opening "O" sound rolls through an entire line again, but not to the speaker's advantage, braced with a touch of alliterative bravado. It is a gesture of mythmaking, isolating the paradisical aspects of primitive dependence upon the island. The gallant tone and rhythm breaks off as suddenly, however, for the "Volcano belly Keeper" of Burning Island is, after all, a fire god ("ash in the eye") and the playful stance is somewhat presumptuous. Nor was the island "lifted" solely for human purposes:

> ash in the eye
> mist, or smoke,

on the bare high limits—
  underwater lava flows easing to coral
    holes filled with striped feeding swimmers

The quick sequence (from laughter to physical irritation to impasses with the place itself) again unbalances the supplicant. He finds himself within a landscape suggestive of Zenga and Nanga painting tradition: the dwarfed human at the edge of the known, faced with looming, impenetrable "mist, or smoke, / on the bare high limits."

Then a dash, and the sudden contemplation of the "underwater lava flows." But why? We are not asked to seek some hidden narrative cause, but to learn a logic of place. Like the speaker, we must honor the event. If we are not impatient for "our" meaning, if we scan with a relaxed eye, we may notice that the antithetical phrases, "bare high limits" and "underwater lava flows," are neatly juxtaposed, one above the other, inviting us to think *in terms of* their opposition. Then we may sense that earlier shift from "lifted" to "sprinkles" as partaking of the same rise-and-fall (exactly like breathing). The entire section, in review, balances around it. Behind, of course, is the opening experience of "cool swimming down," which by this mysteriously impersonal logic is causally related to the Keeper's act of lifting. It is as though everything—the "spirit of place," the islander's response to it, and the poet's language—were immanent expressions of a single dialectical process. (Thus Snyder refuses end punctuation throughout these invocations. The "both-and" of their independence and continuity is nourished by every possible poetic resource.) I have described the oscillation between increasingly farther-flung limits as the poem's "reflex". For the reader, it must earn credibility by its repeated appearance. But even at this point, when Snyder clarifies this law of the poem's proceeding, we should respond to it as a structural expression of that reversal of subject and object which was dramatized at the outset.

The entire second section is "grounded" in the vision of the volcano god's underwater limits, not only formally, but in the harmonious life-fulfillment it exhibits. It is a significantly prolonged glimpse of a peace that does not yet include the poet, a rich calm subtly active at the core: ". . . flows easing to coral / holes filled with striped feeding . . ." Full of richly echoing, backward-harkening sounds within, "filled with" a quiet generosity that hints of a grace at work in things, the passage slows us to a circular sense of life patterns merging where two kingdoms meet. As for the islander, he is not even permitted the settled stance which the god's intimidation might offer, nor can he justifiably expect to share in this generosity out of which the island was "lifted". He (not the island) is still "other".

If we are alert to the poem's signals, the leap to a distant sky kingdom (and to gods who sport recklessly and dangerously with the islanders) will appear as a confirmation of familiar laws. It is the tonal and physical antithesis of the peaceful feeding at the volcano-sea interface: "O Sky Gods cartwheeling / out of Pacific / turning rain-squalls over like lids on us." Yet continuity is there, too, balancing opposed experiences. "Cartwheeling" takes its cue from the preceding assonance of "easing" and "feeding" (the gerundives welcome us into the habitual processes of the island), and those coral holes, peacefully receiving the volcano lava, function like codes for the flowing sky circles that follow. The continuity is also suggested by the *double entendre* of "out of Pacific," the peaceful state from which the Sky Gods are recoiling. As so often in Snyder, word play tugs against the separations of ordinary logic. It is as though the hidden connections of language were passages leading back to the prelogical interplay of creation.

I have described these addresses with an eye to the balance of movement and texture that Snyder has put into motion. Balancing, in fact, is the all-governing law of the poem. If we read attentively, we cannot go far before we suspect that there can be no rest short of an equilibrium that embodies the cosmic wholeness. I state this here, with the Sky Gods' turmoil before us, because the poem exists in its expectations as well as in its concretions. By the very pointed frustration of it, we feel the need for some affirmation of the poet's presence. Having encountered the three gods of water, fire and air, we want to be grounded or completed by an earth god. Saturated with the presence of the male powers, we intuit the counter-balancing strength of the female, waiting. Moreover, the equation of the number four with totality is a common axiom of traditional cultures, and Snyder often employs it to reach the mandala-plane of our psyches, where we still yearn for wholeness (see "The Hudsonian Curlew"). In the peace ("out of Pacific") glimpsed behind the turbulence, we also have a hint of the ultimate respose of the many upon the One. There are other events-to-be as well—like the revelation of the primary forms behind nature's forces, and the human counterpart of the blissful "feeding" of the swimmers—which will satisfy us when they come, as formally anticipated balancings.

As D. T. Suzuki reiterated in book after book, the totality of things is both a temporal continuum and an identity. "Identity belongs in spatial terminology. In terms of time, it is timelessness . . . Time-serialism makes sense only when it goes on in the field of timelessness, which is the Buddhist conception of *sunyata* ("emptiness").[20] Snyder's poetry has always nourished itself on this paradox of Eastern thought, with its defense of the smallest thing's significance—"the real flower in the light of suchness." This "double-seeing" awareness behind

Snyder's dialectical tactics contrasts with the common Western version of dialectics—cancelling things out in the hot teleological pursuit (i.e., throwing away the containers). While "Burning Island" proceeds through its ancient addresses towards a final blessing, the form educates our sense of the whole at work at every point, correcting and balancing, intimating the identity of things. The Sanskrit term for this primal creative intuition is *prajna*, the "self-weaving net," to recall Snyder's favorite metaphor. Thus the poem creates its own experience of the Mahayana way. We need not have read in the Sutras or know how to differentiate the Nara schools to respond to it, although it should be clear even now that real attentiveness is required in the reading. I say this not to revive New Critical axioms, but to suggest the advantage for poetry of a world-view genuinely based on experience rather than concept. We must go to non-Western traditions to find this, as Snyder has shown for over twenty years.

Although the islander has had a hard time of it, being broken through and battered by seemingly alien powers, this has also served as a wise permissiveness, allowing the richness of creation to declare itself through him. His first three invocations, for instance, are not quite sentences. They remain vital appositions, waves of bursting self-enactment from the gods themselves, washing back over him from out of the names. This is all in the spirit of Japanese folk religion, which is continuous with man's oldest customs of nature-worship. In Shinto, the term *kami* is applied to anything evoking awe or respect, although a live volcano ("burning island") would have an especially powerful significance as a focus of cosmic powers. As Motoori Norinaga put it: "Not only human beings, but birds, beasts, plants and trees, seas and mountains and all other things whatsoever which deserve to be dreaded and revered for the extraordinary and preeminent powers which they possess are called *kami* . . . It is not their spirits which are meant. The word was applied directly to the seas or mountains themselves, as being very awesome things."[21] In his study of Japanese mountain worship, Ichiro Hori shows the thorough integration of these prehistoric beliefs into Buddhist customs.[22] The point is that Snyder's fusion of these traditions is not arbitrary. It is a special advantage of Buddhism that it has so comfortably absorbed vital elements of the primitive.

The second half of the Sky Gods section shifts the poem's weight to the speaker himself. When the storm is answered with a rainbow, it passes quickly from the realm of the sky powers to the poet's own body. The recovery of balance is not an effort but a realization of interconnection:

> then shine on our sodden—
> (scanned out a rainbow today at the

> cow drinking trough
> sluicing off
> LAKHS of crystal Buddha Fields
> right on the hair of the arm!)

In "shine," an imperative mood bursts sun-like from the context, intimating the poet's own claims, which are momentarily humbled again in "our sodden—". That phrase offers the poem's first suggestion of earth and community. ("Sudden" is subliminally suggested here, too, slyly enforcing the sense of reversal.)

The parenthetical exclamation is the first active stance assumed by the speaker, and it is full of reversals of what preceded it. It is hardly a resting place, but it begins the poet's affirmation of his place on the island, and its materials suggest an ultimate harmony between remote and intimate presences. Here it answers the fearsome play of the Sky Gods with an astonished, even sacral vision of the dominant elements of air and water. The rainbow exorcizes the perilous spinning of "cartwheels" and "lids," and the line itself returns to the specific past ("today") that opened the poem, reversing the agency. Characteristically, the interaction between far and near works both as a movement in time and as a single esctatic vision. First we experience it in stages, from the rainbow following the rainsqualls to the "cow drinking" water (water for preservation now, but recalling the blissful feeding in the coral), to a sudden vision of the ultimate richness of things "right on the hair of the arm!" The macrocosm has become the microcosm; the smallness that had been humiliated instantly becomes a universe of wonder. We experience the entire parenthesis as a "double seeing," exploding from an explicit Buddhist perspective. "LAKHS of crystal Buddha fields" (the Sanskrit term means "vast multitudes") suggests the great Hwa-yen tenet, that the blissful totality of creation exists in the tiniest of its parts. "In every particle of dust there are present Buddhas without number." "On the point of a single hair the whole Buddha land may be seen."[23] Again, we encounter the mystery of Indra's net.

The opening of the next section marks the decisive break in the poem, its "folding" place, where the present moment punctures recollection: "right on the hair of the arm!) / Who wavers right now in the bamboo: / a half-gone waning moon." "Who wavers . . ." Left open at the front to absorb anything that precedes, the subject purposely misty on that side (and grammatically disconnected from the plural "Sky Gods"), the line itself seems to emerge out of the void, reverberating with the mystery of a single charged presence. Yet it invites all the preceding events of the poem into itself. Quite suddenly, the several manifestations of the island gods are apprehended as a single presence, connected with the moon. We sense

that it is out of this immediate encounter that the invocatory recollections have emerged. We are entrapped by these two lines; they
induce us to hover and circle rather than proceed. It is the first full
stop in the poem, and the "o" and "a" sounds create a luxurious
zone of harmonies. Then we grasp the opening movement of the
poem as flowing into it, climaxing with the echo of "right on the
hair . . ." in "right now". In fact, we are returned to the parenthesis
section with new appreciation. In the sudden collapse of its juxtaposed
dimensions into the physical immediacy of the poet's arm hair, it
anticipates the way the opening addresses collapse into "Who wavers
right now in the bamboo." The effect is of two successive explosions,
the larger upon the smaller, shaking the poem from its roots.

   "A half-gone waning moon" follows the colon. Is the moon the
wavering object? We must be sensitive enough to the poetic arrangement to realize that the moon is not positioned to simply *replace*
"Who". An "empty" presence hovers there, "right now," investing
the moon with its potency. The experience of the many—the various
aspects of the gods—leads to and from this physically arresting
intuition of the One.

   From this pivotal realization in the present, the poem's balance
shifts decisively to the speaker, no longer passive and intimidated,
drinking shochu to the gods. The stance, casual and even a bit reckless,
is possessed by a new momentum.

> drank down a bowlful of shochu
>   in praise of Antares
> gazing far up the lanes of Sagittarius
>   richest stream of our sky—
> a cup to the center of the galaxy!
>   and let the eyes stray
> right-angling the pitch of the Milky Way:
>   horse-heads     rings
> clouds     too distant to be
> slide free.
>   on the crest of the wave.

The vast night sky is charted out in terms of human comprehension—
"lanes," "Antares" (Gary and Masa's patron star) and "Sagittarius
. . . of our sky". This is not, as before, an intimidating, trespassed
kingdom. But the self-confident familiarity here is no more final than
the opening obliteration of human intentions. It assumes its place as
a balancing flow of self, a relaxation into heightened receptivity to
the receding patterns of the cosmos, stretching far beyond our frames
of reference. The shochu helps: "drank down," in happy obedience
to the poem's laws, inspires "gazing far up." The stress is on the

poet's delight and freedom, before the focus shifts to the staggering sights contemplated.

A new sense of harmony and stability, which will govern the remainder of the poem, is achieved through the marvelous euphonies of this passage, as well as through the constant expansion and contraction of its movement. The vowel play sounds ongoing harmonies on "a," climaxing in the final end rhymes. An alert ear will note the presence of end-rhymes throughout, muted at first, then flattening emphatically to strengthen the sense of the poet's own equilibrium, tested at the limits of eye and mind. At right angles to the Milky Way are other galaxies, nebulae, ungraspable flings of space, forms drifting beyond our reference yet somehow continuous with the prevailing harmony. There is a double stop at the close—first for the cloudy patterns receding from the speaker (hence *strangely* earth-like), then for the wave that hefts even them on its crest. (The shift, of course, is from the many to the one: another anticipation.) The wave completes the suggestion of physical momentum in "the pitch of the Milky Way".

The rich, peaceful assurance of the poem's final movement flows out of the satisfactions of the next section. The poet is finally grounded in relation to place and woman, both of which are united in the Earth Mother archetype. The wave-spiral pattern (glimpsed in the starry spaces and embodied in its narration) is repeated here in intimate, tactile terms. Again, the cause is that dialectical reflex that is felt as the poem's guiding presence.

> Each night
> O Earth Mother
>  I have wrappt my hand
>  over the jut of your cobra-hood
>                   sleeping;
>    left my ear
> All night long by your mouth.

Why is this so piercing? We are tempted to abandon the context in deference to immediacies, but much of the force here depends upon its fulfillment of needs frustrated earlier. A tranquil, reciprocal relation between the poet and the island has been long awaited. In the delayed turning to the female power of earth we feel relief and a sense of fitness and completion. The relationship is habitual and intimate, really quite sexual, instead of remote and intimidating. The poet is a native rather than a trespasser, cooperative rather than passive, and steadily in touch with the female rather than subject to tyrannous male gods.

As its opening indicates ("Each night / O Earth Mother"), the address is an assured acknowledgement of the habitually lived connection, the more wondrous for being familiar. Rhetorically, its effectiveness owes much to being the first complete sentence of the poem. And for the first time, the first person subject is explicit. Simple grammatical completenesses satisfy, alerting us that we had missed them. "Jut" hefts its wonderfully tactile suggestiveness into the serpentine flow of the Earth Mother, so that the punning phrase, "cobra-hood," implies both the coiled ambivalence of the mistress of life and death and the *mons veneris* of her human incarnation, the poet's wife.

We are closer now to some understanding of the decisive effect of this passage, which stabilizes the poem. The physical satisfaction suggested in the texture is heightned by the iconic tensions it controls. The Earth Mother's "cobra-hood" may recall the serpentine aspect of Kundalini Shakti in Tibetan lore, where the stress is upon the coiled life energy. But the cobra more likely suggests the dark aspect of Kali, India's primordial chthonic goddess. Erich Neumann cites an especially "frightful" representation of Kali with "phallic animal breasts," delicately fondling one of two cobras at her head: "But with its hooded head, the cobra that is twined round her waist like a girdle suggests the womb—here in its deadly aspect."[24] In the long Tamil verse narrative called *The Ankle Bracelet*, Shalini, the temple priestess of Kali, is praised in conventional terms that are relevant here:

> The virtues of the girl with the golden ornaments
>   are boundless.
> Her pubis is like a cobra's hood.
> She wears the ornaments of Aiyai, goddess of death.[25]

This iconic material nourishes Snyder at a fruitful psychic depth, re-emerging as inspired invention: the speaker "handles" the dangerous power of the Earth Mother by entrusting his body to her erotic and protective aspects. Yet it is pure mythic thinking—there is no compromise of her primordial ambiguity, nor is there any blurring of the sharp line of image and feeling unified. The rich symbolism of the female archetype recurs throughout Snyder's writings—as voice, spiral, muse, earth, lover, and source—but nowhere is it more quietly resonant than here. Functionally, the Earth Mother reconciles place and marriage. The danger of the island powers is absorbed into her, and the faintly submerged image of sleeping lovers becomes an experience of rest in the flow of the life-process.

Finally, the verse form of this astonishing passage guides us into a key theme of the entire island cycle. The lines carry longer, building a wave whose momentum spills into "sleeping". This crucial word of the section, suspended between its two flowing movements, is placed just beneath "cobra-hood," as if to arrest and contain rather than undercut its dangerous potency. "Sleeping" applies to all the persons here. Bodily parts—hand, ear, and mouth—are disposed at the line-ends, simply "left" there, as the poet says of his ear, inviting trusting contact with the Other. Two haunting lines from the Han Shan translations come to mind: "Today I'm back at Cold Mountain: / I'll sleep by the creek and purify my ears." Sleep is a positive, symbolic state for Snyder. ("Rainbow Body" culminates in the same focus—"dazzled ears".) The stress is less on the psychological fact of passive dependence than on the bodily satisfaction of being "in touch" with the source of things. The ear that is "left" all night knows by touching. "Sleeping" so, the ear is sensuously awake, the antithesis of visually distanced knowing: "left my ear / All night long by your mouth." Literally inspired by the breath of the Earth Mother, the poet's craft is itself an extension of the processes everywhere nourishing her kingdom.

The inclusive address that follows is pure abstraction, yet it is poetically earned, poetically expressive.

> O   All
> Gods   tides   capes   currents
> Flows and spirals of
>      pool and powers—

We do not find the leap between opposite realms of utterance odd; it would be odd if abstraction were excluded from the poem's spiraling dialectic, if its totalizing function were not allowed to play its role. (Again, the point is applicable to all Snyder's work. "Anything that works, I'll use.") "All" is capitalized to suggest the oneness the poem has led us to glimpse, behind its own "flows and spirals". Snyder handles the stressed monosyllables like natural events, building them into waves crashing at the line-ends. Thus the entire flow of this little section is a wave, repeating the right-sliding wave-like movement of the preceding sections in its climatic fall. In every way possible, events are resolved into a momentum that spills into a paradoxical emptiness, the One Mind of the controlling presence behind the poem.

That presence, of course, is the tacit subject of the poet's long-awaited prayer. By a familiar intuitional logic, it turns to the immediate context of the gathered community from the most comprehensive and abstract perspective. The secret of this priest-like request is knowing what *can* be given, by being already reconciled to the ways of the island.

> As we hoe the field
>    let sweet potato grow.
> And as sit us down when we may
> To consider the Dharma

> bring with a flower and a glimmer.
> Let us all sleep in peace        together.

The simple force of this opening, with its long "o" and "e" sounds sealing a zone of assured satisfaction, prepares us for the elegantly polite undermining of its syntactic structure in line three. Beyond its religious import, surrendering agency to the mysterious presence the invocations have realized, it is a very Japanese gesture of politeness. (Petitions are usually occasions for indirect expression in Japanese, to avoid coercive suggestions: "let . . . grow.")[26] The short, discrete monosyllables of the third line dramatize the carefully alert, lightly vertical spirits of the supplicants attending to the Dharma, that manifold term whose root is *dhr*, "to subsist or endure." (It means much more than "teachings".) The same receptive temper, with a note of esoterism perhaps, governs "bring with a flower and a glimmer." "Bring" is left open and suggestive on both sides, leaving both subject and object empty. Each possible subject animates it in its own way— the worshippers, the mysterious presence addressed, and even the Dharma—while the ambiguity suggests their interpenetrating identity. ("Both-and" is the prevailing rule, not "either-or") The worshippers bring offerings in the spirit of an ancient custom which Heinrich Zimmer cites from a Tantric source: "One should never approach a deity, image, or sanctuary, unless bearing flowers in one's hands."[27]

One sign of a poem's greatness is that the simplest of expressions acquires sudden weight and significance within its world, as though we had not really heard it before. "Let us all sleep in peace together" resonates so here, with a finality that has the entire poem behind it. The sleep that is the day's end peace of the island community is also the quietly charged receptivity of the poet's sleep at the feminine source of all life. It may seem an oddly passive symbol for a climax of integration and affirmation. In the paradoxical psychology of Zen tradition, one is advised "not to have thoughts in regard to things," but to experience them directly from the unconscious as Suchness, empty of striving, division or conditions. Or as Garma Chang puts it, "Sunyata can be grasped by seeing, hearing, even smelling, but never by thinking!"[28] "All . . . together" recalls the earlier intuition of cosmic Suchness ("O All / Gods tides . . ."), setting the peace of the human community within the larger Sangha of island powers. "Together" is set off to the side to spring this second meaning. Underlining "glimmer" and echoing "flower" as well, its soft, falling recall of the two ritual offerings halts the poem's flow. Their chord reverberates in the surrounding silence.

> Bless Masa and me as we marry
>     at new moon        on the crater
> This summer.

VIII. 40067

This is felt, when we reach it, as that which has been kept back all along, behind the addresses. The personal request has had to wait upon the larger quest, not only because of the diplomacy of ritual supplication but because the prayer for marital blessing must emerge from a balanced, living relation to the surrounding world if it is to be effective. Thinking of primitive society, Eliade declares, "Marital union is a rite integrated with the cosmic rhythm and validated by that integration."[29]

The balance and euphony at the outset of this final section centers in "me". We are meant to recall its opposite role in the poem's first line. The speaker's presence has been revalidated by and through the powers of the island. Formally, "me" breaks the first line into two rhyming movements, followed by equally short phrases which locate the marriage in the simplest of gestures to place and time. Falling end-rhymes ("crater," "summer") echo the closing chord of the previous section ("together"), to enter a larger, richer, more conclusive silence. The date ("40067") enforces what has been tacit throughout the invocations: regeneration through "responsibility and connection" with the living universe returns us to the era of the earliest cave painters. "In the 40,000 year time scale we're all the same people."[30]

## Notes

1. Gary Snyder *Regarding Wave* (N.Y., New Directions, 1970), p. 23.

2. "Open form": see Ekbert Faas, ed., *Towards A New American Poetics: Essays & Interviews* (Santa Barbara, Black Sparrow, 1978), pp. 10–12, 96–99, and Robert Kern, "Recipes, Catalogues, Open Form Poetics: Gary Snyder's Archetypal Voice," *Contemporary Literature*, 18, No. 2 (Spring 1977). "Belief": Charles Altieri, "Gary Snyder's *Turtle Island:* The Problem of Reconciling the Roles of Seer and Prophet," *boundary 2*, 4, No. 3 (Spring 1976).

3. Faas, p. 128.

4. Faas, p. 125.

5. Altieri, p. 770.

6. Gary Snyder, *Earth House Hold* (N.Y., New Directions, 1969), p. 19.

7. "Dance": Stephen Berg and Robert Mezey, ed., *Naked Poetry* (Indianapolis, Bobbs-Merrill, 1969), p. 357. "Mass ego": *Earth House Hold*, p. 122.

8. Public reading at South Quadrangle, University of Michigan, Ann Arbor, April 3, 1971.

9. Gary Snyder, *Myths & Texts* (N.Y., New Directions, 1978), p. viii.

10. *Ibid.*, p. viii; *Earth House Hold*, p. 129 and p. 134.

11. Kern, p. 197.

12. *Earth House Hold*, p. 121.

13. Mircea Eliade, *Cosmos and History: The Myth of Eternal Return* (N.Y., Harper Torchbook, 1959), pp. 4, 23–25.

14. Francis H. Cook, *Hwa-yen Buddhism: The Jewel Net of Indra* (University Park, Pa., Pennsylvania State University, 1977), p. 2.

15. *Earth House Hold*, p. 129.

16. *Ibid.*, p. 142.

17. *Ibid.*, p. 127.

18. Barbara Herrnstein Smith, *Poetic Closure* (Chicago, University of Chicago, 1968), p. 139.

19. *Earth House Hold*, p. 140.

20. William Barrett, ed., *Zen Buddhism: Selected Writings of D. T. Suzuki* (Garden City, N.Y., Doubleday Anchor, 1956), p. 241.

21. Motoori Norinaga (1730–1801) is the most famous scholar of Japanese antiquity. The quotation is from Sakamaki Shunzo, "Shinto: Japanese Ethnocentrism," in *The Japanese Mind*, ed. Charles A. Moore (Honolulu, East–West Center, 1967), p. 25.

22. Ichiro Hori, *Folk Religion in Japan: Continuity and Change* (Chicago, University of Chicago, 1968), pp. 150, 175–178.

23. Garma C. C. Chang, *The Buddhist Teaching of Totality: The Philosophy of Hwa Yen Buddhism* (University Park, Pa., Pennsylvania State University, 1971), pp. 4–6, 224, 390.

24. Erich Neumann, *The Great Mother: An Analysis of the Archetype* (Princeton, N.J., Bollingen, 1963), p. 153.

25. Prince Ilango Adigal, *Shilappadikaram (The Ankle Bracelet)*, trans. Alain Danielou (N.Y., New Directions, 1965), p. 80. I am grateful to Gary Snyder for sending me this reference.

26. Josef Koza, "The Japanese Way of Thinking as Seen Through Its Language," *Hitotsubashi Journal of Arts and Sciences*, 15, No. 1 (Sept., 1974), p. 19.

27. Heinrich Zimmer, *The Art of Indian Asia: Its Mythology and Transformations* (N.Y., Bollingen, 1955), Vol. I, p. 71.

28. Chang, p. 67.

29. Eliade, p. 25.

30. Gary Snyder, *The Old Ways* (San Francisco, City Lights, 1977), p. 33.

# Silence in Prosody:
# The Poem as Silent Form                    Robert Kern[°]

Prosodic innovation in the twentieth century is probably synonymous, for most of us, with the free verse revolution, representing a kind of ultimate innovation, a final departure from classical prosody, an abandonment of the rules or norms of metrical regularity that govern traditional verse in English. Yet the possibilities of innovation are not closed off but rather enhanced by the arrival of free or nonmetrical verse as the dominant post-Yeatsian form. Within the context of

° Reprinted from *Ohio Review* 26 (1981): 34–52, by permission of the author and *Ohio Review*.

liberation from the metrically-determined behavior of traditional poems, poets are free to undertake a more radical kind of tampering— not only with metrical systems (as Hopkins and Bridges had done before the close of the nineteenth century) but with grammar, syntax, and the very discursive structure of language regarded as a communicative or expressive medium. Prosodic innovation, that is to say, shades into a broader kind of innovation that makes the breaking of mere metrical rules quite old-fashioned. What we have now is a whole range of transgressions that radically question the traditional foundations of orderly discourse (though some might say that Whitman anticipates all later experiments).

From a greatly oversimplified historical perspective, we might discern two phases of prosodic innovation: first, a modernist, militantly experimental phase, characterized by the aggressive tone of Pound's resolve to "break the pentameter," and second, a more recent, more casual phase of apparent indifference to metrical matters that seems allied with the radically empiricist presuppositions of postmodernism. In the latter, it is content or reality, the Emersonian "metre-making argument," not the poet-as-creator or tradition, that determines form. And again in the latter, the desire for what Denise Levertov has called "fidelity to experience," demanding a freedom from any systematic, premeditated artfulness or convention, has been the governing motive, one which leads, perhaps, to its own versions of overdetermination of language for aesthetic purposes. Thus in recent writing we find not only a flight from traditional forms but a general tendency to confound expectations about beginnings and endings and about the behavior of the verse line, and a calculated blurring of the distinction between verse and prose. More specifically, we find several varieties of ambiguous or floating or run-on syntax in the work of poets as different as Frank O'Hara, W. S. Merwin, and A. R. Ammons, an increasing use of the prose poem (by such poets as Robert Bly and David Ignatow), David Antin's "natural language genres" or "talk poems," the formal but arbitrary "spontaneous, bop prosody" of Allen Ginsberg, Charles Olson's projectivism and prerational discourse, and Gary Snyder's highly disciplined "riprap," conceived as a way of countering the abstract force of language. Most of these procedures, it seems clear, derive from the general modernist movement away from conventional literary language and patterning toward the rhythms and styles of actual speech, a movement in which actual speech apparently becomes the privileged model for literary utterance. At the same time, and for all its dominance, it seems equally clear that this model is complicated by the competing presence of another one, based on the impulse to get away from language altogether and approximate the effects of nonverbal media like painting and sculpture—the purely presentational style of early twentieth-century Imagism.

If it is the case, however, that actual speech is the reigning style in contemporary poetic discourse, it is still necessary to be aware of differences between such speech in its natural state, so to speak, and the way it is represented or created poetically. The transcript of a taped conversation may be only partly intelligible to a reader, and this suggests the extent to which actual speech, as encountered in a literary text, is an illusion, largely a literary invention. What seems freely and naturally colloquial on the page, moreover, may turn out to be not speech at all, in the sense of overt conversation or voiced, communicative discourse, but a kind of inward, unaddressed meditation, a form of thinking, that depends for its effect on indeterminate patterning and run-on or discontinuous or otherwise unordered syntax—a prosody, we might say, that organizes into verse both voiced speech and the silent speech of thought. The actuality of such meditation or thinking, in fact, seems to depend ultimately on its deviation from speech, the degree to which it can suggest, by verbal and prosodic means, the not exclusively verbal medium of thought; and actuality here means uncalculated, unpolished, even (in theory) unintelligible, since private or interior speech need not meet the same criteria of intelligibility as public or simply voiced utterance. "Communication," as Barbara Herrnstein Smith points out in *Poetic Closure*, "is not the motive of thinking," and so the poem that purports to represent thinking is freed to this extent from the ordinary demands of syntax and logic. The burden of such a poem, as she goes on to argue, thus lies in its obligation to "affect its audience while pretending that it has no audience to affect." Such a poem, that is to say, must accurately reflect the structure of thinking and at the same time maintain its readability as a poem, the problem being, of course, that thinking, which may be only partly verbal, would seem to be at odds with readability.

Put in larger terms, we are dealing here, in an extreme form, with one of the basic problems of the post-Romantic lyric, the poem that attempts to erase the marks of its own production, that seeks to hide its artifice and appear spontaneous, artless, natural. The poem that represents thinking, going a step further, must hide not only its artifice but the very fact that it is a verbal utterance, creating the illusion not merely of spontaneity but of silence. Clearly relevant here also is the distinction, in Heidegger's meditations on language, between "idle talk" and "authentic speech," the latter related both to poetry and silence. In this essentially Romantic conception, poetry reveals the silence that lies beneath idle talk, the depths of unspoken possibility beneath what can be said, and in this sense the language of poetry is ambiguous, breaking silence in order to call attention to it. What is required by the poem as silent form is thus a kind of collapsing of the differences between idle talk and authentic speech, a language that remains itself (for the sake of readability) even as it leads beyond itself (into silence and Being), or a "reticence," as Heidegger puts it in *Being and Time*, that "makes something manifest." A poet like W. S. Merwin often seems to be on the verge of just such a language (one can never be more than on the verge of it), and a younger poet influenced by him, Charles Simic, offers this formulation of its character in some comments on one of his own poems: "I wanted to include in the poem everything that I found unsayable. That is, retain the ambiguity of its origins. It seems to me that poetry aims to stand on that threshold. The poem as the vague figure in the doorway. Ambiguity as whatever still preserves the memory of the other side. Words which still retain the pressure of the unspoken" (from *Fifty Contemporary Poets*).

Far from being an exotic or idiosyncratic effort, then, the poem as silent form actually represents an extension—to an almost terminal point, admittedly—of a lyric mode essential to modern poetry, the poem as act of mind, which continues to be the most prestigious if not the only form of contemporary lyric. Certainly, few poets writing today seem willing to run the hazards of assuming, with any conviction, a public voice. A conservative critic like Paul Fussell acknowledges (in *Poetic Meter and Poetic Form*) that one of the most dominant styles in contemporary poetry is essentially "meditative and ruminative or private . . . a vehicle for themes that are sly or shy, or uncertain, or quietly ironic, or furtive." And a committed open formalist like Denise Levertov continues to promote what she calls "exploratory" poetry, whose value, as she sees it, lies in its ability to incorporate and reveal "the *process* of thinking / feeling, feeling / thinking, rather than focusing more exclusively on its *results*" ("On the Function of the Line," *Chicago Review*, Vol. 30, No. 3)—an understanding of poetry clearly allied with Williams's idea that the poet thinks with his poem, so that poetic structure becomes a medium for thinking as opposed to a display-case for thoughts.

A traditionalist might lament the fact that the contemporary insistence on open form and fidelity to experience ultimately narrows and limits the field of poetic possibility, declaring the illegitimacy of certain historical forms and styles. And he might deplore the fact that what is legitimate often seems to be merely notes for a poem, random jottings, as opposed to any fully achieved statement, precisely the *results* of thought and labor. Yet the analysis of poets like Levertov and critics like Robert Langbaum and others suggests that the poem as act of mind, or mind in action, is the only one that can sustain serious belief or commitment (from both writer and reader) in our current philosophical and cultural context, one in which man as a maker of forms and a creator of order has lost much of his authority. In fact, one meaning of "silence" in contemporary art is the near-abandonment of all efforts to order or make sense of experience, based on the assumption that such efforts can have only fictive results. The problem with a traditional form like the sonnet, as Levertov points out, is that it conveys a sense of conclusion or closure regardless of what it expresses, sealing the poem off from experience that concludes (if at all) neither with the sonnet's structural neatness nor with its underlying implications of certitude. The problem with such a structure, that is to say, is precisely that in its formal implications it is a stay against confusion. On the other hand, a poet like A. R. Ammons can announce, with a programmatic exuberance that almost undoes itself:

> I have reached no conclusions, have erected no boundaries,
> shutting out and shutting in, separating inside
>     from outside: I have
>     drawn no lines. . . .        (from *Collected Poems*)

Of course, the poem without closure *par excellence* is the poem that represents thinking, which, in its fidelity to experience or consciousness, is not provided with any principle of termination. The question raised by such poems is not only how they end but how their necessary conclusiveness as poems can be made consistent with the process that they represent. As for silent poems, we might well ask how they can even begin.

To attempt answers to these questions, I shall turn now to the example of a silent poetry, or at least of a prosody that tries to organize elements beyond the strictly linguistic, that is provided by the work of Gary Snyder, a poet whose anti-conceptual bias compels him to separate actuality from speech and to pursue a poetry that privileges not speech but silence, the latter understood to constitute a reality larger than language can account for. The aim in much of his work is not the modernist dream of the poem that achieves the condition of a thing, however "dumb" or "wordless," but the poem that is more a seeing (or perhaps a thinking) than a saying, a near-mute presentation, without commentary, of the world's ongoing processes. The role of mind or thinking in this work is participatory, not explanatory, judgmental, or form-giving. Decidedly, it is a poetry of meaning rather than being, though the meaning remains unspoken, outside the language which somehow invokes it. As such, and from the point of view of more traditional styles, it is a poetry that thrives on its own poverty, one whose special expressiveness depends on its implied and actual deletions, its several kinds of reticence, the way it seems to cut back on language and device, the extent to which it can efface itself, before the nonverbal reality it wishes to present, and approximate silence—the way, finally, it attempts to eliminate its own ontological status as poetry.

Taken too seriously or literally, of course, such an ambition can only become self-defeating. As Michael Wood remarks of A. R. Ammons's wish for material which "says itself," "a little more of that sort of material would put the poet out of business. The poet, after all, is an interpreter speaking for silent things" *(The New York Review of Books)*. That Snyder understands this is made clear by his conception of the poet as a mediator situated between "the world of people and language and society" and "the non-human, non-verbal world" *(A Biographical Sketch and Descriptive Checklist of Gary Snyder)*. Yet he seems to regard language—in its character as substance rather than function, its tendency to form a systematic web constituting its own reality—as a greater danger than silence, and his craft might be described as an effort to keep language as functional and transitive as possible. Still, the problem of silent forms, as Keats discovered, lies not only in their threat to poetry but in the way they can tease us out of thought altogether. For Snyder, though, this problem becomes a basic poetic strategy, as his poems in this mode seemingly and willingly enact a movement out of thought and out of the self, enabled by a prosody and syntax that disappear or die away into fragments as the poem proceeds. In "Burning the Small Dead," for example, a key lyric in *The Back Country*, the opening block of five lines and parts of lines is the most confident, the most fully voiced, the most continuous in its verse movement in the poem, and even this is slow, hesitant, and grammatically ambiguous, most likely consisting of a dependent clause that simply fails to complete itself in a larger grammatical structure, although it could also be read as a complete sentence with an "I am" phrase omitted at the beginning:

> Burning the small dead
>           branches
>     broke from beneath
>       thick spreading
>         whitebark pine.

The next lines, containing the poem's only verb, do form a complete sentence, though it is somewhat disguised by Snyder's refusal to capitalize and by tricks of spacing:

>       a hundred summers
>   snowmelt   rock   and air
>
>   hiss in a twisted bough.

Serving to set the scene and to initiate the poem's contemplative movement, these opening sets of lines speak in the poem's fullest speech style, based on patterns that are grammatical, or nearly so, in structure. In their hesitancy and brokenness, however, the shifting left margin especially effecting a suspension of enjambment, they are still far from what we might call actual speech. And as the rest of the poem breaks down into a verbless series of phrases and fragments which we must put together for ourselves, we encounter a style that is even less fluent as speech. Yet this becomes the poem's most expressive medium, a scant, elliptical language, nevertheless convincing as a kind of colloquial mental shorthand, whose meaning, like that of most metonymic styles, depends almost entirely on external context:

> sierra granite;
>   mt. Ritter—
>   black rock twice as old.

> Deneb, Altair

> windy fire

Beginning, then, with a focus on concrete physical activity, the poem takes an increasingly inward direction as the speaker shifts his attention from what he is doing to what he is thinking, or at least to the impressions borne in upon him by the fire of small dead branches and the stars. The grammatical indeterminancy of the last several lines—their syntactical discontinuity and freedom from pattern—becomes a rich way of registering the speaker's fluid state of mind, in which a variety of elements and impressions—past and present, rock and fire, the immediately near and the cosmically distant—come together as a unity. Although the tune of something like the classical cretic foot (' $\cup$ ') plays throughout the poem ("whitebark pine," "twisted bough," "twice as old," "windy fire"), it is not meter but grammar and syntax that constitute the poet's means of establishing and varying from pattern. The pattern here is the complete or nearly complete sentence, a form expressing ordinary consciousness and the self's ordinary construction of reality, though the poem barely establishes this form before losing it. As the lines at the end of the poem break up into isolated phrases and fragments that never come together to form grammatical wholes—as those at the beginning of the poem do—they become its intensest signs of inwardness and of awed, silent perception, a subordination of word-order to a larger order outside language, of speech to silence. We are given not a completed thought, certainly, and perhaps not even a complete representation of Denise Levertov's "process of thinking / feeling, feeling / thinking," but the ingredients, the basic elements of such a process. Only the syntax is missing, and the poem implies that it is available, in a different form, outside the poem—in the actual relations of things. The poem, finally, is about that syntax, a celebration of that external system of relations, though it cannot embody it in its own verbal medium.

It is important to understand that syntax breaks down in Snyder's poem not out of allegiance to a naively mimetic theory about the relation of order or disorder in language to order or disorder in the world. This is not an instance of what has been called the fallacy of imitative form. As Donald Justice points out, "it was never the obligation of words or of word-order to imitate conditions so reflexively. Syntax deals, after all, primarily with word-order, not world-order" ("Meters and Memory," *Antaeus,* No. 30/31). And Snyder, it is clear, rather than confusing his poem with reality, maintains the distinction, allowing the inadequacies of language or speech to suggest the external plenitude.

It is by means of its faltering and dwindling speech, then, and the carefully arranged blanks or pauses between its lines and groups of lines, that Snyder incorporates silence into his poem as an expressive element, achieving also in this way a new kind of closure. The poem's ending is not a conclusion but a fade-out; the silence which is organized into its structure becomes increasingly dominant and finally takes over, as language gives way to vision. Thus Snyder offers one answer to Barbara Herrnstein Smith's question about the possibility of closure in a poem that concludes "as a fragment or with the dissolution of its elements." Such a poem both does and does not achieve closure in the sense that its silent, nonverbal element continues to reverberate after its verbal elements cease to function.

We can gauge the originality of Snyder's achievement here if we briefly contrast it with the work of Wallace Stevens, a poet who is equally, if ambivalently, attracted to silence but who does not depart from the conventions of traditional prosody and grammatical speech. Stevens's interest in silence is based on a modernist impatience with the conceptual and representative nature of language and a corresponding desire for unmediated expression, for the thing itself, invoked everywhere in his work. Yet silence remains an ambiguous ideal in that work. In a late poem, Stevens refers to what he calls the "plain sense of things" as a kind of zero degree of existential reality, a quality of bareness or blankness that is essentially nonlinguistic and that implies the excessiveness of language in its relation to the world. "It is difficult," he says, "even to choose the adjective / For this blank cold" *(Collected Poems).* To say anything about this unspeakable condition is to say too much, and Stevens avoids this, and avoids choosing an adjective as well, by punning on "blank." Yet as a poet Stevens is committed to speech—and not only speech but highly organized structures of verse that are persistently and traditionally metrical in their movement. In the early and well-known poem "The Snow Man," this same bare reality is described as "Nothing that is not there and the nothing that is." Again, there is nothing to say about such a reality. Saying is a human activity, but what the snow man beholds has no human content and is therefore unsayable. There is no way of introducing such a reality into a poem without denying or defeating the poem. To a great extent, of course, Snyder would accept these strictures, except that he regards silence not as a submission to the void but as an appropriate response to the fullness of "what is really here," a fullness that renders speech practically unnecessary, a tautological restatement of "what is really here," though language, particularly versified language, can scarcely contain it.

Our analysis of "Burning the Small Dead," in any case, makes possible a broader description of Snyder's prosody. In its general features, it follows upon some of Pound's discoveries and procedures and takes particular advantage of what Donald Davie has described as Pound's achievement of a dismembered line, an achievement based on a prior recognition of the line as the structural unit of verse. One of Pound's earliest uses of the line as a structural or compositional unit was in *Cathay*, his small collection of translations from the Chinese published in 1915, and it is interesting that Snyder arrived at a similar compositional decision not for the specific purposes of translation but as part of a general effort both to adhere to (Poundian) principles of sharpness, economy, and clarity, and to try and write English as though it were Chinese. The value placed on the single line in *Cathay* is closely allied with the replacement of meter by syntax or the use of syntax as a metrical device. Pound, as Davie suggests, was probably influenced by Ernest Fenollosa's argument about the way in which the basic format of the simple sentence reflects natural process and therefore constitutes the most natural vehicle for poetic expression. Thus Pound contrived to produce a verse in which line and sentence more or less coincide. Although variations of movement are possible, the general effect of such a procedure is greatly to slow the verse down. But what is most important is the activity inside the line that this deceleration of verse-movement makes possible. "It was only when the line was considered as the unit of composition," Davie writes in *Ezra Pound: Poet as Sculptor*, "that there emerged the possibility of 'breaking' the line, of disrupting it from within, by throwing weight upon smaller units within the line." It is precisely these "smaller units within the line," phrases and pieces of dismembered larger lines, that constitute the compositional units of Snyder's verse, which thus becomes a structure not of lines, strictly speaking, but of phrases, not of sentences or complete syntactical units but of an atomized syntax.

If Pound's tendency in *Cathay* was to disrupt the line *from within* while maintaining the line itself as a basic structural unit, Snyder's verse displays the literal results of that disruption in its very appearance on the page, a visual or spatial dismemberment of the line into smaller units. Most characteristically, his poems are arranged in patterns with varying left margins that call attention to the integrity of the phrase units as rhythmic units. They demand to be read slowly, with less enjambment than in poems composed in more conventional stichic patterns, since each phrase requires more or less full recognition as a unit. And just as the rhythms are unpredictable, often varying from phrase to phrase (but usually heavily spondaic), so are the syntactical relationships between the phrases—an uncertainty which makes reading these poems a continual process of deciding (and often revising what has been decided) about the extent to which the phrase units are combining to form larger grammatical wholes or maintaining their identity as fragments. It is this sort of structure, in which the rhythmic patterns of the phrase units are fairly prominent, that gives Snyder's poetry its formality despite its grammatical looseness, and that sets it apart from contemporary styles that attempt to adhere more closely to actual speech. In the case of James Wright, for example, as Charles Molesworth points out, we find a verse-movement "which doesn't value the single line so much as the reverberations at the end of the stanza" ("James Wright and The Dissolving Self," *Salmagundi*, No. 22–23), so that we are propelled through Wright's poems toward their often highly-charged endings. In Snyder, on the other hand, our movement through a poem, and even through a line, is continually arrested by the unitary nature of the line and by the frequently heavy stressing in its rhythm, which keeps our attention focused on things and events rather than the logical and linguistic operations of the text. Such closural force as we find in Wright and perhaps also in Robert Bly is deliberately eliminated from poems like "Burning the Small Dead," in which spatial arrangement and fading language are designed to enact the appropriation of voice by silence, and that poem nicely exemplifies the basic structure I have been describing. A more sustained example is contained in this passage from "December," the final lyric of the sequence "Six Years":

> Saiza a quarter to ten
> soup and rice dab on the bench
> feed the hungry ghosts
>    back in the hall by noon.
> two o clock sanzen
> three o clock bellywarmer
>    boild up soup-rice mush.
> dinging and scuffing. out back smoke,

and talk.
At dusk, at five,
black robes draw into the hall.
    stiff joints, sore knees bend
    the jiki pads by with his incense lit,
        bells,
    wood block crack
& stick slips round the room
on soft straw sandals.

Here, in what is essentially a chronological narrative about an intensive meditation session in a Zen monastery—which in itself is remarkable since the poem's style seems more suitable for the expression of simultaneity than for a temporally sequential narrative—enjambment disappears almost entirely as the lines or phrases, syntactically fragmentary as they are, assert their rhythmic autonomy. There is just enough continuity—as in "At dusk, at five / black robes draw into the hall" or "& stick slips round the room / on soft straw sandals"— to tempt us to look for more, though we do so at our peril if we assume, for example, that "bend" in "sore knees bend" is transitive and read on into the next line as though "the jiki" were its object. In fact, there is little syntactical continuity between the lines, and there are only a few instances of lines or groups of lines that assume a complete grammatical form. What we have instead is a paratactic series of elliptical phrases that are autonomous rhythmic units, the style of a mind withholding its own subjectivity and apparently asserting little or no control over its experience, enthralled by an external discipline (though the poet behind the poem, as opposed to the speaker within it, is clearly asserting a great deal of artistic control over the sequences of stressed and unstressed syllables that make up his rhythmic units). The poem, after all, is about the effort to attain enlightenment, the pursuit of a vision of selflessness; the mind that imposes its control over experience in the form of continuous and grammatically-ordered sentences is in a state of suspension. Although the overall impression is that the poem is being composed line by line, with only minimal concern for coherent relationships between lines, the last-quoted stanza displays various kinds of movement and relationship, with the first two lines forming a complete sentence and the fifth, the single word "bells," comprising a unit, as Davie would say, that has broken free from the line of which it was a member. If the whole poem, with its cyclic structure (the end more or less repeating the beginning), exhibits a more conventional kind of closure than "Burning the Small Dead," this is not because it is less a representation of meditation or thinking but because its structure depends on the external organization of the monastery session, a human order instead of a natural one, with a sequential pattern and closure that are highly perceptible. Yet the poet's response is the same. When the activities of the session are over, so is the poem. Without those activities to reflect, he falls silent.

This kind of closure, in fact, is fairly common throughout Snyder's work, suggesting the extent to which his poems, as metonymic structures, depend on external context for their coherence. Yet it also calls attention to the differences between nonverbal experience and the poems it gives rise to, since poems are inevitably aesthetic and structured in a way that experience is not. For all the neutrality, objectivity, and "muteness" of the speaker in "December," the poem ultimately assumes a shape that results from his selection of details and his particular modelling of the experience. The closest Snyder can come to erasing the differences is by blurring them through a fading-out of speech into silence, which amounts to an attempt to avoid closure as much as possible. In a more recent poem, on the other hand, Snyder seems to go to the opposite extreme, offering an explicit, self-conscious instance of metonymic closure that underlines rather than hides the differences between the poem as a poem and its sources in external experience. At the end of "Straight-Creek—Great Burn," the poet sees (or hears) "A whoosh of birds" fly up into the sky. Their flying is "all apart" and yet also "of one . . . mind," and so constitutes an image of unity in anarchy. Finally,

> They arc and loop & then
> their flight is done.
> they settle down.
> end of poem.

The simplest way to read this ending is as a reminder of the close relationship between the poem and the experience it is based on. When the experience ends, as in "December," so does the poem. Yet to say "end of poem" is to call quite explicit attention to the differences between the poem as an aesthetic structure and the experience it reflects, which exhibits no such closure, or at least contains nothing that corresponds to the utterance "end of poem." That utterance, we might say, is in excess of the facts upon which the poem is based, and to that extent violates their silence (as well as the poem's). On the other hand, Snyder could be trying to regard the experience, the flight and settling down of the birds, as itself a poem or aesthetic event. But with this reading we are forced back into the contradiction between the wish for material which "says itself" and the unavoidable knowledge that the poet is an interpreter speaking for silent things. Indeed, that knowledge seems clear in Snyder's explicit interpretation of the birds' unruly flight as an instance, nonetheless, of the essential order of nature.

More than anything else, it is this explicitness and the didacticism

of his recent work, however much demanded by a sense of ethical
and ecological urgency, that signal Snyder's movement away from
the poem as silent form. His poetry has always had an underlying
ethical and didactic dimension, but the work in *Turtle Island* is more
and more addressed to an audience, and to that extent seems increasingly willing to moralize overtly and to take on the status and
style of more conventional kinds of poetic discourse—discourse that
an audience can readily follow even at a public reading. In fact, what
is most striking about many of the poems in this book is the degree
to which they assume the presence of an audience, the sense they
convey of having been expressly composed for oral performance.
Although this alone may account for their oversimplifications of argument, the problems with these poems seem to me to derive mostly
from the fact that Snyder's prosody cannot easily or successfully
accommodate finished, discursive thought and abstract moral reasoning. From the outset, his style was meant to be an anti-style, a
medium for the quick, accurate, and reticent notation of metonymic
detail that would provide no foothold for the subjective ego or analytic
intellect, and this is true even of the early poems in *Riprap*, hampered
as they may be by their reliance on fuller speech patterns and a
prosody that seems torn between more or less conventional metrics
and an urge toward something new but insufficiently worked out. As
Thomas Parkinson has noticed about this early work, it "moves naturally in traditional meters and then tries to deny the movement."
In a relatively weak poem like "Above Pate Valley," for example,
it's important to see that Snyder is in pursuit of effects similar to
the unaddressed meditation and awed silence of "Burning the Small
Dead," but the poem includes more descriptive detail and more talk
than such effects require. Metrically, it starts out with a basically
accentual rhythm, but as it proceeds the rhythm is obscured, not
simply by enjambment but by an increasing tendency of the lines to
yield their rhythmic integrity to the demands of syntactic continuity.
Prosodically indecisive, Snyder seems unclear about how he wants
the poem to be read, and the result is a shapeless line and an awkward
verse-movement:

> We finished clearing the last
> Section of trail by noon,
> High on the ridge-side
> Two thousand feet above the creek—
> Reached the pass, went on
> Beyond the white pine groves,
> Granite shoulders, to a small
> Green meadow watered by the snow,
> Edged with Aspen—sun
> Straight high and blazing

> But the air was cool.
> Ate a cold fried trout in the
> Trembling shadows. I spied
> A glitter, and found a flake
> Black volcanic glass—obsidian—
> By a flower. Hands and knees
> Pushing the Bear grass, thousands
> Of arrowhead leavings over a
> Hundred yards. Not one good
> Head, just razor flakes
> On a hill snowed all but summer,
> A land of fat summer deer,
> They came to camp. On their
> Own trails. I followed my own
> Trail here. Picked up the cold-drill,
> Pick, singlejack, and sack
> Of dynamite.
> Ten thousand years.

As a closural gesture, the line "Ten thousand years" does look forward to the sort of silent realization dramatized in "Burning the Small Dead." In its phrasal and rhythmic autonomy, it contrasts starkly with the volubility of what precedes it, and that contrast, one assumes, is the point of the poem, meant to carry the weight of the speaker's sudden insight. But it is too little and comes too late in the poem to be fully effective as a significant reversal of style. Unassimilated and abortive, it dangles inertly.

A comparison between these poems, however, does suggest the extent to which "Burning the Small Dead" represents a kind of stylistic and prosodic ideal for Snyder, a poetic possibility which he consciously pursued throughout the early period of his development as a writer. What is initially surprising about his recent work, then, is its apparent swing in the opposite direction—toward an audience-oriented rhetoric, strong closure, and forms that, in their frequent closeness to ritualized chant, are highly foregrounded. The movement in many of the poems is toward slogan rather than silence, an acknowledgement on Snyder's part that as he takes up what he calls spokesmanship for nature he is increasingly speaking for silent things and no longer trying to let them speak for themselves. Indeed, *Turtle Island* is the first of his books of verse to include a section of prose statements and essays as a supplement to the poems, as if to make up for their deficiencies in getting his (or nature's) message across. Called "Plain Talk" (as opposed to the poems' fancy or circumlocutory talk?), this section's inclusion is evidence of Snyder's need to address an audience more directly than his exclusive role of poet would seemingly allow. But it also betrays an almost Victorian uneasiness about the social and political inadequacies, the merely aesthetic status,

of poetry. The purpose of the prose is to allow Snyder both to explain
and perform his new role as a representative of "the wilderness, my
constituency." Yet the poems in the book also serve those functions
and are no less open about his social goals and political convictions,
even if these are reduced to bare pronouncements, generalized conclusions attached to brief runs of imagery and lyric commentary,
since it is precisely the reasoning or analysis behind his positions that
his most characteristic style is not suited to contain. The poem "For
the Children," with its slogan-like conclusion of flower-child wisdom—*"stay together / learn the flowers / go light"*—seems the most
egregious example of the naive, utopian generalizing that Snyder
indulges in *Turtle Island,* but a brief catalogue of some typical endings
will suggest the overall tone and closural force of these poems, as
well as the degree to which they are aimed at an audience—an
audience, one might add, of the already initiated rather than one to
be persuaded:

> In the shadow of the bluffs
> > I came back to myself,
> To the real work, to
> > "What is to be done."
> > (from "I Went into the Maverick Bar")

> Behind is a forest that goes to the Arctic
> And a desert that still belongs to the Piute
> And here we must draw
> Our line.                                    (from "Front Lines")

> I would like to say
> Coyote is forever
> Inside you.
>
> But it's not true.                      (from "The Call of the Wild")

> We could live on this Earth
> without clothes or tools!      (from "By Frazier Creek Falls")

> hold it close
> give it all away.                    (from "Up Branches of Duck River")

> Taste all, and hand the knowledge down.
> > (from "Ethnobotany")

> There is no other life.      (from "Why Log Truck Drivers Rise
> > Earlier Than Students of Zen")

Surprisingly straightforward and simplified for immediate reception
by an audience, these endings may be enough to suggest that the

weakness of the poems which they conclude lies in the fact that they give us precisely the results of thinking but not the thinking itself, a violation of contemporary criteria for which Snyder's own earlier work serves virtually as a model. That earlier work, of course, gains its considerable moral authority not from direct didactic statement but from its achievement of a particular vision, a vision that we are implicitly invited to share by adopting the attitudes and values which Snyder firmly but quietly projects as experience. He is still capable of a major poem like "The Bath," whose large cultural significance lies entirely in its devoted massing of specific, observed particulars and whose "morality" emerges directly from concrete actions—so that the family bath becomes a form of prayer and a ritual of recognition of the unity of the family with itself and with the "Great Earth," transcending civilized taboos.

Yet there are sound reasons—primarily a sense of ecological urgency—why Snyder should feel constrained to pursue an expanded, public role for his work, if not to abandon his silent mode completely. The result of his doing so, however, is a deeply divided book, one in which the conflict is not simply between poetry and politics, irresponsible aesthetics on the one hand and committed moral action on the other. Rather, Snyder's political attitudes themselves seem complicated by an underlying feeling in the book that something must be done but that nothing can or need be done, and this emerges on several levels of its contents—in the paradoxical blend of Buddhist quietism and sixties activism that constitutes his ethics and is summed up in his slogan "Knowing that nothing need be done, is where we begin to move from," and, most deeply, in the two opposed senses of nature that lie at the heart of *Turtle Island*. One sense is well conveyed by the poem "The Call of the Wild," in which Snyder imagines the extinction of nature, a "war against earth," and ends with an envoy (quoted above) rejecting the insufficiency, indeed the sentimental fiction, of any merely imaginative preservation of nature: "I would like to say / Coyote is forever / Inside you. / / But it's not true." Nature is seen here as seriously threatened and victimized by man to the point of annihilation, in need of defense and representation in the human world. The other sense emerges most clearly in a poem like "It Pleases," in which the poet, on a tour of Washington, D.C., the very source of violence against nature, has a vision which allows him to see through the monuments of power to the nothingness at their center:

> The center of power is nothing!
> Nothing here.
> Old white stone domes,
> Strangely quiet people,

Earth-sky-bird patterns
  idly interlacing

The world does what it pleases.

Here we encounter a self-sufficient, almost secret nature, serenely indifferent to the human world of politics and history, pursuing its own processes—precisely the reality that Snyder would uncover by exposing all the "arbitrary and inaccurate impositions on what is really here." Yet the visionary insight and spiritual security expressed in this poem are quite at odds with the urgency of environmental problems and the need for action and change to which so much of the rest of the book attests.

Contradictions like these suggest that Snyder's recent problems as a poet go beyond prosody alone. At the same time, those problems seem rooted in the strictness of his adherence to the main tenets of his basic style, one that is radically presentational and nondiscursive, a style specifically fashioned to avoid abstraction and the consecutiveness of logical thinking through its reliance on an atomized syntax and a rhythmic movement that rarely overrides the ends of individual lines or phrases. This style, as we have seen, seems best suited to the dramatization of ecstatic, silent encounters with the natural world. But as Snyder moves from such encounters to the fuller, more self-conscious kind of statement required by his role as spokesman for nature—moves, so to speak, from silence to history—he burdens his style, and increasingly exposes its limitations, by giving it tasks which could perhaps be better served by larger, more continuous verse structures, by a poetry more willing to acknowledge its distance from experience and its status as discourse. Yet he persists with his basic prosody and verse structure even as his work changes its character in other areas, asking to be regarded less as aesthetic construct than as ethically-charged statement—a change clearly underlined by the appearance of the "Plain Talk," supposedly free of aesthetic distortion, with which he now feels called upon to supplement his poems. It is hard, in any case, to avoid feeling that what Snyder needs is a verse structure that will lend greater support to the uses he now wants his poetry to serve, a style more congruent with the fact that his recent poems, no longer mute acts of attention, tend to be utterances in which the poet is present as self-conscious and self-possessed *speaker* rather than the awed witness of something almost beyond the reach of language.

There is still a sense, then, despite its changes, in which Snyder's poetry is less a form of speech than an emphatic instance of versecraft, based on a notion of poetic composition as the physical placing and arranging of words, the Poundian poetry-as-sculpture. To the extent that the presentational and discursive styles, as Helen Vendler has remarked, are the "antipodes of poetry . . . the one all mute, the other all analytic" ("Still Journeying On," *Poetry,* Vol. 133, No. 61), Snyder's persistence with essentially presentational methods keeps his work at a fairly extreme stylistic pitch, distinct from that of his contemporaries who pursue greater fluency and actuality of speech and achieve them largely by mediating between the presentational and the discursive. Thus in Ashbery we find a continual shifting of rhetorics and modes; in O'Hara a chattiness and "personism," especially in his "I do this, I do that" poems, that coexist easily with his Williams-like concentration on urban particulars; while Ammons, close to Snyder in some ways, seems to speak endlessly and even conclusively about not reaching conclusions and about the possibility of things saying themselves. Such mediation is apparent even in so radical an experiment as David Antin's "talk poems," in the light of which, Snyder, with his notion of "Plain Talk" as distinct from poetry, appears to be clinging rather conservatively to the traditional separation between verse and prose. (Once "natural language" is recognized to be a "genre," can any use of language be regarded as "natural" or "plain"?) As a seer, a poet of wilderness, Snyder has few peers. But his recent work suggests that the full registration of experience, both in and outside the poet, calls for a more inclusive style, a broader ranging across the entire spectrum of poetic possibility.

# [Ellipsis and Riprap: Gary Snyder]

Laszlo Géfin°

Of all the poets who have maintained and carried forward the kind of modernism Pound initiated, Snyder is the one who has returned, both in the mental as well as the physical sense, to the Orient, that important source which, through Fenollosa, furnished Pound with the concept of a new creative method. The archaic has been a determining factor in the poetics and practice of all ideogrammic poets, but it is Gary Snyder who has not only adopted and revitalized archaic modes of expression, but refashioned his thinking and life-style to such an extent that they all but exclude *in toto* the values and achievements of Western civilization. He has taken Olson's "archeology of morning" one step further: Snyder not only writes and feels and thinks, but

° Excerpted from *Ideogram, History of a Poetic Method* by Laszlo K. Géfin, © 1982 by the University of Texas Press. Reprinted by permission of the author and the publisher.

actually *lives* as if he existed after a true "dispersion," as if the whole of Western culture and way of life had already crumbled to dust. The "space" of America for him is "Turtle Island," the ancient Indian name for the continent, not expressible in the concentrated actuality of a Gloucester or a Paterson, but only as raw nature, the "wilderness." The community that alone is real to him is the group of people who live outside the norms and structures of postindustrial consumer society—the "tribe" of the new "primitives" living in harmony with nature. Within the nonhierarchic framework of the tribe the function of the poet is equivalent to the shaman, an essentially magical and heuristic activity. The shaman's unique ability gives form to archetypal strata of consciousness. Snyder defines shamanistic poetry as "the skilled and inspired use of the voice and language to embody rare and powerful states of mind that are in immediate origin personal to the singer, but at deep levels common to all who listen."[1] Such a poetic role stems from a vision which stands in complete opposition to the overbearing, rapacious, possessive kind of mentality which characterizes *homo technologicus,* and to the uncontrolled abuse and exploitation of nature and its resources. The vision demands a new (or postlogical) respect and love for nature, which Snyder calls "ecological conscience": "a new definition of humanism that would include the non-human." His poetry is the voice of this new "posthumanism," a revivification of discarded though enduring qualities and achievements:

> As poet I hold the most archaic values on earth. They go back to the late Paleolithic: the fertility of the soil; the magic of animals, the power-vision of solitude, the terrifying initiation and re-birth, the love and ecstasy of the dance, the common work of the tribe. I try to hold both history and wilderness in mind, that my poems may approach the true measure of things and stand against the unbalance and ignorance of our times.[2]

Snyder's archaism is far removed from an illusory, nostalgic "return to the soil." He is astute, sophisticated, learned, and much more. As Thomas Parkinson puts it, "If there has been a San Francisco renaissance, Snyder is its Renaissance man: scholar, woodsman, guru, artist, creatively maladjusted, accessible, open, and full of fun."[3] Other critics have called him the Thoreau of the Beat Generation, and influential force in the poetic community of the fifties and sixties, directing attention not only to sensible, ecology-conscious living but, through this first-hand study of Chinese and Japanese poetry, to poetic techniques best suited to embody the new consciousness. Not surprisingly, Snyder's models for composition included Pound and imagism, Fenollosa and the ideogram. But these influences have been supplemented by his direct study of oriental poetry (Snyder is fluent in Japanese and reads Chinese, and has spent several years in a Kyoto monastery studying Zen Buddhism). He has translated a good deal of poetry into English, chiefly from the work of the T'ang poet Han Shan and the modern Japanese poet Kenji Miyazawa—renderings which utilize and expand Pound's pioneering techniques in *Cathay* and *The Confucian Odes.*

Snyder—scholar, translator, *poeta doctus*—is an heir and continuator of modernism. In one critic's view, he "derives mainly from the Pound / Williams / Projectivist line," i.e., the ideogrammic tradition, and is "the subtlest craftsman of his generation."[4] Yet his method, his own version of ideogrammic composition, does not "derive" solely from his literary masters and predecessors. As with all the poets in the ideogrammic line, the method is equally the fruit of personal experiences and research. In Snyder's case, it characteristically comes from *work,* physical work, into which he threw himself with as much zest, concentration, and perseverance (he was a railroad brakeman, logger, and fire lookout, among others) as into his varied intellectual and artistic endeavors. The method was already at the base of his first published book of poems, *Riprap,* which Snyder has described vividly:

> *Riprap* is really a class of poems I wrote under the influence of the geology of the Sierra Nevada and the daily trail-crew work of picking up and placing granite stones in tight cobble pattern on hard slab. "What are you doing?" I asked old Roy Marchbanks.— "Riprapping," he said. His selection of natural rocks was perfect— the result looked like dressed stone fitting to hair-edge cracks. Walking, climbing, placing with the hands. I tried writing poems of tough, simple, short words, with the complexity far beneath the surface texture. In part the line was influenced by the five and seven-character line Chinese poems I'd been reading, which work like sharp blows on the mind.[5]

In poetry, "riprapping" is the re-creation of an ongoing, ceaselessly unfolding movement of things and events, more correctly, "thing-events," an act of conscious and intuitive participation in the universal scheme of eternal change. The fitting together of perceptual blocks involves both a freedom and an order within which they arrange themselves. But it is an order not predesigned by the intellect—it comes into being from the requirements, the actual direction of energies in each objective particular as it presents itself to the senses. Neither does the imagination soar unbounded; it is held in check by the real presence of the material gathered by the senses. Snyder's method is a realization of process, and the process of riprapping is analogous to Creeley's method of driving. It is a form of proceeding which, as Robert Kern observed, means "moving freely through unknown territory so that not only the form but the very language of the journey will emerge directly from the 'rough terrain' encountered," as opposed to a kind of movement which is self-conscious and follows a prescribed pathway.[6] The very term "riprap" onomatopoeically and morphologically suggests the close juxtaposition of things which are at once different and similar. In certain of their material manifestations, in individual structure and substance they may show a distinct unlikeness to each other, yet they all infuse and diffuse energies according to natural law. The title poem of *Riprap* is Snyder's *ars poetica* where he imagistically sets out the characteristic features of his poetic method. In the poem Snyder makes a notable distinction: the act of riprapping is a laying down of words *before* the mind and not *after* the mind itself has laid down its own rules, a blueprint which the words are then subjected to follow. In other words, perceptual intake and imaginative rendering of the "riprap of things" precedes conceptualization. Actually, the poems do not only precede it but do not even attempt to reach it. Like the real objects in the world (Snyder prefers to call them "people": "Standing Tree People," "Flying Bird People," "Swimming Sea People"), the poems have no predetermined "meaning" or "idea"; they are "only" themselves in their own reality. They are like a road of riprapped stones upon which the "body of the mind" may begin its own journey.

As with all ideogrammic poets, and particularly the projectivists, Snyder does not set himself up as lord and master over the creative act. He does not "force" the song but follows what is "given" in a spirit of obedience. Not that he denigrates closed form, what he calls the "contrived" poem. But there the subjective mind of the maker is seen to be in control, arranging and ordering the particulars of experience and memory as *it* sees fit, taking its cue from a corresponding human metaphysic, an almost visible anthropomorphic cosmology. A poem thus contrived may be a source of pride and accomplishment, but for Snyder the "art" of poetry has an entirely different significance and one opposed to that of the closed poem: "the pure imagination flow leaves one with a sense of gratitude and wonder, and no sense of 'I did it'—only the Muse. *That* level of mind—the cool water—not intellect and not—(as romantics and after confusingly thought) fantasy-dream world or unconscious. This is just the clear spring—it reflects all things but is of itself transparent. Hitting on it, one could try to trace it to the source; but that writes no poems and is in a sense ingratitude."[7] Snyder's "Muse," "the clear spring" which lies underneath or behind things, is the same mysterious presence which Duncan named *It*. It is utterly real and alive, yet cannot be known, and it is in fact presumptuous of us to try and pursue it; for *It* is present and essentially embedded in all existent things. The poet can, and should, do no more than show

forth the things themselves as they are perceived. Their unseen
relations and interdependence allude to *It* without overt human meddling and interference. Snyder's poems are, of course, *human* works,
but in and through them the poet does not want to either copy or
outdo nature. He only sees that the "riprap" of the universe is in
harmony. It is that harmony which he wants to re-create with the
aid of natural yet specifically human resources in the "riprap" of his
poems.

Snyder said, "The poems speak of place, and the energy-pathways
that sustain life. Each living being is a swirl in the flow."[8] His humility
and unassuming naturalness—his "snake-stance"—do not allow him
to even interpret his perceptions. As a result, metaphors of any kind
are seldom present in the poems, with the exception of the "language
beyond metaphor," the compressed, suggestive verbs and the elliptical
juxtapositions of adjectives and nouns like those employed by Ginsberg. The use of connectives is reduced to a minimum. In its una-
dorned, unpretentious simplicity and quick juxtapositions of natural
data, the Snyder poem comes closest perhaps to the Fenollosian
definition of the Chinese ideogram: "a vivid shorthand picture of the
operations of nature." The emphasis is on *operations*, not on mere
outward appearance, and on the poet's own indelible presence in the
"swirl" of the living universe. And when Snyder stresses the merging
of the human with the nonhuman flow of nature, even the frequently
used strong and active verbs are dispensed with and are replaced by
the more pliant gerund, suggesting a transcendence of human control.
Strong transitive verbs Snyder usually reserves for the depiction of
natural things in action. Many of Snyder's juxtapositions have at their
basis the more fundamental opposition of, on the one hand, civilization, society, and the state, often symbolized by the city, and, on
the other hand, forests, mountains, rocks, and animals, subsumed
under the concept of wilderness, as in "Mid-August at Sourdough
Mountain Lookout" in *Riprap*. At times this persistent dichotomy is
presented objectively, but more often than not it is colored by
Snyder's vigorous and committed partisanship.

After *Riprap* Snyder's poems assume an increasingly projectivist
shape, with perception and breath setting the pattern of line length
and position on the page. In the books *Myths & Texts, Regarding
Wave, The Black Country,* and *Turtle Island,* the form is coextensive
with the material. As Snyder comments, "Each poem grows from an
energy-mind-field-dance, and has its own inner grain."[9] The locus of
"creation," as indicated by Snyder's paratactic compression of four
words linked by hyphens, is a process: energy invades the mind,
expands out into a field from which the poem, the dance of words,
comes into being. At the same time, the poem itself contains within
it all four elements, capable of releasing its dance of energies in the

mind of the attentive reader. Though not on the scale of Duncan's almost limitless variety of form, Snyder has used different devices, changing and adapting them to suit his particulars to be expressed. Even strict oriental forms such as the haiku became in his hands singularly Snyderian, for the haiku, the basic ideogrammic form, conforms in structure to the "riprap" of things in nature, and is essentially an open, projective poem. Some of Snyder's best haiku are in a series written in that form, a record of travels playfully titled "Hitch Haiku."[10] All the poems are pieces of two, three, four, or five lines (Snyder naturally abandons the traditional number of lines and syllables of the Japanese haiku), and they capture concrete detail in the simplest language without commentary. As in haiku in general, what remains unsaid in these poems is just as important as the "luminous detail" the poet presents. As Snyder writes in *Earth House Hold*, "Form—leaving things out at the right spot / ellipse, is emptiness."

Elliptic juxtapositions patently dispense with logic. In Snyder's case, his studies in Zen Buddhism have strengthened his instinctive distrust of logic and abstract thinking. As exemplified by the Zen *koan*, or philosophical riddle, the mind is powerless to deal with the world through logic alone. Each *koan* (such as "What is the sound of one hand clapping?" "What was your face like before you were born?" or "When I hear I see, and when I see I hear") is a lesson on the limits of human reason. Snyder's statement that form is emptiness, is just such a *koan*. As a practicing Buddhist he has stepped beyond the pitfalls of assertion and negation, for he knows that in nature there is no negation. The essence and existence of the world is one and inseparable—a fundamental insight transported to the West by Fenollosa and shared by all ideogrammic poets. The paradoxes and nonsensical postulations of the *koan* are meditative devices to prod consciousness to recognize the true oneness of the universe. "The impasse in which 'Koans' place us," writes Robert Linssen in his seminal work *Living Zen*, "cannot be solved by the mind. Before the simultaneity of two contradictory affirmations—opposite but complementary facets of a more vast Reality—logic is forced to suspend its usual process."[11] Logic is detrimental to a true seeing and hearing, to a true knowledge of the world *as it is*—to *gnosis* or, in Buddhist terms, *satori*, enlightenment; that is, to a sensing of the unknowable, what Snyder termed "the clear spring" which is the hidden flow manifested in the interacting and coinhering "riprap" of the material world.

Snyder, with his own independent oriental "archeology," has further enriched the method of ideogrammic composition in its use of nonlogical, "unreasonable" juxtapositions of particulars, as a not-too-distant relation of even such seemingly alien practices as the *koan*.

The aim of juxtapositions is not to point to a reality *beyond* the external appearance of things but to direct attention *inward* into the living thing as an entity. The entity is at once real and transcendental, transcendental not in a humanistic-metaphysical sense but as a thing embodying unceasing motion. It is never still but at all times involved in a transformation of force—a meeting point of metamorphosing energies. The poems in *Myths & Texts* move steadily toward this vision, realized in the final section entitled "Burning." In part 7, for example, the theme of permanence-in-impermanence is delicately presented through a series of juxtapositions from a variety of sources, a device based on the idea of "riprap," the haiku, and the *koan*, but also showing Poundian and projectivist influences. The first section is a complex of heterogeneous elements:

> Face in the crook of her neck
>     felt throb of vein
> Smooth skin, her cool breasts
> All naked in the dawn
>     "byrdes
> sing forth from every bough"
>     where are they now
> And dreamt I saw the Duke of Chow.

In sensuous brush strokes of visual and tactile imagery, Snyder delineates a sleeping woman, probably the beloved. The scene is reminiscent of the medieval alba—hence perhaps the echo of a line of archaic poetry in the mind of the speaker as he gazes at the woman's body in the dawn light. The words "where are they now" seem like the half-conscious thoughts of the speaker as he drifts back to sleep. "They" may refer to the birds in the old poem or, like Villon's *"mais où sont les neiges d'antan,"* may allude to the impermanence of earthly beauty and human existence. The Duke of Chow, whom the speaker sees in the dream, is no less real.

In the second section Snyder presents an image of eternal reality:

> The Mother whose body is the Universe
> Whose breasts are Sun and Moon,
>     the statue of Prajna
> From Java: the quiet smile,
>     the naked breasts.

The following brief section shifts back to human reality and to the transience of human relationships as Snyder quotes the question of a little girl, "Will you still love me when my breasts get big?"— to which the poet answers with a paraphrase of a doctrine from Hindu scriptures, thus ending part 7:

> "Earthly Mothers and those who suck
> the breasts of earthly mothers are mortal—
> but deathless are those who have fed
> at the breast of the Mother of the Universe."

The word "deathless" does not imply the promise of a "heaven"; it does quite definitely signify a *stepping beyond* the dualistic concepts of life and death, real and unreal, finite and eternal, for they are constructs of the mind. An escape from such conflicts can come about if none of the constituent parts of the total reality is disregarded or made to exist separately from each other. In this heightened vision of cosmic relations the earthly woman and the Mother of the Universe are not irreconcilable, mutually exclusive realities, but the one is the other and the other is the one. This is of course my very inadequate rationalization, for the reverse is also true: neither is the one the other, nor the other the one. Snyder's point may perhaps be better illustrated by a Zen *koan* which runs as follows: "At the beginning, the mountains are mountains. / In the middle, the mountains are no longer mountains. / At the end, the mountains are once again mountains." The *koan* describes the steps leading to *satori*. At first, as in the first line of Snyder's poem, the mountains are what we observe through our sense organs: actual rocks, boulders, ravines; stones as stones, earth as earth. But after meditating on this reality, we may suddenly see *into* another reality of the mountain, not as thing, but as motion, something that has come into being through immense forces of energy. These forces are still at play in the mountain, working changes in it from moment to moment, and there will be a time when the mountain will no longer be the thing we now see but transformed into something else. The "thing-ness" of the mountain in this second phase of seeing disappears; its materiality and its actual contours which before were all too real are perceived now as illusory, a mirage. Only those essential forces which are immaterial are now "real." In the third stage, we begin to see that thing and motion are not really different; matter and essence are one: "things in motion, motion in things." The mountains are once again mountains, neither purely material nor exclusively essential and illusory. At this level of true vision we also realize, as Linssen writes, that "the creator of illusions has been finally unmasked: it is none other than our own mind."[12] The attainment of *satori* is seeing things and events in their true relation, acting out their destiny in the vast field of the living universe and seeing our own place in this field as another force among many.

Snyder's poems are steps toward this vision of cosmic unity. They are a testament of nonlogical, posthumanist ways of thinking, feeling, and living. They unify, as Ginsberg's later poems do, the objective and visionary modes of composition. The poetics and ecological writings point to the emergence of a new type of human community, as distinct from "society," a combination of resuscitated archaic values and contemporary exigencies. In this community the poet can once again function as Pound had prophesied: as a teller of the tale of the tribe—not as a kind of "unacknowledged legislator," but as one human being functioning to the fullest potential among equals. Snyder has no trust in the world as he finds it. Rather, his activities and writings seem to be preparations for a saner, more human future, signs of which he already recognizes all around him. As he says, "Industrial society indeed appears to be finished. Many of us are, again, hunters and gatherers. Poets, musicians, nomadic engineers and scholars; fact-diggers, searchers and researchers scoring in rich foundation territory."[13] With this new posthumanist, postindustrial consciousness the poet assumes an age-old role in the community, that of shaman and healer. This poetry is, as Snyder writes, "the kind of healing that makes whole, heals by making whole . . ."[14] He further clarifies his ideas of the poet's work as healing: "I'm obviously not a doctor. I'm not doing magic on anybody's head, either. I'm simply striving to get our heads clear to certain wholenesses that are there anyway; like our oneness with nature, the oneness of mind and body, the oneness of conscious and unconscious, our oneness in society with each other. These are basic and ancient conditions from which we flourish."[15]

Snyder's poetry, then, is a poetry of true transition, the work of a poet who has consciously absorbed and synthesized the most useful elements of Eastern and Western art and philosophy—and by "Western" I do not simply mean European, but Hopi and Navajo in equal proportion. In fact, Snyder's *oeuvre* proves that method is process, and process is conciousness. It is a "new beginning," and thus it does not end the line of ideogrammic composition but makes the method ready and available for use by poets to come.

Notes

1. Gary Snyder, *Earth House Hold* (New York: New Directions, 1969), p. 117.

2. Quoted in David Kherdian, *Six Poets of the San Francisco Renaissance: Portraits and Checklists* (Fresno: Giligia Press, 1967), p. 52.

3. Thomas Parkinson, "The Poetry of Gary Snyder," *Southern Review* n.s. 4 (1968): 617.

4. Alan Williamson, "Language Against Itself: The Middle Generation of Contemporary Poets," in Robert B. Shaw, ed., *American Poetry Since 1960* (Chester Springs: Dufour, 1974). p. 62.

5. Donald M. Allen, ed., *The New American Poetry* (New York: Grove Press, 1960), pp. 420–421.

6. Robert Kern, "Recipes, Catalogues, Open Form Poetics: Gary Snyder's Archetypal Voice," *Contemporary Literature* 18 (1977): 179.

7. Snyder, *Earth House Hold*, pp. 56–57.

8. Snyder, introduction to *Turtle Island* (New York: New Directions, 1974), n.p.

9. Snyder, "Some Yips & Barks in the Dark," in Stephen Berg and Robert Mezey, eds., *Naked Poetry* (Indianapolis: Bobbs-Merrill, 1969), p. 357.

10. Snyder, *The Back Country* (New York: New Directions, 1968), pp. 28–31.

11. Robert Linssen, *Living Zen*, trans. Diana Abrahms-Curiel (New York: Grove Press, 1960), p. 320.

12. Linssen, *Living Zen*, p. 95. For the interpretation of this *koan* I am indebted to Linssen, although the linking of its principles with Fenollosa's ideas is my own.

13. Snyder, *Earth House Hold*, p. 111.

14. Snyder, *The Real Work: Interviews and Talks, 1964–1979*, ed. William Scott McLean (New York: New Directions, 1980), p. 171.

15. Snyder, *The Real Work*, p. 157.

# Gary Snyder: The Lessons of *Turtle Island*

Michael Castro°

> If civilization
>     is the exploiter, the masses is nature
>     and the party
>     is the poets.
> —Gary Snyder, "Revolution in the Revolution
>                           in the Revolution"

## BEING IN NATURE

Gary Snyder is the poet who is best known today for his presentation of the Indian and, more broadly, "the primitive" as important models and sources for the modern world. If Jerome Rothenberg is the contemporary poet who explores to their current limits the implications of Native American forms for a new American poetry, Snyder does the same in making claims for the implications and applications of Native American consciousness for American life. In Snyder's work we can find the culmination of many of the efforts of earlier American poets who sought in Indian cultures alternatives to the fragmented, materialistic culture of modern America and to the cynical, detached irony of its "crafted" poetry. Snyder's poetry and essays develop

° Reprinted by permission from *Interpreting the Indian: Twentieth-Century Poets and the American Indian* by Michael Castro, 139–52. ©1984 by the University of New Mexico Press.

several of the key themes already discussed: relationship to place and to inner and outer nature, holistic awareness as a means to psycho-spiritual health, and, to a lesser extent, the development of a new American poetry based on Native American and other tribal models.

A look at Snyder's poetry should perhaps begin with mention of the fact that his collection of poems and essays, *Turtle Island*, received a Pulitzer Prize in 1974. Its title revives the name for the American continent derived from Native American creation stories. A recurrent theme among its poems and essays is the need for modern Americans to return to the perception of the earth as a living organism to whom we are related; we must break through geopolitical abstractions, he tells us in *Turtle Island*, and begin to see as it actually is "this continent of watersheds and life communities—plant zones, physiographic provinces, culture areas; following natural boundaries." The most important implication of such a renewal of natural perception, Snyder has written, is that it will ultimately enable us to "see ourselves more accurately."[1]

The task of achieving an intimate knowledge of the land for the sake of psycho-spiritual health, of achieving chthonic being, is important to poets like Mary Austin, Vachel Lindsay, Hart Crane, William Carlos Williams, and Charles Olson, but it is crucial to Gary Snyder. For him, it represents a commitment both in poetic stance and life-style. This commitment is reflected in his writing, in his longtime practice of Buddhist meditation techniques, and in his back-to-nature approach to living in California's Sierra Nevada. Through all this, Snyder has never become a recluse like the most influential West Coast literary figure of the previous generation who "went Indian," poet-anthropologist Jaime de Angulo, "the legendary hermit of Big Sur." Instead, Snyder has remained steadfastly concerned in literature and life with the development of an alternative *community*.

Snyder's sense of community includes not just humans, but all living things. Of the poets just mentioned, only Williams approached Snyder's precise attentiveness to beasts and plants as direct sources of the desired chthonic knowledge. Snyder's poems look closely at trout, deer, quail, dolphins, manzanita, mushrooms, and berries and, like Williams's poems on flowers, trees, and animals, Snyder's reflect an acute awareness of living nature, a sense of an intelligence to be found there, and a respectful, observant, participatory relationship with it akin to the Native American's.[2] "You should really know what the complete natural world of your region is and what all its interactions are and how you are interacting with it yourself," Snyder says in an interview. "This is just part of the work of becoming who you are, where you are."[3]

In his best poems Snyder seems to be inside nature, interacting with it, rather than outside talking about it. In "A Walk" (*The Back*

*Country,* 1968), for instance, he takes us with him on a hike, through a sequence of shared impressions that keep reader and poet in the middle of the experience:

> . . . Hopping on creekbed boulders
> Up the rock throat three miles
> > Piute Creek—
> In steep gorge glacier-slick rattlesnake country
> Jump, land by a pool, trout skitter,
> The clear sky. Deer tracks.
> Bad places by a falls, boulders big as houses,
> Lunch tied to belt,
> I stemmed up a crack and almost fell
> But rolled out safe on a ledge
> > and ambled on.
> Quail chicks freeze underfoot, color of stone
> Then run cheep! away, hen quail fussing.

The poem is structured to seem unstructured, a stream of words reflecting a stream of sensations with occasional reflections or realizations, self-glimpses among the views of nature; it moves fast from perception to perception. In its way, this is the kind of writing that Olson called for in "Projective Verse." It "enacts" rather than "describes." The poem ambles, slips, and slides its way along, mimetically re-creating the hike. Its creatures act, but as with the trout and quail in the previous passage, their actions are not elaborately or analytically described but are "snap-said" with a speed and immediacy that recreates the original sensory impression. The poem's "I" moves easily and casually between his senses and his memories, his reflections and their outer natural environment. The poem ends at a natural stopping point—when the hiker stops for lunch. Despite its carefully plain language and cleverly random structure, "A Walk" works convincingly as a poem because it accurately registers impressions in a language appropriate to their immediacy and in a form that synthesizes the natural rhythms of voice, sense, and the experience in nature that is the poem's subject. In this deceptively simple poem, Snyder wrote, as Olson would have described it, with *participation mystique* and he realized what Austin gropingly projected in her concept of the "landscape line": a poem in touch with the interacting rhythms of body, mind, and place.

Elsewhere, Snyder's poems often take the broad view of nature instead of the immediate, close-up look, registering the human interaction with place as continent not as locality. He tried for a "scientific myth," as in "What Happaned Here Before" (*Turtle Island,* 1974), where he traces the evolution of the West Coast region of the continent beginning 300 million years ago. Indians enter the chronological map that organizes the poem at the 40,000-year mark:

> And human people came with basket hats and nets
>   winter houses underground
>   yew bows painted green,
>   feasts and dances for the boys and girls
>     songs and stories in the smoky dark

The white man enters the picture only 125 years ago:

> Then came the white man: tossing up trees and
>   boulders with big hoses,
>     going after the old gravel and the gold.
>   horses, apple orchards, card-games,
>     pistol-shooting, churches, county jail.

The poem is written from the continent's point of view and recounts the evidence of its ceaseless changes. It hopes to broaden its readers' perspective on who we are and where we are by familiarizing us with the historical depth of American life and with the variety of geological, plant, animal, and human forces that have evolved. It presents characteristic images reflecting how human groups have interacted with the land as Olson had planned in "Red, White, and Black"; we see the red people in their "winter houses underground" nurtured in the womb of the earth itself, whom they regard as their mother; in contrast, the white man, "tossing up trees and boulders with big hoses," violently, phallically exploiting the land for its wealth of natural resources. The land is presented as a living, growing, changing thing unto itself:

> First a sea: soft sands, mud, and marls
>   —loading, compressing, heating, crumpling,
>     crushing, recrystalizing, infiltrating,
>   several times lifted and submerged.

Though set in a geological rather than a human time frame, passages in "What Happened Here Before," as in "A Walk," pay close attention to detail and present the interacting elements of nature with precision and immediacy:

> sea-bed strata raised and folded,
>   granite far below.
> warm quiet centuries of rains
>   (make dark red tropic soils)
>   wear down two miles of surface,
> lay bare the veins and tumble heavy gold
>   in streambeds
>     slate and schist rock-riffles catch it—
> volcanic ash floats down and dams the streams,
>   piles up the gold and grave—

Turtle Island is thus presented to us as a vital thing, vaster and longer-lived than man or any of its other species. When we achieve an understanding and an appreciation of the depth and scope of its life, the poem's implicit message states, we can begin to come into proper relationship to our land. To achieve the proper and necessary respect, we must realize, the poem tells us, that "the land belongs to itself," not to us. Only then can we approach a relationship of harmony and balance with the nature around us and begin to develop fully our own inner harmony and a healthy human and American identity. The poem addresses the question posed toward its conclusion by Snyder's sons: "Who are we?" It suggests that we ask ourselves the same question and that its answer requires realizing whether we hear our true voice in the military jets roaring overhead every dawn—the contemporary extension of the early white man uprooting trees, boulders, and people—or in the sounds of the land and its creatures, the nature to which we too belong, whose voice we hear in the poem's final line, "Bluejay screeches from a pine."[4]

Identification with nature—belonging without possessing—is central to Snyder's work. His writing extends the treatment of place found in earlier poets who were interested in the Indian by showing the tangible ecological consequences of our psychological and spiritual alienation from nature. Its main subject is the land itself, but not treated as mere landscape. Snyder's concept of land holds that the development by Americans of a harmonious relationship with their environment is necessary not just for psychological and spiritual health but also for actual survival, physically as well as spiritually. Crane, Williams, and Olson saw from afar the ultimate self-destructiveness inherent in contemporary culture's alienation from nature, but Snyder's camera shows that the whirlwind is nearly upon us as he reports on the exploding ecological crises of the sixties, seventies, and eighties. Snyder's attitudes on this subject, usually implicit in his poetry, are more explicitly developed in his essays. In "The Wilderness," an essay in *Turtle Island*, Snyder wrote, "We are beginning to get non-negotiable demands from the air, the water, the soil."[5] In "Four Changes," another of *Turtle Island*'s essays, Snyder defined and proposed social and political solutions to the four interrelated ecological problems of overpopulation, pollution, consumption, and "transformation." In the latter discussion he summarizes the situation and solution: "Civilization, which has made us so successful a species, has overshot itself and now threatens us with inertia. There also is some evidence that civilized life isn't good for the human gene pool. To achieve Changes we must change the very foundations of our society and our minds."[6] In such urgent need, the Native American becomes in Snyder's work a model for "mind" and for living stably, respectfully, and nonexploitatively with a natural environment. In *The Old Ways* (1977), a collection of six essays exploring relationship

to place, Snyder cited the example, as described in ecologist Eugene
Odum's paper "The Strategy of Ecosystem Development," of certain
Native American societies' relationship to their environment, as contrasted with that of contemporary white America. Odom suggested
that exploitative and exhaustive use of land, as found in the United
States, was characteristic of a "young" ecosystem culture. Snyder, in
"The Politics of Ethnopoetics,"[7] extended Odum's discussion by tracing the exploitative tendency back to early civilizations and to the
development of a centralized state in cities like Babylon and Rome,
which spread their economic support systems far enough that they
could afford to wreck one local territory's ecology and keep moving
on. The development of America, he suggested, through the gradual
settlement of an ever-expanding frontier, has followed a similar pattern.[8] In a relatively early poem, "Oil" (*The Back Country*, 1968),
Snyder likened the ultimately self-destructive reliance on nonrenew-
able resources characteristic of this process to the self-demeaning
behavior of an addict. He described the oil tanker he was a laborer
on:

> bearing what all these
> crazed, hooked nations need:
> steel plates and
> long injections of pure oil

Older Native American cultures, he suggested, represented a historical
alternative. Snyder pointed to Indian societies in general, and to
traditionally sedentary ones like the still viable Pueblo tribes in the
Southwest in particular, as models of human organization that do not
self-destruct by exploiting and exhausting their resources. In Odum's
terms, they are "mature" ecosystem cultures. Their relationship to
the land is characterized by protection rather than production, by
stability rather than growth, by a concern for quality rather than
quantity. Snyder proposed this model as a guide to America's ecological survival. The radical shift that it implies is to a relationship
of stewardship rather than exploitation and to a regional rather than
a global approach to resource usage, particularly of energy resources.

   Though dismissed as unrealistic by many, Snyder's position is
that such an approach, however drastic, is necessary and imperative
given the crisis we face; the "poet's" analysis agrees with those of
prominent ecologists ("scientists") who, like Odum and Barry Commoner, draw similar conclusions.[9] Thus, the importance of the Native
American model becomes even more urgent in Snyder's work than
in that of his poetic predecessors: for those predecessors, the message
was that reform of the spirit was necessary to our salvation, but
Snyder showed the hell into which our present path will shortly lead
us. Previous poets told us that to recover Eden we must become as

Indians. Snyder asserted that unless we become true Native Americans we will make America hell on earth.

Snyder, of course, is no mere doomslinger. His poems and essays point to models of the kind of respectfully knowing attitude toward nature that would ensure survival in a good land. One such model is found in "Prayer for the Great Family" (*Turtle Island*, 1974), his adaptation of a traditional Mohawk prayer:

> Gratitude to Mother Earth, sailing through night and day—
> and to her soil: rich, rare, and sweet
>     *in our minds so be it.*
>
> Gratitude to Plants, the sun-facing light-changing leaf
> and fine root-hairs; standing still through wind
> and rain; their dance is in the flowing spiral grain
>     *in our minds so be it.*
>
> Gratitude to Air, bearing the soaring Swift and the silent
> Owl at dawn. Breath of our song
> clear spirit breeze
>     *in our minds so be it.*

As Olson instructed in "Projective Verse," "Prayer for the Great Family" is "objective," concerned as it is with relationships, and with conveying a distinctly process-conscious "stance toward reality."

Like other poets discussed earlier in this book, Snyder believed that renewed understanding of ourselves and our land can come from communing with Indian peoples, whose traditional relationship to nature and whose techniques for meditative and visionary explorations offer hope for the deeply disturbed earth / body and spirit / mind of modern man. "The primitive world," he told me in a 1979 interview, "measures us in terms of final physical and psychological health." Further, it can lead us to take "the next great step of mankind . . . to step into the nature of his own mind," to answer "the real question . . . just what is consciousness?"[10] Native American cultures, Snyder suggested, have been dedicated to exploring this question for thousands of years, and though they have not developed a technology comparable to the West's, they have exceeded us in developing as "technicians of the sacred."[11] Poets like Snyder, Rothenberg, Olson, Williams, and Austin, who espoused or practiced an organic, relativistic poetics, sought a similar type of development: contact with the truly spiritual, truly poetic consciousness to be found in the human mind and the "mind" of nature. Snyder suggested that "very simple cultures who are really trying to find out what the possibilities of the mind are" often are far more physically and psychologically stable than more technologically advanced societies. Like most of the writers we have discussed, Snyder's work challenges the Western myth of progress through the industrial and technological development associated with civilization. Snyder went so far as to wonder aloud if "all civilization is just a very recent and somewhat eccentric sidegrowth that will find itself at a dead end likely, and then come back to the main line again."[12]

## "Original Mind"

Snyder views the study of Native American cultures and their literature as a way for poets to reconnect with this "main line" and with the shamanic roots of their own craft. To the degree that poets can integrate the perspective that they find in their study of Indian peoples into their own minds and lives, they can feed it back to their own culture through their work. Native American sources, if so employed, Snyder says provide "an exercise in locating yourself concretely in the world, and . . . an exercise in getting deeper down into your own mind."[13] But Snyder does not advocate in his poetry and prose, as many of his critics believe, nostalgic return to a past that is forever gone. Like Olson, he is an avid student of modern science and the closing informational circle of the twentieth-century world. Beginning with the essays collected in *Earth House Hold* (1969), he has been tracing the development of a new set of attitudes and assumptions in the West as our culture draws on ancient Asian and Native American models of reality as well as the discoveries by our own physical and environmental scientists. In "Four Changes," Snyder wrote that we must "master the archaic and primitive as models of basic nature-related cultures—as well as the most imaginative extensions of science—and build a community where these two vectors cross."[14]

Ultimately, Snyder envisioned an interpenetration of primitive and civilized states of mind that will return modern man, at least periodically, to the experience spoken of by the Buddhists as "original mind"; this is roughly equatable with the intelligence found in all nature, which ecologists call "biomass." Snyder has been interested in the point where these correspondences between exterior and interior landscapes merge.[15] Many of his poems strive for an image or a voice that can capture this interpenetration. In "Magpie's Song" (*Turtle Island,* 1974), for instance, Snyder described a sudden, magical encounter with a magpie and recorded the message that the bird communicated:

> "Here in the mind, brother
> Turquoise blue.
> I wouldn't fool you.
> Smell the breeze

It came through all the trees
No need to fear
What's ahead
 Snow up on the hills west
 Will be there every year
 be at rest.
 A feather on the ground—
 The wind sound—

 Here in the Mind, Brother,
 Turquoise Blue."

The capitalized "Mind" in the next to the last line suggests the "original" or "biomass" mind. The poem itself should be seen as a modern attempt at a "shaman song" that tries to put us into contact with that "Mind." It brings back from the mystical experience the voice of the nonhuman or extrahuman and shares it with the community, as has been the practice of shamans over the centuries.[16] Though Snyder refrained from claiming that title, this is one of the few poems that he literally sang at public readings, using the musical and inflective power of his voice to convey the poem's strange otherworldliness and power, much as a shaman would. As Snyder told Gene Fowler in a 1964 interview: "A reading is a kind of communion. I think the poet articulates the semi-known for the tribe. This is close to the ancient function of the shaman. It's not a dead function."[17] "Magpie's Song" is one of Snyder's most purely "primitive" poems. Paradoxically, it represents an evolution from the "shaman songs" found in the early work, *Myths & Texts* (1960). There, the shamanic experience was filtered through the interpretive commentary of the poet-speaker. Here, the experience is sung directly, as if from its original source, nature itself. Such "direct treatment of the thing itself," as Ezra Pound put it in 1913, represents one of the important convergences of primitive and modern poetics.

 In "Poetry and the Primitive" (*Earth House Hold*, 1969), Snyder quoted the anthropologist Claude Lévi-Strauss, who predicted the further development in the twentieth century of a type of consciousness "which is neither the mind of savages nor that of primitive or archaic humanity, but rather mind in its untamed state as distinct from mind cultivated or domesticated for yielding a return."[18] Snyder compared this untamed state to a wilderness area, calling it "wild mind."[19] The poet, he said here and elsewhere, was its apt spokesman, for from the beginnings in Neolithic shamanism down through the works of specific poets in the Western tradition the poet's role has been to represent the hidden forces of nature within and without. In our own age, characterized by dissociation, alienation, and a destructiveness toward nature of unprecedented proportions, the need for this "wilderness" consciousness, Snyder suggested, was more acute than ever. His poem "What You Should Know to Be a Poet" (*Regarding Wave*, 1970) speaks to its reacquisition. Snyder recommended that the aspiring poet learn "all you can about animals as persons," as well as the names of trees, flowers, weeds, and stars; planetary and lunar movements; dreams; the darkness within; human love; the six senses, including the intuitive sense; the ecstasy of the dance; and the "enstasy"[20] of "silent solitary illumination." These elements represent keys to recovering holistic awareness and the "original mind" within each of us, which can counteract the dissociative tendencies inherent in modern society. Snyder's work suggests many doors into this holistic consciousness: through the formal discipline of meditation; through the types of total involvement and attention required by hunting or other forms of nonalienating work; through the investigations of surrounding and interior landscapes demanded by poetry itself. The poet is, by profession, Snyder said, a representative of nature and of "original mind." The poet who returns to his archaic shamanic roots actively seeks this original mind, and when he or she finds it, tries to speak from it to the rest of us, and to speak to it as it exists within the rest of us.

Snyder, like a number of other poets in this century, has come to believe that this "original mind" was open to and sung through the Native Americans on this continent, speaking for all of us to nature and the cosmos, and speaking to us from nature also. This, of course, sounds vague and maybe even silly. But before we dismiss it, let us consider a poem of the contemporary Native American writer Simon Ortiz, "Speaking," which seems to me to do exactly what I have just described, that is, what Snyder suggested was done by Native American shaman-poet. Here, in its entirety, is "Speaking":

> I take him outside
> under the trees,
> have him stand on the ground.
> We listen to the crickets,
> cicadas, million years old sound.
> Ants come by us.
> I tell them,
> "This is he, my son.
> This boy is looking at you.
> I am speaking for him."
>
> The crickets, cicadas,
> the ants, the millions of years
> are watching us,
> hearing us.
> My son murmurs infant words,

speaking, small laughter
bubbles from him.
Tree leaves tremble.
They listen to this boy
speaking for me.[21]

The poem is notable for its simplicity and its lack of flashy rhetoric. It depicts a shared communion between father and son and the things alive in nature and in time. The father in the poem is, in effect, initiating the son into the "original mind" in nature and in himself by having the boy stand in its midst—"on the ground"—and listen to its voice in the timeless sound of the crickets and cicadas. The poem seeks to contact in its readers a similar sense of the community and continuity of life within time. It concludes with the infant boy's "small laughter"—an expression of his "original mind"—speaking both to and from nature, and for the poet.

This book has attempted to reveal how a similar sense of the community and continuity of life has struck poets in this century as lacking in our culture yet as being vitally necessary. Often independently of one another, these poets have sought to translate and interpret the Native American in ways designed to begin the process of returning the American mind to a fullness that would connect us to where we are and restore a holistic awareness that would enable us to feel, once again, holy and whole. Snyder's work is all directed toward this restoration of inner and outer unity. At times it contains a trenchant critique of American and Western civilization, but this is intended as a "Control Burn," after the Indian practice, as Snyder maintained in a poem of that title in *Turtle Island.* Its purpose, as that poem suggests, is to allow the manzanita seed buried under the razed foliage—that is, the human spirit and spirit of place underneath civilization—to come into flower.

In "Through the Smoke Hole" (*The Back Country,* 1968), Snyder contemplated the smoke hole of the ceremonial kiva of the Pueblo peoples as an image of the ultimate sort of unity that we need to seek. The metaphor is not original with Snyder. He had in fact adapted the metaphorical dimensions the kiva holds for Indian peoples—its living poetry—to the printed page. In Pueblo cultures the smoke hole atop the kiva represents the passage between worlds, the unity of time and timelessness, worldly and spiritual beings, life and death:

Out of the kiva come
masked dancers or
plain men.
      plain men go into the ground.

The masked dancers referred to here are the spirit beings (kachinas) depicted by ceremonial dancers. But the word *or* in this passage is significant, for the Hopi and other Pueblo tribes believe that the masked dancer is literally transformed into the kachina that his mask represents. His identity as man or spirit is a fluid one. The last line of the quoted passage—"plain men go into the ground"—describes the descent of the dancers into the kiva preparatory to the dance, but at the same time it emphasizes the fact of death. "Through the Smoke Hole" drifts with apparent randomness, like smoke itself, from one image sequence to another—from descriptions of cave paintings depicting the magical figures of tribal myth, to descriptions of actual, earthy women deemed equally magical, to

>thirty million years gone
>    drifting sand
>    cool rooms pink stone
>worn down fort floor, slat sighting
>    heat shine on jumna river
>
>dry wash, truck tracks in the riverbed
>coild sand pinyon
>
>    seabottom
>    riverbank
>    sand dunes
>the floor of a sea once again.

The poem, as this characteristic passage suggests, establishes the depth of time and its circularity, senses of which form the foundation of the Native American view of life.[22] "Through the Smoke Hole" itself ends with a line that completes a circle: "Plain men come out of the ground." Here the emphasis is not on death, but on emergence and rebirth. The normal, linear time process has been meaningfully reversed. For the poem has shown us that in the timelessness within which time exists all things occur and recur, shift identities from one reality to another like smoke drifting from the world below of the kiva to the world above. The two planes of existence are revealed as interpenetrating and one.

We exist as "plain men" within this same ticking timelessness on this same living, shifting landscape. Snyder, in this poem and elsewhere, points us to Indian cultures that, like the shamanism he urges poets to emulate, can heal us of our social, psychological, and spiritual ills by helping to restore the unity of life that has been shattered. He reads various attempts by poets in this century to translate the Indian as a fortuitous linkage, an expression of the "antennae of the race," of our need to "reconnect." In "Why Tribe" (*Earth House Hold*, 1969), he wrote of the importance of contemporary poets' interest in Indians and shamanism: "we have almost unwittingly linked ourselves to a transmission of a gnosis, a potential social order, and techniques of enlightenment surviving from prehistoric times."[23]

## Notes

1. Gary Snyder, *Turtle Island* (New York: New Directions, 1974), p. 1.

2. There are many sources that provide a sense of how important knowing and observing nature were to Indian peoples. One excellent place to start would be with Charles A. Eastman's *Indian Boyhood* [1902; rpt. Greenwich, Conn.: Fawcett, 1972], especially the chapter entitled "An Indian Boy's Training." In this chapter, Eastman, a Santee Sioux, recounts how his uncle, who was responsible for his education until he was fifteen, would send him out into the woods early in the day with the injunction, "Look closely at everything you see." When Eastman returned in the evening, his uncle would test him for an hour on what he had observed and learned. "He did not expect a correct reply at once to all the voluminous questions that he put to me on these occasions," Eastman wrote, "but he meant to make me observant and a good student of nature."

3. Interview with Gary Snyder in *Road Apple* (1969–70) by Doug Flaherty, reprinted in Gary Snyder: *The Real Work: Interviews and Talks 1964–1979* (New York: New Directions, 1980), p. 16.

4. As Carter Revard observed in a May 1981 conversation, for Whitman, America's first great poet who tried to express the "voice of the continent," both voices are "ours." Snyder took only half of Whitman's territory, at most.

5. Snyder, "The Wilderness," *Turtle Island*, p. 108.

6. Snyder, "Four Changes," *Turtle Island*, p. 99.

7. Snyder originally delivered "The Politics of Ethnopoetics" as a talk at the first annual Ethnopoetics Conference, a gathering of scholars, ethnologists, poets, and native songmen and -women organized by Jerome Rothenberg and Dennis Tedlock at the University of Wisconsin–Milwaukee in the spring of 1975. The essay also appears in *The Old Ways* (San Francisco: City Lights Books, 1977), pp. 15–43.

8. For a cogent analysis of this process and of the image making and militarism associated with it, see Richard Drinnon, *Facing West: The Metaphysics of Indian Hating and Empire Building* (New York: New American Library, 1980).

9. See Barry Commoner, *The Politics of Energy* (New York: Alfred A. Knopf, 1979). Commoner, after studying the energy problem from many angles over many years, recommends conversion to self-renewing solar-energy sources. He cites "the importance of the most distinctive feature of solar energy—that it is diffusely spread across the surface of the entire planet . . . This means that the present pattern of building huge, centralized power stations is inherently uneconomical if it is applied to solar energy" (p. 44).

10. See Jan Castro and Michael Castro, "Interview with Gary Snyder," *River Styx* (1979), p. 38.

11. This term, which Rothenberg borrowed for the title for his anthology of tribal poetry, was coined by Mircea Eliade to describe the shaman. See Eliade, *Shamanism: Archaic Techniques of Ecstasy*, trans. Willard R. Trask (New York: Pantheon Books, 1964).

12. Castro and Castro, p. 38.

13. Castro and Castro, p. 41.

14. Snyder, "Four Changes," p. 102.

15. See *The Real Work*, p. 5. For a good discussion of the intelligence in nature from the point of view of a contemporary scientist, see Lewis Thomas, "Debating the Unknowable," *Atlantic Monthly*, July 1981, pp. 49–52. Thomas writes here of the contemporary scientific debate of such issues as animal intelligence, cooperative intelligence between animals and between animals and plants, and the "Gaia Hypothesis" of Lovelock and Margulis, "which is, in brief, that the earth itself is a form of life."

16. This is not to suggest that the words of Snyder's poem represent what he literally heard in his encounter with the magpie. As Kenneth Lincoln, editor of the *American Indian Culture and Research Journal*, has written in his essay, "Native American Literatures: 'old like hills, like stars,'" in *Three American Literatures: Essays in Chicano, Native American, and Asian-American Literature for Teachers of American Literature* (New York: Modern Language Association, 1982), pp. 108–9:

> There seems to be consensus among holy men, scholars, and translators that the visionary truth of the other world, regardless of time or culture, can enter this world only through the special concentration of dream images, a language of many tongues speaking in one, and a fleeting sense of witnessing more than the ordinary mind can see or comprehend or tell. John Neihardt, Black Elk's intermediary, remembers "half seeing, half sensing" the blind man's story, translated across languages, cultures, and time itself, as if he were seeing "a strange and beautiful landscape by brief flashes of lightning." The dreamer's language remains sacred and symbolic, *wakan* the Lakota says, and not to be understood as ordinary words.

17. *The Real Work*, p. 5.

18. Quoted in "Poetry and the Primitive," *Earth House Hold* (New York: New Directions, 1969), p. 118.

19. Castro and Castro, p. 53.

20. The term *enstasy* was apparently coined by Snyder to mean "within a condition of stasis or balance." The word has intentional overtones of ecstasy, for meditative enstatic communion can involve a calm yet ecstatic experience.

21. Simon Ortiz, "Speaking," *A Good Journey* (Berkeley: Turtle Island, 1977), p. 52.

22. Black Elk said, "The Power of the World always works in circles, and everything tries to be round" (John G. Neihardt, *Black Elk Speaks* [Lincoln: University of Nebraska Press, 1979], p. 164). Lame Deer: "I point my peace pipe toward all these directions. Now we are one with the universe, with all living things, a link in the circle which has no end" (John [Fire] Lame Deer and Richard Erdoes, *Lame Deer: Seeker of Visions* [New York: Simon and Schuster, 1972], p. 107.

23. Snyder, "Why Tribe," *Earth House Hold*, p. 116.

# [The Political and Poetic Vision of *Turtle Island*]
Charles Molesworth[*]

We can take Snyder's *Turtle Island* as the most complete expression of his political and poetic vision, not only because it is his most

[*] Reprinted from *Gary Snyder's Vision* by Charles Molesworth, by permission of the University of Missouri Press. © 1983 by the Curators of the University of Missouri.

recent finished volume, but also because it contains the fullest mediations of the themes and concerns of all his work. I propose to
look at the book as incorporating three mediations. First, *Turtle Island*
serves Snyder with a chief metaphor for a physical environment and
a utopian vision. As he puts it in the "Introductory Note," Turtle
Island is the "old / new name for the continent, based on many
creation myths of the people who have been living here for millennia."
The metaphor of the continent floating on the back of a giant turtle
serves as a cosmogonic emblem of archaic knowledge and future
hopes: "Hark again to those roots, to see our ancient solidarity, and
then to the work of being together on Turtle Island." This work,
another version of the real work, extends beyond North America to
"the earth, or cosmos even," because Turtle Island is another version
of the "idea found world-wide" of a "serpent-of-eternity," the *uro-
boros* familiar to all students of world mythology. Turtle Island thus
combines the immanent awareness of a space occupied for thousands
of years with the historically transcendent space of the planet rei-
magined as the seat of the species.

Secondly, Snyder uses Turtle Island as a way of mediating between
an ethics of responsibility and an ethics of ultimate ends. I take these
terms from Max Weber's well-known essay "Politics as a Vocation"
(1918).[1] Weber distinguishes between these two "fundamentally differing and irreconcilably opposed" senses of value, since those who
formulate or pursue ultimate ends are unlikely to take pragmatic
consequences into consideration. But Weber is quick to add that the
ethics of ultimate ends need not produce actions that deny or evade
all consequences, and likewise the ethics of responsibility should not
be equated with "unprincipled opportunism." Snyder includes in
*Turtle Island* a section, called "Plain Talk," of prose essays, the most
extended of which is "Four Changes." This essay contains "practical
and visionary suggestions" and is the fullest statement in expository
prose of Snyder's aims and beliefs. Here he advances several radical
ideas: the world's population should be cut in half, alternative family
structures should be explored, the world should be divided into
"natural and cultural boundaries rather than arbitrary boundaries"
(thereby eliminating nation-states and most existing political structures), we should seek a reliance on unobtrusive technologies and
energy sources, and so forth. The arguments for each proposal mix
appeals to scientific and technological fact and research with attacks
on the ideology of consumption and private property. All of the
proposals, however, are for a new ethics, and this new ethics stands
in relation to our current ethical standards and behavior in a way
that is based on both immediate responsibilities and ultimate ends.

The third major mediation in *Turtle Island* presents a sense of
the lyric poem that has dominated literature for the last century and

a half, together with a future model of the lyric poem as more committed to enhancing an awareness of cosmic scale and cosmic forces and the need of the community to heighten and preserve such awareness: "The common work of the tribe." The dominant current model of the lyric poem originated with the postromantic sense of the isolated artist and the autotelic theories of aesthetic experience. This model was made more or less canonic by such anthologies as F. T. Palgrave's *Golden Treasury* (1861) and by such critical studies, some generations later, as I. A. Richard's *Principles of Literary Criticism* (1925).[2] Snyder is indebted to this model, as is virtually every postromantic poet, and his riprap poetics can be seen in part as an extreme development of one aspect of the art-lyric, the dictum against ornate or merely decorative imagery. But Snyder's more recent work is set against several other dicta of the art-lyric, chiefly the strict avoidance of intellectual content and didactic intentions. Snyder attempts to celebrate the common work of the tribe, and so his poetry has a didactic role, as well as a concern for group consciousness and social value (although more often of a desired rather than an actual sort) that mitigates against the art-lyric's concentration of the single, exacerbated sensibility. In a poem like "Anasazi," which opens *Turtle Island,* there is little or no trace of an observing subject or a lyrical ego; everything is subordinated to an almost phenomenological rendition of the Anasazi's tribal existence. More like an ethnographic field report than an art-lyric, this poem relies on an understood valuation that praises any social grouping that relates harmoniously to its physical environment. The ending of the poem blocks out in stark imagery the tribe's conditions of existence, and the ambiguity of reference equates the landscape with the tribe itself:

> trickling streams in hidden canyons
> under the cold rolling desert
>
> corn-basket                wide eyed
>         red baby
>         rock lip home,

Anasazi

The "streams" can be the water that nourishes the Indians' crops or metaphorically the Indians themselves; the corn-basket can contain either the cereal that is the staple of their diet or their infants; their homes are made in and of the rock lip, the "clefts in the cliffs." The poem does not directly address any inner state or dramatize any emotional tension; it records and names rather than enacts or addresses its subject matter. It applies to us only insofar as we can see ourselves as products of, and preservers of, a physical environment.

Each of these three mediations helps to center Snyder's poetry and to support the other two; the mediation of poetic ends is, however, perhaps the most important. Snyder has talked about shamanistic songs and about the use of poetry and art that extends back to the Pleistocene era. Though the anthropological evidence is slim in these matters, there is a social use for poetry that extends beyond that of the art-lyric and the privatized reader. Some of this use function was once partly fulfilled by epic poetry, and today some have suggested it is fulfilled by advertising copywriters, who are the most successful, or at least widespread, mediators of our common dreams and our social reality. But Snyder returns to some of the functions of epic poetry while preempting the role of advertising. Here, from *The Old Ways*, is a description, written in 1975, of the new model of poetry Snyder envisions:

> We're just starting, in the last ten years here, to begin to make songs that will speak for plants, mountains, animals and children. When you see your first deer of the day you sing your salute to the deer, or your first red-wing blackbird—I saw one this morning! Such poetries will be created by us as we reinhabit this land with people who know they belong to it; for whom "primitive" is not a word that means past, but *primary*, and *future*. They will be created as we learn to see, region by region, how we live specifically (plant life!) in each place. The poems will leap out past the auto-mobiles and TV sets of today into the vastness of the Milky Way (visible only when the electricity is turned down), to richen and humanize the scientific cosmologies. These poesies to come will help us learn to be people of knowledge in this universe in community with the other people—non-human included—brothers and sisters.

For me the key term here is "salute," for that is the mode of address in the Anasazi poem quoted above. Salutation involves recognition but also a well-wishing, a call to and for the forces of health and safety. Salutation, of course, also has a social dimension, and it communizes both its speaker and the person addressed. By this complex act of naming, well-wishing, and social placement, Snyder is less concerned with interior states than with environmental harmony. Learning to live "specifically . . . in each place" means knowing the plant life, knowing how the immediate physical environment makes available and uses its weather, soil, and other conditions to produce food, and this knowledge is necessary for the community to sustain its biological life as well as its cultural identity. Such localism and regionalism are not grounded in xenophobia or philistinism; rather they draw on and lead to a scientific understanding of the importance of place. Thus, Snyder's new poetry is as likely to include facts as it is to draw on so-called primitive or archaic knowledge and culture.

The second section of *Turtle Island* begins with a poem called "Facts," and in its ten numbered prose sentences it moves as far from the model of the art-lyric as would seem possible. Here are some samples:

1. 92% of Japan's three million ton import of soybeans comes from the U.S.
2. The U.S. has 6% of the world's population; consumes ⅓ the energy annually consumed in the world.

. . . . . . . . . . . . . . . . . . . . . . . . . . . . . . . . . . . . . . . . . . . . .

6. General Motors is bigger than Holland.
7. Nuclear energy is mainly subsidized with fossil fuels and barely yields net energy.

These formulations can be further understood, beyond their self-explanatory factuality, in the larger contexts of Snyder's recurrent concerns. But such an integration into a larger vision does not make "Facts" a good poem. Certainly no argument will convince a reader who expects or desires an art-lyric to like "Facts." Thomas Parkinson has identified two modes in Snyder, one that is "measured, dramatic, definite . . . in design, formal, and contemplative," and another that is "fluent, wise, witty, mediative and hortatory." For Parkinson the first mode is clearly the best, while the second produces work that is "prepoetic."[3] *Prepoetic*, of course, would also describe most oral poetry, primitive chants, mantras, and other forms that, from the perspective of the art-lyric, lack the dramatic and contemplative features we associate with postromantic poetry. "Facts" can be seen as prepoetic not only because it lacks a dramatic or formal structure but because it clearly reads as prose and uses the language of mundane reality in nonstylized ways. But Snyder bids us to recall all the specificity of our world of prose; not every song can be a salutation, yet each poem can address a fact that informs the community about an essential aspect of its identity. By including the prepoetic (or the unpoetic, though this word has been largely outlawed since W. C. Williams objected to Wallace Stevens's use of it in describing Williams's poetry), Snyder at the very least implicitly acknowledges that a chant or song will not of itself alter social reality.

Another way to see "Facts" is to recognize that Snyder's ethics of responsibility does not get obscured by an ethics of ultimate ends, that the pressures and constraints of a very real social structure create an inescapable obligation to keep a vision alive with actual consequences.[4] Another poem, from the first section of *Turtle Island*, is closer to the art-lyric tradition, and its dramatic, anecdotal structure might be seen by a programmatic avant-gardist as old-fashioned. This is "I Went into the Maverick Bar," which vividly captures the de-

spairing lack of social possibility that is a minor but important theme
counterpointing Snyder's utopian vision.

> I went into the Maverick Bar
> In Farmington, New Mexico,
> And drank double shots of bourbon
>                 backed with beer.
> My long hair was tucked up under a cap
>
> I'd left the earring in the car.
> Two cowboys did horseplay
>     by the pool tables,
> A waitress asked us
>     where are you from?
> a country-and-western band began to play
> "We don't smoke Marijuana in Muskokie"
> And with the next song,
>     a couple began to dance.
>
> They held each other like in High School dances
>     in the fifties;
> I recalled when I worked in the woods
>     and the bars of Madras, Oregon.
> That short-haired joy and roughness—
>     America—your stupidity.
> I could almost love you again.
>
> We left—onto the freeway shoulders—
>     under the tough old stars—
> In the shadow of bluffs
>     I came back to myself,
> To the real work, to
>     "What is to be done."

The allusion to Lenin's revolutionary tract in the last line of the
poem, along with the use of what is one of Snyder's key phrases,
"the real work," poses this anecdote on an edge of ambiguity that
in many ways resembles that prized in the art-lyric. Yet the ambiguity
here—the unspecified commitment, the feelings of rejection and fear
mingled with nostalgia and fondness—actually dissolves with the
phrase "I came back to myself." Here Snyder realizes how far his
values are from those of many of his ordinary fellow citizens, but he
also realizes he must and will maintain those values. Unlike the art-
lyric, which traditionally strives for an image of closure that focuses
and yet heightens ambiguity, this poem closes with an opening vista
of resolution to pursue an ethically formed, intellectually shaped goal.
    The most important supposition of the art-lyric, namely that
momentary emotion, heedless of larger consequences, has a self-

justifying truth grounded in its very intensity, is here embodied in the flow of the verse. The dancing couple breaks in on the song celebrating repression, and this triggers the memories of work and class-affiliation, which are then shattered by an image impacted with contradictory emotional values ("short-haired joy and roughness"); this causes the speaker's consciousness to crest with a large abstract image, followed by the unconcealment of his emotional conflict. As a phrase, "I could almost love you again" refuses to indulge its lyric impulses, and instead the poem turns away from the immediately present community to a larger, less present, but more "real" commitment. So the verse, with its dashes and line breaks, not only enacts the process of discovery but also registers the speaker's self-denial and self-correction. The poem is about promise-within-failure, and it must take its recognition of the "common work of the tribe" away from the immediate source of its song.

Much of the tension present in "I Went into the Maverick Bar" pervades the whole of *Turtle Island*. The book is divided into four sections, three of poetry and one of prose. The sections of poetry— "Manzanita," "Magpie's Song," and "For the Children"—could respectively be considered a poetry of prayer and ritual, a poetry of instruction, and a poetry of hope. But this sort of classification will not hold firmly, and it is better to see each section as containing some poems from each of the three modes, though dominated by a specific set of concerns. Perhaps we can best see this organization, loose as it is, by looking closely at the shape and subjects of one section, noting some exceptions, and then glancing at the other two sections. In the section called "Manzanita," for example, the first two poems, "Anasazi" and "The Way West, Underground," are clearly salutations, the second being a poem about bears that recalls the Coyote poem that opened *The Back Country*. Then there is a poem that reads very like a doxology from a religious ritual: "Without," which argues that singing is "the proof of the power within." This poem announces one of the volume's chief themes, that all energy must be internally graceful in order to be truly powerful. Harmony relies on the path having "no / end in itself" but rather recircling in both inner and outer realms. The poem is written in simple language, virtually without imagery, and draws on the philosophical bent we saw in *Regarding Wave* (for which it could serve as a fitting epigraph). Other poems in this section, namely "The Great Mother," "No Matter, Never Mind," and "Prayer for the Great Family," resemble "Without," and together they can be read as Snyder's creation hymn and doxology. As a group they strongly influence the feeling of this section as one preoccupied with prayer and ritual. There is even an exorcism poem, "Spel against Demons," which contributes to this feeling. In turn this feeling pervades a poem like "The Bath," with its refrain of

*"This is our body"* and its description of an ideal erotic and familial union among Snyder, his wife, and his sons, Kai and Gen. The exceptions to this dominant mood are poems such as "I Went into the Maverick Bar," "Front Lines," and "The Call of the Wild." With a little ingenuity we could see these three poems as broken rituals, places where the "common work of the tribe" breaks down into alienation and mistrust. "Front Lines" recalls the poems in the "Logging" section of *Myths & Texts,* and here we see a

> bulldozer grinding and slobbering
> Sideslipping and belching on top of
> The skinned-up bodies of still-live bushes
> In the pay of a man
> From town.

Since Snyder has written this poem before, and generally better, the best reading of its inclusion here would argue that the problem of alienated labor has not gone away, and recognition of the problem is demanded even in a group of primarily celebratory poems.

The last two poems in the section contribute to the salutational atmosphere. The poem that lends the section its title, "Manzanita," is clearly a song of plant life that mediates between Coyote as a mythical figure and the plant itself, with its transformative power and its connections to the net of what Snyder calls "ethnobotany," the use of vegetative life in human culture. "The longer you look / The bigger they seem," says the last stanza of the poem, describing the manzanita bushes. This poem then concludes by citing the etymology of the plant's name, "little apples." The final poem, "Charms," looks back to the mode of "The Song of the Taste" in *Regarding Wave,* but its subject is the "dreamlike perfection / of name-and-form" incorporated in female beauty. Snyder says that such beauty evokes "the Delight / at the heart of creation" and even avers that he could be "devastated and athirst with longing / for a lovely mare or lioness, or lady mouse." To the vegetable kingdom of "Manzanita" this poem exuberantly adds the animal kingdom, and where "Manzanita" is local and specific, "Charms" is universal; where the one celebrates the immediate physical environment, the other makes a hymn to a utopian sense of "another world," the Deva Realm as Snyder calls it. Read together the two lyrics not only help to complete our sense of Snyder's new poetry but they also show how the reinhabitation of the land will be aided by songs of knowledge and community. In a sense both of these poems are postpolitical, since they speak to a consciousness built of a total harmonization of man with nature and man with man.

As a section, then, "Manzanita" is heavily weighted with poems that salute principles of harmony and growth, though there are also poems, such as "Front Lines," that try to face up to the "Rot at the heart / In the sick fat veins of Amerika." The book's next section, "Magpie's Song," has several longer poems that seem concerned with conveying information, somewhat in the manner of Thoreau's natural historian who is content to let a fact flower into a truth. "Mother Earth: Her Whales," "Straight-Creek—Great Burn," and "The Hudsonian Curlew" take delight in descriptions of natural processes and rhythms and seek little metaphoric resonance beyond the awareness of immanent order and shapeliness. Again, this feeling is determined in part by the section's opening poem, "Facts," but it is also counterpointed by an ethical longing or predilection that arises in some of the shorter poems. I am thinking here of the conclusions to poems like "Ethnobotany" ("Taste all, and hand the knowledge down") and "Up Branches of Duck River" ("hold it close / give it all away"). These ethical principles are, as I have suggested, sometimes versions of a Buddhist-like wisdom and sometimes a practical field-knowledge. This particular mediation, between ultimate ends and local responses, has been a goal of Snyder's poetry all along, of course, though it seems to be more self-conscious and more aesthetically successful in *Turtle Island* than in, say, *Riprap*. In this section's closing poem, "Magpie's Song," Snyder begins with a specific place and time and then alludes glancingly to the tutelary or totemic figure of Coyote, but here the creature is seen naturalistically. One might expect the following figure of the magpie to also operate in a naturalistic manner, but instead the poem ends with a message of hope and the poet's integration of and with natural forces and his own disciplined mind.

> Six A.M.
> Sat down on excavation gravel
> by juniper and desert S.P. tracks
> interstate 80 not far off
>     between trucks
> Coyotes—maybe three
>     howling and yapping from a rise.
>
> Magpie on a bough,
> Tipped his head and said,
>
>     *"Here in the mind, brother*
>     *Turquoise blue.*
>     *I wouldn't fool you.*
>     *Smell the breeze*
>     *It came through all the trees*
>     *No need to fear*
>     *What's ahead*
>     *Snow up on the hills west*
>     *Will be there every year*
>     *be at rest.*

*A feather on the ground—*
*The wind sound—*

*Here in the Mind, Brother,*
*Turquoise Blue"*

The magpie's instruction recalls the Rinzai sense of the mantras that are to be found in the patterns that result from natural forces: the blowing snow, the sounding wind. The poet has been fraternalized by this initiation or instruction scene, and the jeweled mind corresponds once more with the jeweled net of interconnected systems. The Amerindian West and the Buddhist East are brought together as the local and the cosmic open to one another.

The third and final section of poetry in *Turtle Island* is called "For the Children" and obviously deals with that new sense of the primitive that Snyder strives to establish, the primitive as both "primary" and "future." But the section also contains one of Snyder's boldest historical poems, "What Happened Here Before," which moves, in a little over three pages, from 300 million years ago to the present. The *here* refers to the area around Snyder's homestead in the Sierra Nevadas, and the poem ends with the challenge: "WE SHALL SEE / WHO KNOWS / HOW TO BE." This challenge refers to the ethos of Snyder and the reinhabitants of Turtle Island, with their specific knowledge of county tax rates and local history as well as of their cosmic and prehistoric vistas, as opposed to the people who pilot the "military jets [that] head northwest, roaring, every dawn." Preceding this poem in the section is "Tomorrow's Song," which begins with the radical notion that because America "never gave the mountains and rivers, / trees and animals, / a vote," it has "slowly lost its mandate." This is Snyder's most challenging, most "untraditional" notion, that animals and trees should be represented by government and accorded rights. Part of his hope for the preservation of the wilderness and natural resources, this notion may also be seen as Snyder's final mediation between his reverence for nature and his socialist-humanist political vision. Snyder says that "We look to the future with pleasure" since we can "get power within / grow strong on less," and in this new political-natural order he imagines a people living on Turtle Island who will be "gentle and innocent as wolves / as tricky as a prince." By inverting the Hobbesian sense of man as predatory and by playfully invoking Machiavelli's *The Prince,* Snyder redraws two of the Western political tradition's main metaphors and uses them to redefine what he means by being "At work and in our place." The real work is knowing what is to be done, but knowing also the ground—in all the senses of the word—on which it can be done. "Tomorrow's Song" is Snyder's salute to the future and contains one of his fullest descriptions of the ethos of Turtle Island.

The poem that lends its title to this last section of poetry, "For the Children," concludes with a simple testament of faith, a gesture that catches up elements of salutation and instruction to form a final set of ethical principles.

> In the next century
> or the one beyond that
> they say,
> are valleys, pastures,
> We can meet there in peace
> if we make it.
>
> To climb these coming crests
> one word to you, to
> you and your children:
> *Stay together*
> *learn the flowers*
> *go light*

Political community, reverence for nature, and an ascetic graceful-ness—all of Snyder's values are reflected in these three injunctions. The simplicity of the diction and the images recalls Blake, and the whole tradition of the literary ballad, in which a sophisticated poet adopts a simple framework to say something that is at once primitive and essential. Snyder's "one word" is the equivalent of what Kerouac called the "final lesson," and in each case the sublime is domesticated, brought home by bodily knowledge and mental harmony.

Taken together, and with the remarkable prose essays as well, the three sections of poetry in *Turtle Island* form a whole that advances Snyder's work well beyond the objectivist poetics of the early books and the political suppositions of *Earth House Hold*. Supplemented with the essays of *The Old Ways*, some of which are contemporary with *Turtle Island*, Snyder's vision is as full and distinctive as that of any of his contemporaries, including the slightly earlier generation of Lowell, Berryman, and Jarrell. Only Olson, I believe, compares with him in terms of a mythic imagination, and only Levertov has as broad and deep a political consciousness. But can Snyder claim for his art (or can his readers claim on his behalf) any authority other than that of the aesthetic realm? Take his notion that trees and animals should be represented in Congress. While this neatly ties together his ecological awareness and his political concerns, can the average reader see it as anything but an amusing conceit? Perhaps we can glimpse through this "literary" notion, this play with meta-phors and contexts, a twitting of the serious tradition of representative democracy. Or can we better see it as a serious critique of representational government if we realize that banks and corporations command a share of representative power in our legislatures, and they are no more capable of speaking for themselves, without human mediation, than are trees and animals? If humans can find a way to define the rights of a corporation, why can they not do the same for the forest?

As for *Turtle Island* as a literary work, its language goes against the grain of several canonic tenets of modernism, and it flies in the face of once fashionable styles such as confessionalism. Like much genuinely innovative work, Snyder's poetry resorts to some quite ancient strategies and rhetorical gestures. Without the resplendent imagery of neo-surrealism, or the tight dramatic irony of academic poetry, or the display of an exacerbated sensibility, Snyder has reduced and yet enlarged the range of the lyric poem. But only a reader with at least a political awareness, if not a like-minded political will, can extensively respond to that range. Snyder has not solved the problem (how could he?) that animated so much of the theory of the autotelic art-lyric in the first place, namely, should not the extra-literary considerations of political or ethical belief be separated from the judgment of a poem on purely literary grounds? Snyder's work implicitly rejects the autotelic, formalist solution which said that only strictly structural and technical criteria should determine the worth of a poem, "as poem." This rejection is etched in the apparent lack of formal expertise in much of his poetry (though in fact his prosody can be quite sophisticated if judged from a nontraditional vantage point). Whether his language use can bring about a broad revival of, or even limited respect for, such forms as a poetry of salutation or instruction is an intriguing possibility. As early as the 1952 "Lookout's Journal" in *Earth House Hold,* Snyder asked:

> —If one wished to write poetry of nature, where an audience?
> Must come from the very conflict of an attempt to articulate
> the vision poetry and nature in our time.
> (reject the human; but the tension of
> human events, brutal and tragic, against
> a non-human background? like Jeffers?)

It is to the credit of *Turtle Island,* and the whole of Snyder's work, that he has not rejected the human, and indeed has avoided Jeffer's solution by refusing to subordinate the human to the nonhuman. On the other hand, what separates Snyder from many traditional poets is his refusal to appropriate the nonhuman (or natural) realm as no more than a dramatic or illustrative backdrop to the "tension of human events." This is what gives Snyder a legitimate claim to be operating as much outside or beyond the contexts of traditional literary values as any other contemporary poet. What *Turtle Island* finally mediates is the tension in mythical speculation that sees the world as supported and yet free-floating. Literature in such a mediation can try to be both self-grounded and ethically normative. But no modern poet would ever think such a dual burden could be easily lightened. Snyder says in the closing poem of *Turtle Island* that

> A Mind Poet
> Stays in the house.
> The house is empty
> And it has no walls.
> The poem
> Is seen from all sides,
> Everywhere,
> At once.

We have to realize the "house" is both the cosmos and the imagination, and that a poem whose perspective is panoptic and omnipresent can be understood both as an art-lyric poised on the vanishing point of self-reflective irony and as a cosmic hymn of all-embracing belief. Here Snyder's vision, or at least his desire for a healing vision, is as full as possible.

## Notes

1. In *From Marx to Weber: Essays in Sociology*, trans. and ed. H. H. Gerth and C. Wright Mills (New York: Oxford University Press, 1946), pp. 77–128.

2. See Christopher Clausen's essay on Palgrave in *Georgia Review* 34.2 (Summer 1980): 273–89. Viewed from a radical perspective, this essay supports the view of Oakeshott mentioned in Chapter 1 of *Gary Snyder's Vision*.

3. "The Theory and Practice of Gary Snyder," *Journal of Modern Literature* 2,3 (Winter 1971): 451. Parkinson's earlier essay, "The Poetry of Gary Snyder," *Southern Review* 4 (1968): 616–32, was largely positive and did much to win critical respect for Snyder, though now the piece seems rather thin. The later essay tries to deal with arguments against Snyder and shows a greater sense of the struggles involved in refining the vision.

4. See Charles Altieri, "Gary Snyder's *Turtle Island*: The Problem of Reconciling the Roles of Seer and Prophet," *boundary 2* 6.3 (1976): 761–77. Altieri's sense of reconciling prophet and seer overlaps with my sense of mediation in Snyder. For Altieri, the prophet's vision is communally directed while that of the seer is intensely private; for him Snyder's *Turtle Island* veers close to stereotype in some poems and is insufficiently charged with personal drama. In a sense, my argument about the new modes of poetry in Snyder is an attempt to address Altieri's telling criticism.

# Gary Snyder and the Curve of Return

Robert Schultz and
David Wyatt°

I

Gary Snyder was born in San Francisco in 1930. He grew up in Washington state and in Portland, hiking the woods and sometimes logging in them. After a brief early marriage, the Reed graduate interspersed work on a trail crew in Yosemite with study of Oriental languages at Berkeley. He was on hand the night in 1955 when Ginsberg first read "Howl" and later shared a cabin with Kerouac in Mill Valley. At 26 he left America for Japan, married again, and spent much of the next 13 years there, traveling and studying at its Zen monasteries. In 1967 he married his third wife—Masa Uehara—on the lip of an active volcano. They returned to California in 1968 and moved to San Juan Ridge in the hot, pine-studded foothills of the Sierra Nevada. There they continue to build their home, Kitkit-dizze, and to raise two sons, Kai and Gen.

Snyder's career has been expressed through two motions at once unique and complementary: turning and returning. Turning emphasizes all that is unique, passing, lost; returning, all that is collective, located, able to be held. The choice is as simple as one between the road and home, though at its most exalted it becomes one between transcendence and a life lived in time. The strongest poem in Snyder's latest book, *Axe Handles* (1983), beautifully captures the tension between the urge to be out and away and the need to settle and stay. It is called "True Night."

As the poem begins, the sleeping poet is suddenly awakened by the clatter of raccoons in the kitchen. He chases them outdoors only to find himself caught by the temptation of permanent escape:

> As I stay there then silent
> The chill of the air on my nakedness
> Starts off the skin
> I am all alive to the night.
> Bare foot shaping on gravel
> Stick in the hand forever

Stripping away history like clothes, the early Snyder had often sought for a moment such as this in which the self, lost to all others, commits to a moment of pure vision or sensation. The poet stands a long moment, listening to crickets "Faint in cold coves in the dark." But he has long since accepted the pull of a contrary motion:

° Reprinted by permission from *Virginia Quarterly Review* 62, no. 4 (1986). 681–94.

I turn and walk slow
Back the path to the beds
With goosebumps and loose waving hair
In the night of milk-moonlit thin cloud glow
And black rustling pines
I feel like a dandelion head
Gone to seed
About to be blown all away
Or a sea anemone open and waving in
Cool pearly water.

Dispersal into space and of self: these remain the attractively threatening possibilities that haunt even this conservative turning back. Time has conspired, however, to transform the poet's life into a series of repetitions he ruefully and quietly accepts: "Fifty years old. / I still spend my time / Screwing nuts down on bolts." It is the choices made in time that now continually pull him back. When he mentions what lies within the shadowed house, it is as if poet and reader agree to remember what they have temporarily agreed to forget:

At the shadow pool,
Children are sleeping,
And a lover I've lived with for years,
True night.
One cannot stay too long awake
In this dark

Dusty feet, hair tangling,
I stoop and slip back to the
Sheath, for the sleep I still need,
For the waking that comes
Every day
With the dawn.

Snyder's *Axe Handles* returns to love and work. How he achieves this utter and yet gently reluctant resolve is the story of his career.

Published when he was 29, Snyder's first book empties the mind of the "damned memories" that clog it in an ascesis that marks the beginning of his quest. In *Riprap* (1959) he turns from America toward the East and begins the motion out and away that will preoccupy him for 15 years. *Myths & Texts* (1960) promotes Snyder's emerging vision of process in a dialectical structure which resolves that all form is a momentary stay, "stresses that come into being each instant." In a world where "It's all falling or burning" the experience of place is only a fiction, and there can be therefore nothing to return to. *Mountains and Rivers without End* (1965–) will contain 25 sections and is as yet unfinished. This may prove the major work of Snyder's career, though, as in Pound's *Cantos,* the poet can seem more committed to the theory than the poetry of this poem. The theory holds, in Snyder's words, that "every poem in *Mountains and Rivers* takes a different form and has a different strategy." A poem built upon the impulse of turning away from its own realized structures, *Mountains and Rivers* would seem a work about journeys, about "Passing / through." Its fascination however with what Snyder has called the "focal image" and with a realm above the Blue Sky also reaches toward permanence. These growing tensions as well as the poem's quality as a running rumination on all that Snyder holds dear place it at this point beyond any developmental model of Snyder's career.

*The Back Country* (1968) is in this argument the pivotal book, the one most openly engaged with Snyder's own history of turning. What begins as a reprise of *Riprap*—in "Far West" Snyder amasses his reasons for moving and forgetting—proceeds by discovering an opposing impulse to return and remember. A poem like "Dodger Point Lookout" bears comparison to "Tintern Abbey" in its acceptance of meaning as a function of elapsed time. The return of the poet to a beloved spot five years later "brings it all back," and he admits that the conserving power of memory is what keeps him "sane."

*Regarding Wave* (1970) shores up the position gained in *The Back Country* by valorizing a new and conserving pattern—the wave—capable of storing and releasing the energy which Snyder had earlier discovered in the stream. A book about "What's Meant by Here," *Turtle Island* (1974) registers Snyder's emerging commitment to a structure that stays in place. Homesteading replaces hitchhiking as the privileged human activity as Snyder's act of settlement in California expands into a sense of stewardship over the entire planet.

This rapid summary brings us back to *Axe Handles,* Snyder's first book of poems in nearly a decade and one in which he celebrates the whim and wisdom of middle age. In *Axe Handles* Snyder begins with work around the house and ends with journeys. Travel is now seen as the venturing out from a hearth, and thus the controlling metaphors ("Loops" and "Nets") are of structures that return or contain.

## II

*Axe Handles* is divided into three parts, "Loops," "Little Songs for Gaia," and finally "Nets," which itself contains four sections. At first glance, the book may seem too intricate or arbitrary in its structure, but with further reading sections and subsections reveal important groupings of Snyder's current concerns. The book follows the poet's movement of mind as he attempts to discover a coherence among commitments that are personal, familial, and cultural in scope.

"True Night," the book's central poem and the concluding poem of the first section, most succinctly dramatizes the choice Snyder has made in favor of returning and settling. But the poems which surround it show the full content of the poet's choice. *Axe Handles* is a declaration of affiliations to an ideal of "home," an ideal that has grown in Snyder's imagination to include the full range of a life's attachments, from the most personal and local to the most public and distant. At the personal level, Snyder takes firm possession of his own biography, noting memories which reveal patterns of self-definition ("Look Back," "Soy Sauce," "Delicate Crisscrossing Beetle Trails Left in the Sand"). He writes of family and community with ideals of mutual support and teaching ("Changing Diapers," "Painting the North San Juan School"). He writes about the possibilities and limitations of government ("Talking Late with the Governor about the Budget"). He returns again and again to the mooring certainties of hard physical labor ("Working on the '58 Willys Pickup," "Getting in the Wood"). And, as ever, he writes with great attention to a natural order seen through the particularities of his home region (the book is dedicated "To San Juan Ridge").

Memory, family, community, teaching, government, and natural process: the subjects of *Axe Handles* necessarily involve Snyder in time and recurrence. The poet who began by relishing the obliterating sense of timelessness as he peered down alone through miles of air from Sourdough Lookout now gives special emphasis to the loops of cultural transmission, and *Axe Handles* begins with a coincidence which dramatizes for Snyder the "craft of culture." His son has asked for a hatchet handle, and while carving it with an axe Snyder remembers with a shock of recognition the Chinese phrase, "When making an axe handle the pattern is not far off." The lesson, first read in Ezra Pound and then studied again under Snyder's Japanese teacher, Chen, is now lived by the poet, and he writes:

> . . . I see: Pound was an axe,
> Chen was an axe, I am an axe
> And my son a handle, soon
> To be shaping again, model
> And tool, craft of culture,
> How we go on.

The book's second poem reinforces the theme, as the spirit of Lew Welch returns from the dead to tell Snyder: ". . . teach the children about the cycles. / The life cycles. All the other cycles. / That's what it's all about, and it's all forgot." And indeed, subsequent poems deal

with integrities created by recurrence: the water cycle; the life cycle
of a Douglas fir; loops of personal memory that illuminate present
moments; and a pilgrimage of return to Japan to renew ties with
Masa's family and, incidentally, to crisscross the path of Snyder's own
earlier travels.

In "River in the Valley"—a poem about cycles—one of Snyder's
boys asks, "where do rivers start?" and the poem answers:

> in threads in hills, and gather down to here—
> but the river
> is all of it everywhere,
> all flowing at once,
> all one place.

Instruction is at the heart of this book, emphasized in its beginning
and returned to frequently. "What Have I Learned," a poem near
the end of the book, concludes: "Seeing in silence: / never the same
twice, / but when you get it right, / you pass it on."

And what, at age 53, is the knowledge the poet would pass on?
In "What Have I Learned," Snyder modestly claims to know only
"the proper use for several tools," how to recognize the "yellow
petals, the golden hairs" of the Colachortus flower, and to enjoy
contemplation while sipping wine "between hard pleasant tasks." But
in *Axe Handles* as a whole Snyder communicates admiration for the
economy of nature's transactions, respect for the wisdom of primitive
cultures, disdain for an economy doomed by its dependence on oil,
and disgust for the "poisons" of ownership, greed, and waste. He
also explains his belief in the work done by arts councils and expresses
a bond of sympathy with those who live by physical labor. Most of
all, however, Snyder seeks to pass on glimpses of the severe and
beautiful economies he sees in nature and which provide him with
patterns he applies in his own way of life.

In "Among," Snyder notes the presence of one Douglas fir among
Ponderosa Pines at 3,000 feet near the Yuba River in California, and
he is fascinated by the combination of events that has allowed it to
thrive there. Conditions are unfavorable, but the fir has propagated
by discovering the minutest niche of opportunity in the local ecology:

> Every fall a lot of little seedlings sprout
> > around it—
>
> Every summer during long dry drouth they die
> Once every forty years or so
> A rain comes in July.
>
> Two summers back it did that,
> The Doug fir seedlings lived that year

The next year it was dry,
A few fir made it through.
This year, with roots down deep, two live.
A Douglas fir will be among these pines.

This is the harsh, yet precise and finally beautiful natural order which informs Gary Snyder's moral sense. Within such an order, the law of the land is ground to a fine, sharp edge.

Imbued with a sense of nature's rigor, Snyder has chosen to live apart from what he takes to be the extravagance of his contemporaries. He frets comically about the $3.50 worth of kerosene required to soak his fence posts and wonders at the amount of fuel burned in displays of power by air defense jets. His alarm at our civilization's utter dependence upon a diminishing oil supply, in fact, arises in no fewer than five poems, making it one of the book's most insistent concerns. In "Alaska" he describes a trip to the oil pipeline, where he read the question, "Where will it all end?" spray-painted on the elevated tube. Later, dozing with his colleagues in a small plane, he suddenly noticed out the window "the mountains / Soaring higher yet, and quite awake."

The eerie presence of those mountains, immense and watchful, looms for Snyder as a premonition of inevitable retribution. According to the poet's sense of natural law, unnatural acts call forward inevitable consequences, and in several poems Snyder sounds a note of judgment. In "Money Goes Upstream," he is in a lecture hall, daydreaming about greed and corruption. Money, he thinks, is "an odd force . . . in the world / *Not* a power / That seeks to own the source." It behaves unnaturally—"It dazzles and it slips us by. / It swims upstream." Therefore, those who place it too near the center of their lives become unmoored, possessed. Against this insidious influence Snyder poses his own ability to summon the corrective presence of nature: "I can smell the grass, feel the stones with bare feet / though I sit here shod and clothed / with all the people. That's my power." This power is two-fold: Snyder's firsthand knowledge of nature and its sufficiencies inoculates him from avarice, and his ability to summon what is not present keeps him ever close to the natural law from which he borrows his authority.

Snyder could hardly have traveled farther from his early absorption with moments of pure vision or sensation to the instinct for teaching—and judgment—so apparent in *Axe Handles*. The former experience is solitary and held out of time by its novelty and intensity, while "passing on" is communal and temporal. Yet the poet still holds that our most fundamental knowledge is discovered in moments of experience which stand out of time. And, as if to reaffirm this fact, Snyder includes at the center of *Axe Handles* a sequence of lyrics which presents a gallery of such moments.

## III

"Little Songs for Gaia," issued in an earlier version as a Copper Canyon Press chapbook (1979), is addressed to the earth goddess of Greek mythology. In it Snyder descends from the more general point of view which allows him to be discursive elsewhere in the book to write here with an unmixed particularity. The ecological point of view expressed in *Axe Handles* has grown out of a thousand individual experiences, and here Snyder reestablishes contact, zooming down to the thing, itself:

> Red soil—blue sky—white cloud—grainy granite,
> and
> Twenty thousand mountain miles of manzanita.
> Some beautiful tiny manzanita
> I saw a single, perfect, lovely,
> manzanita

> Ha.

Snyder, like Antaeus, renews his strength by touching ground, and that is what he does in this middle section, absorbed in description of his home region and his daily domestic life.

Elsewhere in the book readers may sometimes balk at Snyder's prose-like rhythms, which often conform only to the poet's clipped, trochaic manner of speech. But "Little Songs for Gaia" features some of the most accomplished lyric writing of Snyder's career, whether he is presenting a dream of corn goddesses or a deer hit by a car:

> Dead doe lying in the rain

> on the shoulder
> in the gravel

> I see your stiff leg

> in the headlights
> by the roadside

> Dead doe lying in the rain

The circularity of this brief lyric fixes our attention, beginning and end, on the unfortunate deer, with the assonance of the spondee, "Dead doe," hammering home the image. In between, the four prepositional phrases are exactly parallel in rhythm, relentlessly locating the dead animal. And in between them, the kernel sentence, "I see your stiff leg," particularizes the doe efficiently and with poignance.

Elsewhere, Snyder even uses end rhyme to good effect:

> Log trucks go by at four in the morning
>     as we roll in our sleeping bags
>         dreaming of health.
> The log trucks remind us,
>     as we think, dream and play
>
> Of the world that is carried away.

The surprise of the closural rhyme, which suddenly links the family's dreams and play with eventual loss, is largely responsible for the power of this brief lyric. Contributing to the effect, three consecutive anapests speed the final line, creating a sense of the poet's world quickly slipping away.

"Little Songs for Gaia" is made of glimpses—heightened moments of perception or feeling communicating an intimacy of contact with things which spices and sustains the life of the poet. Everywhere in this section Snyder is intent upon the particular and absorbed in the moment, attending to everything as to the flickers' call: "THIS! / THIS! / THIS! / in the cool pine breeze."

Snyder moves back from knowing to doing in the book's final section, "Nets," in which each of the four clusters of poems forms a rather loosely organized Poundian "ideogram." Taken together, these four clusters portray the "nets" of contemplation and activity in which Snyder is currently enmeshed.

The first, a bridge from the Gaia sequence, presents Snyder active and reverent in a natural world that flashes glimpses of deity. Walking a Yellowstone meadow, for instance, he observes its graceful creatures and ambiguously records the perception of a goddess-like presence: "And I saw: the turn of the head, the glance of the eye, / each gesture, each lift and stamp // Of your high-arched feet." Part II of "Nets" probes the possibilities and shortcomings of government. Snyder is skeptical (he seems to long for a more expansive governmental perspective when he notes that "The great pines on the Capitol grounds [in Sacramento] / Are less than a century old"), but he is willing to participate, and former California governor Jerry Brown, who appointed Snyder to the State Arts Council, is a sympathetic character in the book. Adding another piece of the cultural puzzle, part III juxtaposes "civilization" with more primitive ways of life, marking chiefly their differing relationships to the ecosystems which support them. In "Dillingham, Alaska, the Willow Tree Bar," pipeline workers are "Drinking it down, / the pain / of the work / of wrecking the world." By contrast, in Australia Snyder feels cleansed by a ritual which carries him to an aboriginal oneness with an arid landscape ("Uluru Wild Fig Song"). Closing the book, part IV once again celebrates nature's health and ends with Snyder's wry pledge of allegiance:

> I pledge allegiance to the soil
>     of Turtle Island,
>     one ecosystem
>     in diversity
>     under the sun
> With joyful interpenetration for all.

The allegiances pledged in *Axe Handles* are many—to family, community, culture, and planet. And to make such pledges Snyder has turned considerably from his earlier conception of the world as "all changes, in thoughts, / As well as things" ("Riprap"). Within this earlier view, the poet's only recourse was to attempt to fix in words moments plucked out of the careering flux.

In *Axe Handles* there are many heightened moments seized out of time by language, but these are now seen to take their place within a broader continuity. Snyder still prizes moments when the self loses itself entirely in sensation, and a poem like "Getting in the Wood" shows how that early experience of transcendence survives into its new context. This passage in mid-poem contains no subject because the self is utterly absorbed in its work:

> The lean and heave on the peavey
> that breaks free the last of a bucked
>     three-foot round,
>         it lies flat on smashed oaklings—

Departing from the usual subject-predicate structure, Snyder's noun phrase presents only the effort itself and the object worked upon, with internal rhyme and skillfully managed rhythms communicating the strain of the job. The poet is happily lost in what he elsewhere calls the "relentless clarity at the heart of work," an experience which is for Snyder virtually a kind of meditation. At peace in his work, his attention is enthralled by

> Wedge and sledge, peavey and maul,
> little axe, canteen, piggyback can
> of saw-mix gas and oil for the chain,
> knapsack of files and goggles and rags.

Snyder could be writing about his early logging days in a poem like this, which captures in words the grit and strain of sensation. But the distance he has traveled since those early days is revealed in the final stanza, in which the task at hand is shown to be a collective one, and in which Snyder emphasizes the continuities of family and community which the work helps to develop:

> the young men throw splits on the piles
> bodies hardening, learning the pace
> and the smell of tools from this delve
> in the winter
> death-topple of elderly oak.

This is a community task, with the young men learning and hardening to the jobs they will inherit when their elders pass, like the toppled oak. Here is the sense of continuity and cultural transmission which Snyder has acquired as a husband, father, and homesteader, a sense which has changed him over the course of his career from *dharma* hitchhiker to domestic visionary.

# The Importance of Nothing: Absence and Its Origins in the Poetry of Gary Snyder

Jody Norton°

> When everything has stalled, when thought is immobilized, when language is silent, when explanation returns home in despair—then there has to be a thunderstorm.
>
> —Kierkegaard

> Summer lightning!
> Yesterday in the East,
> Today in the West.
> —Kikaku

### THE ELLIPTICAL MODE

> form—leaving things out at the right spot / ellipse, is emptiness
> —Gary Snyder[1]

In his early wilderness poetry, Gary Snyder builds absences into the structure, imagery, and syntax of his texts in order to inscribe the essential Zen Buddhist perception of the identity of sunyata (Emptiness) and tathata (suchness, objective reality) in the form itself of each poem.[2]

In the West, we are accustomed to conceiving the world dual-

° Reprinted from *Contemporary Literature* 28, 1 (1987): 41–66, by permission of the University of Wisconsin Press. © 1987 by the Board of Regents of the University of Wisconsin System.

istically. We define both material objects and ideas in terms of binary oppositions (rough / smooth, good / evil). We oppose the real to the ideal, valorizing one at the expense of the other or, with Plato, redefining the one *as* the other. Buddhism subverts such definitional projects by questioning the capacity of abstract thought to comprehend or articulate reality in any except misleading ways. Mind (Oneness), being inseparable from itself, cannot be understood in dualistic terms (Absolute / conditional, for example).[3]

Gary Snyder's poems sheer away from abstractions, delineating the material world boldly in series of concrete images. Matter-of-fact as they appear, however, Snyder's lyrics depend as much on what they omit as on what they include. Honeycombing his poems with syntactical and structural ellipses, and refusing to fully determine his imagery, Snyder seeks to disrupt our complacent relation to our own experience by short-circuiting our customary ways of dividing and conquering that experience, the chief of which is language.

Grammars, books on usage, manuals of style, and the like seek to make language systematic and reasonable. When conventionally required elements are omitted from linguistic structures, be these structures lines, sentences, or poetic forms, they become unreasonable, and their meanings are consequently problematized. But Snyder's procedures are aimed at more than merely confounding the understanding. His purpose is to use the grammatical, syntactical, and semantic spaces that permeate even language, the model for all structuralist enterprises, to make possible a kind of immediate knowing that language is not theoretically designed to produce.

Because language must make provisional use of names, Zen Buddhist teachings refer to an ultimate reality, by one word or another, in attempting to help the student of Zen to his own direct spiritual experience. But such words do not mean, in the ordinary sense, because the "meaning" they intend escapes enclosure within any particular term. To speak of the One as though it were an entity among other entities is precisely (and wrongly) to *constitute* it as such an entity. Snyder thus avoids any explicit reference to an Absolute.

By eliding the solitary speaker as well as the One in many of his poems, Snyder follows Buddhism in tacitly asserting the illusory nature of the self. Elision of the subject is often accompanied by a replacement of verbs with verbals. Use of these two forms of ellipsis enables the poet to present activity not in terms of an "I" who takes action but simply as action that is taking place.

Wishing, however, to avoid simply substituting an inverted hierarchy for the one he seeks to put in question (nothingness for objective reality, let us say, or Absence for Presence), Snyder fills his poems with palpable natural imagery—earth, plants, animals—

which is strongly sensuous but at the same time generic in its conception. This generalization of imagery accomplishes two ends: it denies the reality of individuation (the proper) without refusing particularity (the common), and it implies that the embodied experience of the poem is neither personally nor historically unique.

Never fully present, Snyder's poems enable, rather than provide, an indefinite number of actualizations—actualizations that the reader can produce only by refusing to be merely the receiver of the text. The poems demand that their reader exceed rational and discursive approaches and engage his imagination, and ultimately his intuition, actively in the completion of the poetic experience.[4]

Snyder's poetry incorporates, in addition to the Buddhist (non)conception of the Void, which constitutes its unstated ontological ground, numerous elements of the poetics and stylistic procedures of the shih poetry of T'ang Dynasty China and the Japanese haiku. Snyder combines these assumptions and practices with his own experience, imagination, and voice to compose a characteristic elliptical mode, whose aim is to make form not an extension, but an expression, of content.[5]

## THE T'ANG DYNASTY SHIH

I write because I do not want the words I find: by subtraction.
—Roland Barthes[6]

While Buddhist ontology is an originary component of Snyder's poetics, his elliptical stylistics are more immediately ascribable to the influence of the shih and other formal and linguistic antecedents. The shih, a song / poem of unspecified but relatively short length, in syllabic meter, was the standard lyric form of the T'ang Dynasty.

Numerous characteristics of the shih are attributable to the nature of the Chinese language itself. Chinese is uninflected, and its nouns lack gender and number as well as case. The nouns of the T'ang shih, in turn, tend to be concrete, denoting objects rather than abstractions, but are typically not individualized.

Verbs in Chinese lack tense in addition to person, number, voice, and mood. They are autonomous, requiring neither subject nor object. Because of this, personal pronouns are rarely used, though they do exist in the language. Frequently, a five-character shih line contains no verb at all:[7]

| 雞 | 聲 | 茅 | 店 | 月 |
|----|----|----|----|----|
| cock | crow | thatch | inn | moon |
| 人 | 跡 | 板 | 橋 | 霜 |
| man | trace | wood | bridge | frost |

These lines lack not only verbs and verbals, but connectives, prepositions, and articles as well. They consist of a selection of nominal elements organized in a highly elliptical syntactical relation which "strongly suggests the actuality of the situation" (Yip 25), but for which a fixed imaginative synthesis has not been prescribed. Wai-lim Yip suggests the following possible translation (purely for the sense of the passage):

> (At) cockcrow, the moon (is seen above) the thatched inn;
> Footprints (are seen upon) the frost (covering) the wooden bridge.
> (Yip 25)

Yip describes the method of the T'ang Dynasty shih as "vigorously unanalytical presentation" (Yip 20). It is a poetry of image rather than idea, in which the images are neither fully drawn nor explicitly located, and in which the precise nature of their interrelationships is not defined. As Burton Watson notes, T'ang Dynasty landscape poetry "offers us a landscape which is not really a landscape at all . . . but rather a blank canvas . . . inscribed 'tree,' 'bird,' 'mountain,' 'water' in the appropriate areas, upon which we are asked to execute our own realization of the scene."[8] Spaces are created both in the figuring forth of the imagery and in the poems' syntactical and structural chains, in order to draw the reader into an imaginative actualization of situations and events that have been minimally suggested by the selected, juxtaposed images of the text. Such imaginative activity may, in turn, lead on to a wordless recognition of the true nature of what is thus envisioned.

Looking back to the lines

| cock | crow | thatch | inn | moon |
|------|------|--------|-----|------|
| man | trace | wood | bridge | frost |

one is struck by the tangibility of the objects but equally strongly by their lack of particularity. Generalized imagery is common in Snyder's poetry as well. "August on Sourdough, A Visit from Dick Brewer" provides numerous instances: "Meadows and snowfields, hundreds of peaks," "summer mountain rain" (*BC* 25), and so on.

As a grammatical accompaniment to this nonspecificity of imagery, Snyder frequently elides definite and indefinite articles, so that a field is neither *a* field nor *the* field, but rather *field*, a generic sign that the imagination must materialize. Here, for example, are the opening lines of "Across Lamarck Col":

> Descending hillsides in
> half morning light, step over

>       small down pine,
> I see myself as stony granite face. (*BC* 106)

As one would expect, given the broad outlines of their imagery, T'ang shih poets tend to qualify their nouns simply and economically: "green willow" is a fair hypothetical example, whereas "delicately tinctured foliage shimmering with an aquamarine refulgence" is not. Snyder's poems exhibit a similar economy of modification. The following section from "The Spring" provides a particularly clear instance of the firmly nominal character of his imagery:

>       the foreman said let's get a drink
>       & drove through woods and flower fields
>               shovels clattering in back
>       into a black grove by a cliff
>               a rocked in pool
>               feeding a fern ravine
>                       tin can to drink
>       numbing the hand and cramping in the gut
>       surging through the fingers from below (*BC* 18)

"Black" is the only true adjective in the passage. "Flower" and "fern" are nouns used adjectivally, "rocked in" a neologized past participle. These lines, however, are more apt as a sample of technique than as an example of the open-endedness that the use of generalized imagery in shih poetry tends to create, for the mood of this passage is quite intimate and particular (one is lightly reminded of that part of "This Lime-Tree Bower My Prison" in which Coleridge writes of that "dell, o'erwooded, narrow, deep, / And only speckled by the mid-day sun").

Snyder's use of sparely modified, generalized imagery indirectly reflects the Zen Buddhist conviction of the pointlessness of intellection. An insight into the nature of Mind cannot be passed on by means of elaborate descriptions, dense figuration, or esoteric allusion, because all such devices depend on the understanding—which is inherently discriminatory and hence powerless to comprehend the Void. Such "in-sight" cannot, in fact, be passed on at all. At best it can be coaxed out, elicited; and to accomplish this, both Snyder and his models seek to provide the reader with a maximum of imaginative freedom.

Another mark of this imaginative latitude, in the shih, is the absence of a lyric "I." The elision of a subject through whose eyes and in whose terms nature is perceived invites the imaginative entry of the reader into the poem, and at the same time prevents the suggestion of an anthropocentric, dominant / subordinate relation between man and nature. Human beings and human activities, so overbearingly—and transparently—central in much of Western poetry, from the *Aeneid* to Shelley to Ginsberg, are deemphasized, not in order to produce a theologized Nature at the cost of a reductive version of human possibilities, but in order to bring those possibilities and their halting enactment into a harmonious interplay with other elemental processes of life. The vision implicit in this formal procedure is exactly congruent with the Zen Buddhist perspective on the place of man in nature reflected in Gary Snyder's poetry.

If "Riprap" is not the crucial statement on poetics Sherman Paul would have us believe, the poem nevertheless can serve as a summative example of the Chinese origins of Snyder's elliptical management of imagery.[9] Without sharing Fenollosa's extravagant and misguided assessment of the significance of Chinese ideograms, we can comprehend the visual as well as syntactical sense in which T'ang Dynasty shih do, as Snyder puts it, "Lay down . . . words / Before your mind like rocks" (*RCM* 30), and Snyder's practice in the poem— his choice of concrete but generic nouns, sparingly modified—is clearly a conscious adoption of these characteristics of the Chinese. Like Hui-neng pounding rice in the temple of the Fifth Patriarch, or like the Zen injunction to "make your work your meditation," Snyder's speaker does not languish in a self-indulgent spiritual aporia; he selects stones, and builds trails.

In addition to syntactical ellipses, and ellipses in the articulation of imagery, the shih displays significant elisions and disjunctions in its formal structure. The essential structural component of the shih is the five- or seven-character line.[10] There is very little enjambment: each line is typically a complete sense unit. There is thus an ellipsis of transition between each line and its successor, in lieu of which structural cohesion is achieved by the rhyming of even-numbered lines.

The following form of the five-character line exhibits a paratactical organization that Gary Snyder frequently employs:

| 國 | | 破 | | 山 \ | | 河 | 在 |
|------|------|--------|-----|-----------|-----|-------|--------|
| empire | (is) | broken | (:) | mountains | and | rivers | remain |

| 城 | | 春 | | 草 | | 木 | | 深 |
|--------|------|------|-----|-------|-----|-------|--------|--------|
| spring | (in) | city | (:) | grass | and | trees | (grow) | thick |

(Yip 18)

In each line, the two segments are parallel and independent. Snyder's use of this kind of structure is the more striking since in English one generally subordinates ancillary clauses to a main clause, a tendency that is evident in this structurally inaccurate translation by W. J. B. Fletcher: "A nation though fallen, the land yet remains. / When spring fills the city, its foliage is dense" (Yip 18). Wai-lim Yip comments: "in the original, the two phases of perception, like two cones of light, cut into one another simultaneously. Any attempt to reconnect them even syntactically will destroy the simultaneity and fall back on the logic of succession" (Yip 19). There is no coherent narrative / discursive sequence in the Chinese. The very structure of the poem rejects an ontology that conceives of natural objects as chained in a dependent relationship one to another, and successful translation must reject the logic of English syntax equally firmly.

Lines 6, 9, and 12 of "August on Sourdough" illustrate the influence of this paratactical construction on Snyder's line:

> You hitched a thousand miles
>         north from San Francisco
> Hiked up the mountainside    a mile in the air
> The little cabin—one room—
> 5          walled in glass
> Meadows and snowfields,    hundreds of peaks.
> We lay in our sleeping bags
>         talking half the night;
> Wind in the guy-cables    summer mountain rain.
> 10    Next morning I went with you
>         as far as the cliffs,
> Loaned you my poncho—    the rain across the shale—
> You down the snowfield
>         flapping in the wind
> 15    Waving a last goodbye    half hidden in the clouds
> To go on hitching
>         clear to New York;
> Me back to my mountain    and far, far, west. (BC 25)

Snyder carefully avoids creating a dependent relationship between the parallel elements of these lines. Neither portion is rendered as a subordinate clause or prepositional phrase modifying the other. No verbs or conjunctions join them. And once again, Snyder uses typographical space, as well as hyphens, to emphasize the disjunctive nature of these intralinear relationships. Like the guy-cables, each line is composed of separate strands—it is neither only one nor fully two.

Another characteristic of shih poetry, the avoidance of direct expression of emotion—in effect, an elision of sentiment—is manifest in this poem in Snyder's handling of his central theme, the union friendship, and tension between this shared human feeling and the self-reliance that both protagonists implicitly value. Constructed around the encounter of the speaker and his friend Dick Brewer, the poem follows Brewer from San Francisco up to the speaker's mountaintop where the two friends converse half the night, then to the cliffs, next morning, whence Brewer heads down the snowfield to New York and the speaker "back to my mountain     and far, far, west." The encounter itself is thus centered in the poem in three ways: geographically, on a mountaintop between San Francisco and New York; dramatically, as the crux of the anecdote; and structurally, as the six middle lines of the poem (7–12). In his apostrophe to Brewer, his silent auditor, the speaker moves back and forth between Brewer and himself, dramatizing the bond of friendship between them through the intertwining of personal references: "You hitched a thousand miles," "We lay in our sleeping bags," "Next morning I went with you," "Loaned you my poncho—," "You down the snowfield," "Me back to my mountain." The first line begins with "You," and the last with "Me."

There is a feeling of impermanence embodied in the poem—not simply in the content of the anecdote but in phrases such as "Wind in the guy-cables," "summer mountain rain," and "half hidden in the clouds"—which both intimates the inexpressible, the Void, and underscores the bittersweet mood of the meeting and parting friends: on the one hand devoted and compassionate (one going a thousand miles out of his way, the other parting with his poncho), and to that extent interdependent, and on the other resolute, self-reliant, and utterly independent. The poem (the action of which takes place the summer before Snyder began serious study of Asian languages at Berkeley, preparatory to traveling to Japan to study Zen Buddhism) leaves one with a sense that the speaker has real, though possibly unacknowledged, reservations about the ultimate validity of a personal decision—and, by implication, the philosophy motivating it—that in a certain sense involves the subordination of the individual and his human relationship to the pursuit of Emptiness.

Although several of its lines are enjambed, Snyder's poem "Water" exemplifies the practice of shih poetry in that each line contains an image complex which, while it may lead on to the next line / image (and almost must in such a roiling, vigorously kinetic poem) is also complete in itself:

> Pressure of sun on the rockslide
> Whirled me in a dizzy hop-and-step descent,
> Pool of pebbles buzzed in a Juniper shadow
> tiny tongue of a this-year rattlesnake flicked,
> I leaped laughing for little boulder-color coil—
> Pounded by heat raced down the slabs to the creek
> Deep tumbling under arching walls and stuck
> Whole head and shoulders in the water:
> Stretched full on cobble—ears roaring
> Eyes open aching from the cold and faced a trout. (*RCM* 10)

"Pressure of sun on the rockslide," while it runs into "Whirled," is a fully realized image on its own. "Pounded by heat raced down the slabs to the creek" does not require the next line to complete its statement, nor does "Stretched full on cobble—ears roaring." The seventh line, ending with the verb "stuck," is the most violently enjambed but even this line contains its own complete image. The poem very skillfully plays off the incredible energy compressed into its verbs and verbals—"Whirled," "buzzed," "flicked," "leaped," "raced," "tumbling," "stretched," and so on—against the relatively static shih line upon which it is based.

Structural ellipsis in T'ang shih poetry is fairly limited in its range of possibilities due to conventions of the form, the more so in comparison to Snyder's open form poetics. Nevertheless, some kinds of ellipsis Snyder employs, which do not occur in shih poetry—such as multiple unconnected images—reflect Chinese influence in their syntactical characteristics. For instance, consider the final eight lines of "Burning the Small Dead":

```
6                    a hundred summers
              snowmelt       rock       and air
              hiss in a twisted bough.
                  sierra granite
10                    mt. Ritter—
                  black rock twice as old.
              Deneb, Altair


                  windy fire (BC 22)
```

Here Snyder makes a calculated use of space, both visually, in his placement of the poem on the page, and syntactically, in his elision of connectives. First of all, the blanks in line 7 slow the pace of the line—the eye simply cannot travel as fast from "snowmelt" to "rock" to "and" as it could if the words were conventionally spaced. Secondly, of "summers," "snowmelt," "rock," and "air," only "air" is linked by either word or punctuation to the noun preceding it; and one suspects the "and" is included more for the sake of rhythm— lines 6–7 form a fully regular line of iambic pentameter—than because of any particular need felt by the poet to express overtly a logical or grammatical link between the final object in the series and its predecessors. Lines 6–8 could have been rendered, more conventionally and succinctly, "A hundred summers (snowmelt, rock and air) / hiss in a twisted bough." Snyder's choices in layout and syntax have obviously been made in order to avoid such a facile discursive relation and to force the reader's eye to pause over each object and consider it independently. Another glance at the shih line "cock crow thatch inn moon" leaves little doubt as to the source of Snyder's syntax. "Burning the Small Dead" closes with three more unconnected images: "Deneb, Altair" (really a single image cluster), and "windy fire." Here again, connectives are elided, and the signs are enclosed in emptiness.

Snyder's ellipsis of overt logical and grammatical links between images magnifies the significance of juxtaposition as a structural mechanism. Juxtaposition creates a de facto connection between two elements of a poem: at the least, they are related through contiguity. This structural proximity, in turn, can tacitly suggest a semantic similarity. "Deneb, Altair" and "windy fire," for example, engage in a particularly rich play of equivalence and difference. Deneb and Altair literally *are* windy fire, on one level, but "windy fire" is also less (the brush fire in the poem) and more (a Vulcanic archetype of generation and annihilation) than the stars. To understand the full role of juxtaposition in "Burning the Small Dead," however, it is necessary to be familiar with a poetic form that makes the conjoining of disparate images an architectonic principle, and that has had considerable influence on Gary Snyder's poetic practice—the haiku.

## THE HAIKU

> Uttering a word is like striking a note on the keyboard of the imagination.
>
> —Wittgenstein[11]

The haiku is a Japanese form consisting of one line divided into three segments of five, seven, and five character-sounds (roughly equivalent to syllables).[12] In the hands of Matsuo Bashō (1643–94), the haiku was legitimized as a vehicle for serious artistic expression. His poems, grounded in the ontology of Zen Buddhism, employ oblique, radically elided image constructs to represent intuitive experiences of Emptiness. Bashō's frog haiku is characteristic:"The old pond: / A frog jumps in,— / The sound of the water" (Blyth 1:340).

By proposing—almost always in the present tense—one, two, or three objects, alone, juxtaposed in a tableau, or interacting, usually in a natural environment flavored with the associations of a given season, the author of a successful haiku suggests to the mind of the reader the psychological event through which he himself has attained an immediate perception of things-as-they-are. The reader comprehends the poem only to the extent that he himself is able to achieve a similar intuitive perception through the re-created experience of the poem.[13]

The diction of haiku is spare. Few modifiers are employed, and some haiku contain no adjectives, adverbs, or even verbs. Such economy of means, enforced in part by the sheer brevity of the form, is not so much a function of grammar (cf. the shih) as it is of method. The haiku poet does not deal in abstract ideas; he presents simple, sensuous images.[14] These images are brought together without any overt narrative or figural connection. Consequently, there is little need for, or use of, adverbial clauses, prepositional phrases, conjunctions, or other connecting and subordinating devices.

Many of these stylistic attributes have been mentioned as typical of the shih. But whereas the shih, laconic as it is, covers a certain textual and temporal duration (many of Han Shan's shih are eight lines long), the haiku experience is momentary. In addition, while the silent metaphor in the shih line "cloud mist stopover visitor('s) feeling" (Yip 20) is readily apparent, haiku often almost aggressively yoke radically unlike images in order to pressure the reader into breaking out of the logic of oppositions and through to a likeness more profound than any logic. Thus, the function of similar kinds of ellipsis in the two forms is often quite different, and these disparate functions, in turn, reflect themselves and their particular sources at distinct points in Snyder's oeuvre.

One of the most characteristic structural devices of the haiku is what Kenneth Yasuda calls the "thought-pause." This anacoluthic interval, coming at the end of the first or second "line," divides the poem into two segments, usually also two images. It is a syntactical and imaginative interstice, similar in function to the empty space in sumi painting.

In a typical haiku, an initial generalized image invokes the reader to flesh it out and expand its context; with this process in motion the poem itself is abruptly cut short by the thought-pause, while the reader's imagination continues to evolve the material with which it has already been presented. The second image, arriving abruptly, creates a comparison or contrast with the initial image and at the same time resolves the imaginative and rhythmic movement of the poem. Mind is thus led toward an intuitive recognition of Mind— the Buddha-nature as undifferentiated Oneness—through the fusion of two ontologically equivalent yet manifestly diverse images, across the thought-pause, into a powerful, aesthetically complete haiku moment. The following haiku by Buson illustrates both the structure and function of the thought-pause: "Tilling the field: / The cloud that never moved / Is gone" (Blyth 2:167) Here, "tilling the field" provides the sparest linguistic indication of the archetypal human activity in which the speaker is engaged. In order to enter the poem, the reader must use his own imagination to create a view in the direction toward which this poetic sign points. The thought-pause is a formal horizon bounding this view. Yet in going beyond this formal (and temporal) horizon, the reader finds himself returning with the speaker to a place and time *anterior* to the poem itself, in which there appeared to exist a "cloud that never moved." In the midst of his perpetual motion, the speaker had an illusory perception of permanence (the permanence of a cloud, of all things!). But the third line, "is gone," enacts a return from the return—to a place and a present that are now both the same and different. The effect of this line is to dissolve view and horizon, permanence and transience, sameness and difference, and to precipitate in the reader an intuitive recognition of the folly of boundaries.

Gary Snyder's "Hitch Haiku," "A truck went by," demonstrates the use of the thought-pause in his poetry: "A truck went by / three hours ago: / Smoke Creek desert" (*BC* 29). Here, as in Buson's haiku, a tension is created between motion and stillness, and between the temporal and the timeless. But Snyder's haiku contains an additional dimension: a humbling contrast between the "real world" of human affairs and a nature symbolic of absolute reality.

"A truck went by": what could be more mundane? Yet the familiarity of such an event and such a statement is unsettled when we discover that the temporal "familiarity" of the event is not what we would assume from such a casual remark. In fact, the truck passed not "just now" but three hours ago. And this unanticipated extension of time, together with the implication that no other vehicle has passed meanwhile, urges us to a dramatically diminished re-vision of the status of man and machine in the desert. The apparent continuity, even inexorability, of human motion and motivation is suddenly called in question. The hitchhiker presumably hopes for a quick and easily managed ride—a willed outcome which, if achieved, will reinforce his tacit assumption that what intentionally *does* controls what unintentionally *is*. Instead, he comes face to face with an emptiness powerful enough to wither all such pretentious intentionality.

Critical explication of a haiku unavoidably pours it into a narrative / descriptive mold that can never do justice to the crystalline character of the poem itself. However we (mis)read this particular haiku, the necessary point is the absolute undeniability of the desert. In its midst, complacent concepts such as "community" and "progress" lose their meaning, and the lone individual feels his loneness.

Returning to "Burning the Small Dead," one can see that Snyder uses a thought-pause in the haiku-like lines 9–11, and he in fact expands this structural device into a formal principle that shapes the text as a whole:

> Burning the small dead
> branches
> broke from beneath
> thick spreading
> whitebark pine.

> a hundred summers
> snowmelt          rock          and air
>
> hiss in a twisted bough.
>   sierra granite;
>       mt. Ritter—
>       black rock twice as old.
>
> Deneb, Altair
> windy fire (*BC* 22)

The poem consists of a series of images, in one case complicated by an uncharacteristic metaphor, building by association from a small trail fire through Deneb and Altair (stars of the first magnitude) to "windy fire," an image suggesting the fiery origin / termination of the universe. Spacing and punctuation control the movement of the poem outward through a group of image clusters toward an implied infinite. The poem subdivides into five sections, the first four of which end in a break that is in effect a thought-pause. After each of these breaks (at "pine," "bough," "old," and "Altair") the poem takes a quantum leap in temporal scope from the present to "a hundred summers," to the thousands-of-years-old Sierras, to the incalculably old stars, to a timeless and ambiguous image mutually symbolic of creation and destruction the temporal shifts accompanied by parallel increases in physical dimension. These geologic faults in the poetic structure function, as do thought-pauses in haiku, to fragment syntax and to separate imagery so that a smoothly sequential reading becomes impossible.

As Charles Altieri points out, "windy fire" is not only "a continuation beyond the stars to a kind of essence of fire," but also "a return to the limited space of the burning branches." Altieri posits, finally, "a third windy fire that unites the two spaces in the back country of the poet's mind."[15] The first two of these interpretive statements seem accurate and necessary, and together with the third they comprise a reading that has the advantage of providing the poem with a satisfyingly circular closure. But we can do at least equal justice to the poem's formal development and to the Buddhist perspective underlying it if we dispense with Altieri's "third windy fire"—which leaves the poem within the realm of the conditional—and include instead the blank space, or margin, following the final line of the printed text. "Burning the Small Dead," as I have pointed out, is a series of beyonds. The passage following each succeeding thought-pause, is however, shorter than the one before it. As the poem's imagery expands in physical and temporal scale the scope of its language diminishes. Beyond creation and destruction there is only

All. Beyond "windy fire" as language there is nothing. The poem suggests we would do well not to see a difference.

"August on Sourdough, A Visit from Dick Brewer," "Sixth-Month Song in the Foothills," "The Spring," and "Riprap" all illustrate the kind of generalized imagery that I have compared to the practice of T'ang shih poetry. As in the shih haiku imagery though it tends to be more prismatic in quality and somewhat more precise in its outlines, is often deliberately underdetermined.[16] The lightest, sparest descriptive strokes suffice to prompt the reader's imagination, strokes so delicate, and at the same time so unconstraining, that the reader is led effortlessly toward their full accomplishment.

"Sixth-Month Song" demonstrates both generalized images ("saws," "door," "rakers," "eaves," etc.) and sparse modification ("low hills," "white mountains," "new grass"). Many of its formal features derive specifically from haiku, and it may thus be worth examining in some detail:

> In the cold shed sharpening saws.
>     a swallow's nest hangs by the door
> setting rakers in sunlight
> falling from meadow through doorframe
>     swallows flit under the eaves.
>
> Grinding the falling axe
> sharp for the summer
>     a swallow shooting out over.
> over the river, snow on low hills
> sharpening wedges for splitting.
>
> Beyond the low hlls, white mountains
> and now snow is melting. sharpening tools;
>     pack horses grazing new grass
> bright axes—and swallows
>     fly in to my shed. (*BC* 17)

The poem comprises a series of interlinked haikulike image complexes that evoke both haikai, the linked-verse form from which haiku sprang historically, and the sequences of haiku on a single theme composed by poets like Shiki. The speaker is elided, with the exception of the possessive adjective in the final line, and gerunds and participles frequently take the place of verbs. The omission of logical and syntactical connectives between lines, in most cases results in an open series of juxtaposed images / actions, many of which function freely with both those preceding and those following. The line "swallows flit under the eaves," for instance works equally well as the third line of "setting rakers in sunlight: / falling from meadow through doorframe / swallows flit under the eaves" or as the first line of "swallows flit under the eaves: / Grinding the falling axe / sharp for the summer."[17] Lines 6–7 can work with the swallow image that occurs in line 8 as well as with that of line 5. "Sharpening wedges for splitting" combines with line 9 and 11 as follows:

> over the river,
> snow on low hills:
> sharpening wedges for splitting:
>
> sharpening wedges for splitting.
> Beyond the low hills,
> white mountains.

"Pack horses grazing new grass" may be combined with either "sharpening tools" or the two concluding lines of the poem, nor does this exhaust the possibilities for recombination.

As one would expect in a poem that can be divided into a variety of haikulike configurations, the thought-pause is a basic mechanism in "Sixth-Month Song," although, unlike the practice of haiku, the reader is here allowed some leeway as to how many thought-pauses he brings into operation in reading the poem, and precisely where they are located. One can, for example, read in a thought-pause after every gerundial or participial phrase, with the exception of "Grinding the falling axe," but of course would not do so in every case (though where one did might vary with different readings of the poem).

The key to an account of "Sixth-Month Song" as amounting formally to a haiku sequence is its imagery, and specifically the patterns of repetition and exchange into which it falls. Images of the speaker preparing his woodcutting tools for summer and of swallows inhabiting their newly-built nest dominate the poem. These seasonal activities take place in a shared home—expressed in the cluster of "shed" images: "cold shed," "door," "doorframe," "eaves," and the closing "swallows / fly in to my shed"—and in the larger shared home of nature. In their home-in-nature neither being interferes with the other, bird and man pursuing separate works, separate ends without destructiveness or hostility. Moreover, the poem makes it clear that these works and ends are not, in fact, so very separate. As the summer solstice approaches, the speaker prepares to take to the woods, bringing with him the manmade tools he needs. The swallows, meanwhile, are already lodged in his dwelling, having brought with them such bits of the earth and woods as they needed to build their own home within a home within a home. Householder, denizen of the wilderness: the one becomes the other while remaining itself, an interchangeability mirrored in the poem's structure.

Of course this dancelike interpenetration of man and nature

involves not only an exchange and a retention but also a return. Throughout the poem, references to the speaker alternate with references to the swallows and in each case a series of similar activities is depicted: the speaker is "sharpening saws," "Grinding the falling axe," "sharpening wedges"; the swallows "flit under the eaves," and "fly in to my shed."

In its crossing of winter and spring, "Sixth-Month Song" is at once a processional of life and a harbinger of death. The seasonal motif traditional in Japanese haiku appears here in references to "cold," "snow," and "white," contrasted with "sunlight" "summer," "melting," "new grass," and "bright axes." What at first reading may appear to be a temporally static lyric portrait turns out on closer inspection to be dynamic. The approach of warm weather is first explicitly referred to in strophe two, and it is only in strophe three that the snow is described as "now . . . melting," the pack horses as "grazing new grass," and the axes as being "bright," i.e., sharpened and ready for use. An increasing emphasis on the warmth, brightness, and fecundity of spring through the three strophes gives us the impression that spring is in fact bursting into bloom before our very eyes, rather like the process of germination of a flower filmed through time-lapse photography. At the same time, this palpable articulation of growth and change only adumbrates more vividly the continued revolution of the cycle—to the time when speaker and snow, swallows and sun will all execute their obligatory returns, as the dance of the seasons comes to a close.

In accordance with the teachings of Zen, we cannot force the poem to assert either absolute sameness or absolute difference. It simply points to a certain commonality of being that possesses its own truth, despite—or rather in conjunction with—the transience that the poem simultaneously insists on.

The nondiscursive, presentational nature of haiku poetry is apparent in its syntax as well as its structure. Most significant is the frequent ellipsis of subject and / or verb, rendering the haiku an incomplete grammatical unit. Where there is no main verb, action is often expressed participially or gerundially, rather than as a transitive—necessarily dualistic—relation in which a does b to c: "Rice planting; / Ripples, / The wind blowing up behind" (Blyth 3:120).

Omission of an overtly postulated speaker or subject, as in this haiku by Taigi, has the effect of universalizing the experience of the poem and, as R. H. Blyth puts it, of teaching "the egolessness of things" (1:358). In the following haiku, Buson represents man obliquely, as an elided transparency in and of nature, rather than as a subject, with all the ontological privilege such a role entails: "In the morning mist / The sound of striking a stake, / Smack! Smack!" (Blyth 3:373).

As I have indicated, ellipsis of the speaker is a formal trademark of Gary Snyder's poetry. "Trail Crew Camp at Bear Valley, 9000 Feet. Northern Sierra—White Bone and Threads of Snowmelt Water," for instance, opens "Cut branches back for a day—," follows a trail up to "a stone / cairn at the pass," balances for a visionary moment ("strippt mountains hundreds of miles"), and concludes

> sundown went back
> > the clean switchbacks to camp.
> bell on the gelding,
> stew in the cook tent,
> black coffee in a big tin can. (*BC* 20)

The trail has been cleared, but no "I" has cleared it. Some of the signs of human activity in the poem harmonize with nature—the manmade trail follows the natural trail of the creekbed, "a stone" is enjambed into a "cairn." But trails, shareable by man and animal, can precede highways which are not shareable, and the woodsman who cuts branches for a day and thinks of trees in both abstract and particular terms—"timber white pine"—prefigures the lumber companies who strip whole mountains over a period of years and think only of board feet. The one can easily evolve into the other. No simple syntactical removal of the "I," then—or willed self-abnegation in the practice of a spiritual discipline—can safely separate us from the errors of becoming. Even enlightened we are no less being, with all the creative and destructive potential it contains—simply, perhaps, more farsighted.[18]

"Sixth-Month Song in the Foothills," discussed above, illustrates a different but equally characteristic means of eliding the speaker. The poem begins, "In the cold shed sharpening saws." It is a theme with variations, in which human actions are expressed as haunted gerunds—present participles modifying an absent "I"—here freed from the customary diminishing modifier / modified relation: "sharpening," "setting," "Grinding," and so on. The processes are emphasized, and we are prevented from conceiving of the doer as primary.

For many of Snyder's poems it would be difficult to establish conclusively whether the shih or the haiku is more significant as a stylistic source of his ellipsis of the speaker. However, where the ellipsis of the "I" is accompanied by the elision of verbs and the employment of participles or gerunds, a pattern of poetic procedure becomes manifest that can be clearly traced from its origins in Japanese haiku poetry through haiku of Snyder's and on into more elaborate exemplifications of the same stylistic cluster in his longer poems. First of all, a haiku by Ryuho: "Scooping up the moon / In the washbasin, / And spilling it" (Blyth 3:388). Compare this to the following "Hitch Haiku" by Snyder:

> Drinking hot saké
>               toasting fish on coals
>    the motorcycle
>   out       parked in the rain. (*BC* 31)

Then examine a slightly more ambitious poem, "North Beach Alba":

> waking half-drunk in a strange pad
> making it out to the cool gray
>    san francisco dawn—
> white gulls over white houses,
>    fog down the bay,
> tamalpais a fresh green hill in the new sun,
> driving across the bridge in a beat old car
>    to work. (*BC* 69)

And to all these, finally, compare "Sixth-Month Song," which I have described as amounting formally to a series of linked haiku.

Not only does Snyder frequently elide verbs in favor of verbals, there are passages in his poetry where neither human actor nor action are to be found, as in "The Late Snow & Lumber Strike of the Summer of Fifty-four": "Chainsaws in a pool of cold oil / On back porches of ten thousand / Split-shake houses, quiet in summer rain" (*RCM* 2), or in the "Hitch haiku," "Cherry blossoms at Hood river": "Cherry blossoms at Hood river / rusty sand near Tucson / mudflats of Willapa Bay" (*BC* 31).

The Zen Buddhist perception of sunyata as tathata and tathata as sunyata is essential to haiku poetry, but Emptiness is never explicitly referred to, since to refer to the Void as a concept is automatically to fall into the error of distinguishing the indistinguishable.[19] This ellipsis of the Void, in poems shadowed by its "presence," is so characteristic of Gary Snyder's poetry that it is difficult to limit one's examples. "Piute Creek" is one instance, but a flawed one because it leans toward statement rather than presentation. The burden of "Words and books / Like a small creek off a high ledge / Gone in the dry air" (*RCM* 6) for example, is much more effectively conveyed in Snyder's haiku "*Over the Mindanao Deep*": "Scrap brass / dumpt off the fantail / falling six miles" (*BC*, "Hitch Haiku" 29). Here a two-part image places the unimaginable before us with a dramatic effect far greater than any explanatory analysis or routine simile could hope to achieve.

"Mid-August at Sourdough Mountain Lookout" provides a sparkling example of the same kind of ellipsis, the project of the poem being precisely to locate its speaker in the Void:

> Down valley a smoke haze
> Three days heat, after five days rain
> Pitch glows on the fir-cones

Across rocks and meadows
Swarms of new flies.

I cannot remember things I once read
A few friends, but they are in cities.
Drinking cold snow-water from a tin cup
Looking down for miles
Through high still air. (RCM 1)

Within its marvelously economic form the poem employs virtually
every kind of ellipsis discussed in this essay. The first strophe is very
reminiscent of shih poetry. No speaker is posited: we are presented
with a handful of selected objects within a roughly sketched climatic
and geographic environment. The lines (unenjambed except for line
4) propose concrete but nonparticularized images in a language dominated by nouns. "Glows" is the only verb. There is little use of
articles, and besides the adjectival numbers, "new" is the only true
adjective in the passage. The lines themselves do not function paratactically, strictly speaking, but each line contains a balanced pair
of nouns and hence creates a similar parallel effect.[20] How akin the
line of this section is to the five-character shih line (especially if one
reads line 5 as the second half of line 4) may be seen by comparing
four lines of Han Shan's shih, translated by Snyder as "#8" in *Cold
Mountain Poems:*

The long gorge choked with scree and boulders,
The wide creek, the mist-blurred grass.
The moss is slippery, though there's been no rain
The pine sings, but there's no wind. (RCM 44)

Use of the present tense in both poems entices the reader into
creatively elaborating the quickly drawn scene in his imagination,
taking the generalized images as starting points.

Lines 6–7 of "Mid-August" parenthetically place a speaker in
the landscape. The effect of these lines is emphatically not, as Richard
Howard would suggest, "heartbreaking."[21] Rather, the lines indicate
that the speaker is following the Zen ideal of formlessness—that is,
nonattachment to the objective world while living in its midst. He
has overcome his reliance on both books ("No dependence on words
or letters," exhorts a famous T'ang Dynasty quatrain)[22] and people.

The final three lines of the poem return to the egoless mode of
lines 1–5. They constitute in themselves a very effective haiku, with
the thought-pause at the end of line 8 separating a sharply specific,
vividly tactile action—the drinking of ice-cold snow-water—from an
almost eerily insubstantial act of vision, both expressed gerundially.[23]
The speaker is represented as simultaneously engaged with the objective, the commonplace, the functional, and with the unknowable,

the indefinable, the "seeing [that] is no-seeing,"[24] to neither of which he is attached.

The poem thus passes through three phases. In the first five lines an environment is suggested to the reader's imagination. In lines 6–7, the state of mind of the speaker—with whom the reader has been imaginatively conflated until this point—is expressed as an aside that suggests to the reader, in turn, its appropriateness for himself. The final three lines, in which speaker and reader are again conflated, *do* what lines 6–7 *say:* they express through contrasting images a state of mind wholly conscious at once of the many and the One. Emptiness, as is ever the case in haiku, is not overtly expressed but is nonetheless manifest, in the combination of mountaintop location, the seemingly boundless vision of the speaker, and the inherent feeling of calmness and sublimity attaching to his situation, as well as through the very tissue of ellipses of which the poem is constructed.

> Many people are afraid to empty their minds lest they may plunge into the Void. They do not know that their own Mind is the void. The ignorant eschew phenomena but not thought; the wise eschew thought but not phenomena.
>
> —Huang Po[25]

By the term "elliptical mode," applied to Gary Snyder's poetry, I have intended to designate not a consistent poetic form, but a ruled play of absences that has allowed Snyder to cause the most conditional of conditional realities—language—to signify that for which no words are adequate. The very absoluteness of this inequivalence has led Snyder to level the usual structural hierarchy of poetic texts, so that his poems take place as much within their lacunae as within their language.

Snyder's metaphor of poetry as "riprap of things" is doubly pertinent as a description of his stylistic procedure: rocks, and other concrete objects, are tangible and easy to get around, as the water of Bashō's pond "gets around" the frog; and no matter how well fitted the cobble, there is always space between the stones.

The haiku presents itself as a formal paradigm for Snyder's poetics of absence. Not only is the ultimate object of the poetic act unnamed, the actor himself remains grammatically nameless, as he must if he is to succeed. Linguistic ventures into the conditional world take place, to be sure, but ventures whose rational progression is constantly dispersed by transitional crevasses. The mind cannot plod heavily across a thought-pause: it must leap.

Shih poetry, in its refusal to abstract man from his natural environment and then, in turn, to reconstitute him as a concrete but privileged subject (as does much of postromantic Western poetry), provides a useful corrective for formalized anthropocentrism. Its systematic disjunctions between images, phrases, and lines provide Snyder with another useful model of the poetic composition of absence.

Snyder's poems strive to be, and are, aesthetic wholes, while simultaneously perforating themselves with holes of a different sort—holes that in a certain sense remain unfilled by either poet or reader. For ultimately, Snyder's poems function to transfer to the reader more than a specific content, as attractive as that content often is; they present a possibility of seeing, a means of comprehending Mind, that non-entity which is both—and neither—"that which you see before you," and the "void which cannot be fathomed" (Huang Po 29). As Snyder expresses it in "Piute Creek": "A clear, attentive mind / Has no meaning but that / Which sees is truly seen" (RCM 6).

## Notes

1. Editions of Gary Snyder's poems cited here are as follows: Riprap, & Cold Mountain Poems (San Francisco: Four Seasons Foundation, 1965), hereafter cited as RCM; and The Back Country (New York: New Directions, 1968), hereafter cited as BC. "Water" and "Mid-August at Sourdough Mountain Lookout" from Riprap, & Cold Mountain Poems reprinted by permission of Gary Snyder. Poems from The Back Country copyright 1957, 1966, 1968 by Gary Snyder. Reprinted by permission of New Directions Publishing Corp. The Kierkegaard quotation comes from Repetition, trans. and ed. Howard V. Hong and Edna H. Hong (Princeton: Princeton UP, 1983) 212. Kikaku's haiku appears in Haiku, trans. R. H. Blyth, 4 vols. (Japan: Kamakura Bunko, 1949) 3:71. The Snyder passage is taken from "Lookout's Journal," in Earth House Hold (New York: New Directions, 1969) 5.

2. By "wilderness poetry" I mean a crucial segment of Snyder's oeuvre that includes poems set in nature, often wilderness, locations in the American West. Snyder's numerous poems dealing with his logging, fire lookout, and trail crew experiences are archetypal examples. I would group all of Myths & Texts, all of Riprap except the tanker and Japanese poems, and most of the "Far West" section of The Back Country under this heading. Technically, not all of the poems discussed in this essay would qualify as wilderness poems ("North Beach Alba," for example, would not), but all share a definable poetic.

3. The Zen masters of the T'ang Dynasty had various idiosyncratic ways of designating ultimate reality, and translators have been equally idiosyncratic in rendering the Chinese terms into English, the aim of both groups being to avoid misleading their audiences into forming an intellectual conception of an Absolute. In Zen literature, the terms "Mind," "no-mind," and "original mind" are synonymous. In this essay, they are also equivalent to One, Oneness, the Buddha-nature, the Void and Emptiness.

4. I use the term "imagination" only in the following sense (from the OED): "that faculty of the mind by which are formed images . . . of external objects not present to the senses and of their relations." I use the term "intuition" in an equally limited sense (again from the OED) as denoting "the immediate apprehension of an object by the mind without the intervention of any reasoning process." "Apprehension," in turn, signifies the aesthetic apprehension embodied in haiku and the ontological apprehension experienced in satori, which are essentially similar, differing in degree of spiritual profundity rather than in mode of psychological cognition.

5. In addition to Snyder himself, a number of critics have written usefully on

ellipsis in Snyder's poetry, including Robert Kern, Sherman Paul, Charles Altieri, and Maurice Yaofu Lin. Bob Steuding's observations, in *Gary Snyder* (Boston: Twayne, 1976), are among the most pertinent to the topic of this paper.

6. Roland Barthes, *The Pleasure of the Text*, trans. Richard Miller (New York: Hill and Wang: Farrar, 1975) 40.

7. Wai-lim Yip, *Ezra Pound's Cathay* (Princeton: Princeton UP, 1969) 25. My discussion of the formal characteristics of the T'ang Dynasty shih relies largely on Yip's excellent first chapter, "The Chinese Poem: Some Aspects of the Problem of Syntax in Translation."

8. Burton Watson, *Chinese Lyricism: Shih poetry from the Second to the Twelfth Century* (New York: Columbia UP, 1971) 8.

9. Sherman Paul, "From Lookout to Ashram: The Way of Gary Snyder," *The Iowa Review* 1 (1970): 76–89. See especially 85–86. Paul speaks of "the imperatives of art set forth in the poetic directive of 'Riprap' " referring to the latter as "a poem that exemplifies [Snyder's] skills and remains his test of art." See Steuding 34–35 for a different assessment of the poem's significance.

10. Classical Chinese is a monosyllabic language. One character = one syllable = one word.

11. Ludwig Wittgenstein, *Philosophical Investigations*, trans. G. E. M. Anscombe, 3rd ed. (New York: Macmillan, n.d.) 4e.

12. In English translations these segments are usually transcribed as three separate lines.

13. Otsuji describes this "haiku moment" as "the instant when our mental activity almost merges into an unconscious state—i.e., the relationship between the subject and object is forgotten" and one "becomes one with nature" (qtd. in Kenneth Yasuda, *The Japanese Haiku* [Rutland VT: Charles E. Tuttle Company, 1957] 12–13). Yasuda, on the other hand, ascribes to the haiku moment "the realization of what the object is . . . in and for itself . . . so that it becomes unique" (13). Thus, at the haiku moment, just as in the experience of satori, we may see the many in the One (the sense of becoming one with nature) but we may also see the One in the many.

14. Because the object of haiku is to enable the reader to attain an intuitive recognition of things-as-they-are, haiku poets tend to avoid figures of speech, paradox excepted. Yasuda states, "Nothing is like something else in most well-realized haiku" (50); and Bashō himself advised, "Learn of the pine from a pine" (Yasuda 50).

15. Charles Altieri, *Enlarging the Temple: New Directions in American Poetry during the 1960s* (Lewisburg, PA: Buckness UP, 1979) 138.

16. In *Haiku*, vol. 1, R. H. Blyth speaks of haiku as both an expression of unity and "an enumeration of differences, the slightest of infinite importance" (318). To the extent that he is speaking of the imaginative participation of the reader, he is correct in stressing the importance of subtle differences. The actual language of the poems, however, is more often remarkable for its broad range of suggestiveness than for its precision of definition and distinction.

17. I have, perhaps unfairly, rearranged the layout of these and the following passages, and altered their punctuation, in order more pointedly to suggest their similarity to haiku.

18. See Derrida's brilliant meditation on trails as initial writings in *Of Grammatology*, trans. Gayatri Chakravorty Spivak (Baltimore: Johns Hopkins UP, 1976), 107–8.

19. See the first section of this paper, "The Elliptical Mode." Hui-neng, the Sixth Patriarch, laid great stress on the fact that our very nature is the Buddha-nature, and that the one thing necessary for enlightenment is to experience this identity.

"From the first not a thing is," was his way of emphasizing that to strain after an elusive spiritual Other (Mind) is simply to defer the critical task of severing our covert but tenacious attachment to the realness of the personal self (that is, the self conceived as proper name) (qtd. in Daisetz Teitaro Suzuki, *Zen Buddhism: Selected Writings of D. T. Suzuki,* ed. William Barrett [Garden City, NY: Doubleday, 1956] 160).

20. See Maurice Yaofu Lin, "Children of Adam: Ginsberg, Ferlinghetti and Snyder in the Emerson–Whitman Tradition," diss. U. of Minnesota, 1973, 224. Lin notes the parallelism of word groups such as "down valley" and "smoke haze," and "three days heat" and "five days rain" as a shih influence, though his explanation of the nature of this influence is somewhat different from my own.

21. " 'To Hold Both History and Wilderness in Mind': The Poetry of Gary Snyder," *Epoch* 15 (Fall 1965): 90.

22. Daisetz Teitaro Suzuki, *The Essentials of Zen Buddhism,* ed. Bernard Phillips (New York: Dutton 1962) 19.

23. The grammatical status of "Drinking" and "Looking" is complex. Technically they are gerunds, but the ghost of the subject explicitly present in 11. 6–7 pulls them toward the participial, or toward a transformation of full verbal status, i.e., the present progressive "[I am] drinking." But when we recall the ontology grounding the grammatical structure we are moved to exorcise the ghost and reaffirm the gerund. Nevertheless, a certain ambiguity designedly prevails. Cf. "Sixth-Month Song."

24. Suzuki, *Selected Writings* 163.

25. *The Zen Teaching of Huang Po,* trans. John Blofeld (New York: Grove Press, 1958) 48.

# The Pattern which Connects: Metaphor in Gary Snyder's Later Poetry
Julia Martin°

What pattern connects the crab to the lobster and the orchid to the primrose and all the four of them to me? And all the six of us to the amoeba in one direction and the backward schizophrenic in another? (Bateson, 16–17)

With one or two exceptions, critical readings of Gary Snyder's poetry have argued that he makes little use of metaphor. On this point critics have taken their lead from Thomas Parkinson, whose comments in 1968 seem to have set the trend for many later readers [his essay is reprinted in this volume]. Following Parkinson's emphasis

° Reprinted from *Western American Literature* 22, no. 2 (1987): 99–123, by permission of the Western Literature Association.

there have been several very useful commentaries which I do not wish to question here.[1] The problem with this kind of analysis is, however, that it tends to overlook the appearance in the poetry of structures which I can only term metaphoric. This is particularly clear in the later poetry, which has so far received rather scant critical attention.

Robert Kern has shown how Snyder's use of syntax and open forms is intrinsic to the "ecological consciousness" which the poetry proposes. My reading suggests that the use of metaphoric structures is as important in this respect. The view which Snyder once rather whimsically called the "Avatamsaka (Flower Wreath) jewelled-net-interpenetration-ecological-systems-emptiness-consciousness" (*The Old Ways* 64) is surely his most significant contribution to the reconciliation of personal, political and religious models.† And in the later poetry this view of things is often most clearly expressed by means of metaphoric structures.

The Avatamsaka model has been discussed at some length—what has been variously called Snyder's "ecological consciousness," or his idea of "interbirth," "True Communionism," and so on. But it is still useful to identify its main features. In a paper given at the Ethnopoetics conference in 1975, Snyder made what I consider to be his most intriguing comment on the subject: "From the standpoint of the 70's and 80's it serves us well to consider how we relate to those objects we take to be outside ourselves—non-human, non-intelligent, or whatever" (TOW 9–10). The phrase "objects we take to be outside ourselves" refers here to everything which, in an epistemology of oppositional relations, is habitually defined as "other." From the position of phallocentric culture then, this has meant: nature, women, "other" races, animals, the body, the "primitive," etc. The corollary of this sort of division is an idea of the individual (person, species, community, etc.) as being a self-contained unit, existing in opposition to other such entities.

Working as I do in apartheid South Africa, one is confronted every day with some of the political implications of this sort of binarism. In Snyder's work this aspect is an important one, but his analysis does not originate in a study of ideology. His critique of oppositional epistemology derives largely from his studies in ecology, systems biology and Buddhism. These disciplines also propose an alternative view which informs the poetry. Recent work in ecology and biology has shown that the relation of an individual organism to its environment is that of one open system to another, and that to conceptualize these systems as being "closed," in competition, or in opposition to each other is to falsify the necessary exchange between them. Buddhism similarly stresses the deficiency of a dualist model in which the skin-bound observer is separated from a world to which s / he stands in opposition. Consequently one commentator defines the term "maya," illusion, as "the power whereby the individual consciousness, distinguishing itself from others, considers itself separate from them" (Woodroffe, 101). If this oppositional separation is illusory, then the practice of mediation, "koan" study and so on, which seeks to "go beyond" dualism, is motivated by a conviction that all things are interdependent, mutually interpenetrating. One of Snyder's earliest metaphors for this pattern of interdependence is the "vast 'jewelled net' " in which all are "interborn" (EHH 129), an image from the Avatamsaka sutra of Hua-Yen Buddhism.[2] His later work proposes further metaphors (the Great Family, the goddesses Vak and Gaia, etc.) but the same emphasis remains.

Altieri has called the concept of interbirth or Communionism Snyder's fundamental religious insight (*Enlarging the Temple* 132). Molesworth goes a step further when he examines it as an innovative political term (85–87). This seems more accurate, since for Snyder the religious, political and personal are not meaningfully separable domains: each informs the other. In *Earth House Hold* he criticized the "ultimately uncompassionate and destructive" tendency of institutional Buddhism to "ignore the inequalities and tyrannies of whatever political system it found itself under" (EHH 90). In rejecting an epistemology of binary oppositions, the poetry and prose question both some of the fundamental assumptions of Western metaphysics and their ideological manifestations.[3] Snyder recognizes in the epistemological error which opposes "self" and "other" an implicit hierarchy with "us" at the top. This allows for the systematic exploitation of "other" for whatever gains, and has (in religious terms) frequently led to the denigration of physical, material, worldly things, in favor of what is "otherworldly." Like several other writers, Snyder considers this error to be at the root of the present ecological crisis.[4] Consequently his work seeks to articulate a metaperspective on dualistic oppositions: what might be called a systems view.

In this essay I will also call it a *metaphoric view* of things. However, in order to do so I must define some terminology. "Metaphor" as it is ordinarily understood denotes a transfer of meaning from one semantic domain to another. This is the first sense in which I will use the term. As several critics have pointed out, this transfer indicates a relation of, say, "tenor" and "vehicle" that seems inappropriate to the state of undifferentiated or ecological consciousness that many of Snyder's poems seek to evoke. In this respect it is often similar to Chinese landscape poetry. Wai-lim Yip makes the point very clearly: "The view that landscape qua landscape is Nature's Way points to the merging of vehicle and tenor: the tenor is contained in the vehicle, or the vehicle is the tenor, the container is the contained, the thing named is the thing meant. This explains why a large proportion of Chinese poetry is non-metaphorical and non-symbolic. Because of the merger, it does not require human intellect to interfere or mediate" (Yip 218). Other critics have made similar comments about Snyder's "distrust" of metaphor (for example Altieri and McLeod). It should be clear that he has good reason to be wary of the kind of metaphoric transfer that appears in the writings of many Western mystics, and of the metaphors and symbols characteristic of so much Romantic and Modern poetry. Nevertheless the later work does make important use of metaphors. Molesworth acknowledges this briefly, showing that the significance of a metaphor is affected by the context of belief in which it appears. Given the Buddhist metaphor of the jewelled net, ". . . no metaphor is possible, since all is contained in all to begin with. More precisely, in such a view metaphor will not have the transgressive or daring quality it has in, say, modernist or surrealist writing. Metaphor will be healing and corrective rather than normative, disruptive, or innovative" (89).

In addition to the usual understanding of the term I will also make use of Jakobson's definition of metaphor. This concerns the way in which a discourse is constructed, how the constituent elements are combined—whether on the basis of their similarity (metaphor) or their contiguity (metonymy). Jakobson's distinction between metaphoric and metonymic discourse derives from his identification of two distinct processes, "selection" and "combination" of semantic items, that take place in any speech act. Metaphor involves combination of items in terms of similarity, while metonymy involves combination in terms of contiguity. According to this definition a "metaphoric" piece of writing will tend to be highly patterned in structure, exhibiting contrasts, repetitions, parallels, contrasts and so on.[5] Given Snyder's view, a patterned structure of this kind is analogous to the patterned structures which connect all things in the jewelled net (both in the present and in history). For this reason I consider his model to be a metaphoric one.

In this respect, I am following Lévi-Strauss. Using Jakobson's terminology, he extended it to describe the difference between a "mythic" world view (which sees history and the present in terms of timeless patterns of correspondence) and the more linear "historicism." By analogy, he identified these views with the metaphoric and metonymic poles of discourse respectively (Altieri, "Objective Image" 103–4). Clearly, the traditions which Snyder favors belong to the first category. For example, in *The Real Work* he describes appreciatively the Plains Indian view according to which trees, animals and mountains are in a sense "individual turbulence patterns of the energy flow that manifest themselves temporarily as discrete items playing specific roles and then flowing back in again" (TRW 44). This idea is comparable with the Buddhist view of nature as a complex of interdependent patterns which cannot exist or be interpreted in isolation, and is easily compatible with the proposals of systems biology. In each case the model may be termed a metaphoric one.

In this essay I will give particular attention to *Regarding Wave* and *Axe Handles*. Part 1 examines the function in *Regarding Wave* of what I call *metaphoric patterning*—as in Jakobson; part 2 is a brief discussion of *Turtle Island;* part 3 considers the effect in *Axe Handles* of particular *metaphors*—in the ordinary sense of the word; and part 4 draws some conclusions. In each case the use of metaphor seeks to establish a metaperspective on binary oppositions. In place of the Romantic or Modernist "mythmaker," this supports Snyder's idea of the poet as "myth-handler-healer" (TRW 172).

I

*Regarding Wave* is probably Snyder's most successful articulation of the theme of interdependence. As the syntactically ambiguous title suggests, the collection is directly concerned with the potentially revolutionary significance of experiencing oneself as a participant in a dynamic universe. Both structurally and thematically the book reflects Snyder's preoccupation with the goddess Vak who becomes the focusing metaphor.

In *The Old Ways* Snyder alludes to the tradition of Sanscrit poetics, according to which poetry originates in the sound of running water and the wind in the trees. According to this idea, human language (and particularly the poet's use of voice) derives from "the sense of the universe as fundamentally sound and song," that is, from an experience of Voice. This Voice is the goddess Vak (or Sarasvati, "the flowing one"). She is associated with rhythmic pattern, and is described as "the universe itself as energy, the energy of which all sub-energies are born" (TOW 35).[6] As the flyleaf of *Regarding Wave* suggests, the linking of energy, sound and the feminine which Vak represents is precisely what Snyder is aiming for in the collection. The poetry is presented as the vehicle of a vision of the community or interdependence of all phenomena. According to this all things are perceived in terms of their participation in Vak—that is, in energy (what I call here "waveness") and sound ("voice"). This view is articulated most clearly in the poems "Wave" and "Regarding Wave" which frame the seminal first three sections of the book, Regarding Wave I, II and III.

Snyder's first discussion of Vak appears in the essay "Poetry and the Primitive" in *Earth House Hold*, where "Voice" is presented as one of the Buddhist Three Mysteries. The section "The Voice as a Girl" emphasizes the significance of the goddess Vak with respect to the notion of "woman as nature the field for experiencing the universe as sacramental" (EHH 124). In *Regarding Wave* the correspondence of "woman" and "nature"—Vak and the pattern of interpenetrating energies—is made repeatedly.

This emphasis centers on the correspondence of "wave . . . wife" in the opening poem, "Wave," which presents the mind's apprehension of pattern or "waveness." The poem is, in Jakobson's terms, a strikingly metaphoric piece (see diagram in Appendix). Appropriately, the structure serves to convey the quality of this pattern and the interrelatedness of phenomena which it implies, as well as the orientation of the perceiver that this order of experience requires. Like many of the others in *Regarding Wave* this poem is a celebration, in this case a celebration of the mind's interaction with the patterned texture of the world—"those objects we take to be outside ourselves." Playing with the phonetic expectations set up by the core word ("wave"), the poem proposes the correspondences that may be perceived to exist, at many levels, between apparently separate natural phenomena. The final climactic invocation calls for the speaker to be caught and thrown out of the narrow selfhood, his imaginary autonomy, into the "dancing grain" of the world, the pattern of the "wave." Significantly, the pattern dances, not only in "things" out there, but in the mind of the poet as well. In this way, the last two lines make explicit the relative status of mind and objects that the poem proposes. The corollary of perceiving the waveness of all phenomena is both a recognition of their interrelatedness, and a sense that the human "I" is also a participant in this environment.

The significance of these aspects of the poem becomes clear when it is read in the context of the rest of the collection. For the poems that follow, "Wave" functions as the primary source of imagery and subject matter, the association of the feminine with water, the sea and rhythmic process being made repeatedly. The purpose of this is, on the one hand, to confirm the connection of "wife," the maternal sea, with energy and voice, and consequently with fertility and creation. At the same time, the possibility of sexual union with the feminine "other" reveals, metaphorically, the possible interpenetration of mind and Mind, the voice of the poet and the Voice of the Goddess which the concluding lines of "Wave" suggest. It is therefore appropriate that the central experiences in *Regarding Wave* should be those of love-making, marriage, conception and birth, and that these should take place in a non-hierarchic island community.

The thematic cohesion of the collection makes for a structure that is not accounted for by what is usually written about Snyder's work, although some of his own statements are very explicit. In *The*

*Real Work* he compares the structure of his poetry with that of the raga and tala in Indian music: "These give me a model, analogous in some senses to my own work, of a longer range sense of structuring with improvisatory possibilities taking place on a foundation of a certain steadiness that runs through it. So one poem has of itself the periodicity of a line, one structuring, and a number of poems to get a scene together will form a construct that is like one whole melodic thing. The model that underlies that also is the sense of the melodic phrase as dominating the poetic structure." (TRW 45–6). *Regarding Wave* is the clearest example of this sort of construct, and appropriately so, given its major concerns. The structure remarkably resembles that of a piece of music composed of repetitions around a single note or theme. This prevalence of parallels, contrasts and repetitions (phonetic, syntactic, lexical) makes it in Jakobson's terms a highly metaphoric document: the elements are usually combined by virtue of their similarity.

I describe the collection as a single document deliberately. While several poems (such as "Wave," "Seed Pods," etc.) are certainly metaphoric in this way, patterning of this kind is more marked across the collection as a whole. This means that a single poem simply cannot function fully as a separable, discrete item, since the "longer range sense of structuring" demands that it be read in relation to the others to which it is connected. Each poem (like a living organism) is necessarily an "open system." Particularly with respect to the use of metaphor, the single poem is not the main focus, as this comment from Snyder asserts: "As for metaphor, the definition (and use) of metaphor can be vastly shrunk or expanded. Almost all the poems in *Regarding Wave* respond to a subtle underlying thematic metaphor. The same for all my other books. Metaphor is not trotted out as a short term device section by section in poems but amounts to subtle controlling imagery that binds whole cycles of poems together" (Letter 8/20/84).

After "Wave," the most obvious poem for discussion is "Regarding Wave." Snyder's frequent claim that a text should be a "scoring" for an oral performance is particularly applicable to a poem such as this, being as it is an account of "Voice." A text that is metaphorically cohesive as this one (or "Wave") is, functions very much like a piece of music in which themes are repeated and varied. However it is only when the two poems are considered together (the second informed equally by the connections that have been established in the intervening poems) that their full sense begins to appear. For this reason I have printed the poems together in the Appendix.

In the earlier poem Snyder examined the texture of natural objects and the sense of correspondence this evokes. The focus is close, the attention to the "dancing grain" suggesting the flow of matter at a molecular level. This is reversed in "Regarding Wave." The field of vision has widened. The "flow" is now perceived on an extended scale, recalling the earlier poetry and its similarity to Chinese land-scape painting. Nevertheless the concerns of the two poems, the acts of mind they represent, are very similar. The later poem serves to establish that the relations in "Wave" remain: after the climactic central events (the birth of Kai and the new life this brings) "The Voice / is a wife / to him still." In order to be understood this sentence draws on the correspondences between "wave" and "wife" that the first poem establishes and subsequent poems reinforce. This infor-mation serves to clarify the reference to "wave" in the title of a poem ostensibly concerned with "Voice."

The appended parallel reading of the two poems reveals their structural, phonetic, lexical, thematic correspondences at a glance. It should be clear that the coherence of each depends on its relation to the other. In framing the "Regarding Wave" sections of the book, these poems inform the others, defining the patterns according to which they are to be read. The effect of this metaphoric patterning is a linguistic mimesis of a metaphoric view of things—that is, mimesis of the omnipresent patterned grain—with which the poems are con-cerned. Similarly, the interdependence which attention to grain and wave reveals is reflected in the open system which the poems together comprise. However, instead of being in any sense distinct from, or in opposition to, nature (which mimesis would usually imply), the mind which makes these linguistic patterns, and the voice which sings the songs, are seen as participants in a Voice and a Pattern that includes this mind, these poems, and yet goes beyond them.

So far I have used terms such as "framing," "open system" and "cohesion" without comment. Both poems exhibit a highly cohesive verbal structure, which nevertheless resists closure. By the most inconclusive of conclusions Snyder seeks in each case to extend the experience of reading the poem into a deeper interaction with "those things we take to be outside ourselves," and therefore with Self, Vak, Mind. The speaker's invocation at the end of "Wave" is extended in "Regarding Wave" in the linguistically more dramatic transition from English to mantra. This is an intriguing development of the "new kind of closure" that Kern identifies in the earlier work ("Silent Form" 41), and is worth some attention. It should be sufficient here to note that mantra is often described as the closest human articulation of mystic sound—Snyder's "shimmering bell / through all."[7] In con-cluding a poem (and a cycle of poems) in this way, Snyder is doing something rather unusual, which is at the same time very appropriate. Since the function of a mantra is precisely the dissolution of dualistic oppositions, the use of mantra in the poem invites the reader to participate, not in ideas *about* Vak, the interdependence of "self" and "universe," but rather in direct experience of these.[8]

If the encounter with wilderness in Snyder's earlier poems signified on the intrapsychic level meeting with unconscious areas of the self, then making love with the feminine represents another aspect of the same process: "As Vak is wife to Brahma . . . so the voice, in everyone, is the mirror of his deepest self" (EHH 125). In *Regarding Wave,* however, because the voice-wave-wife is experienced as permeating all phenomena, the epiphany is not only an intrapsychic event. It involves rather "becoming one" with whatever is considered to be *outside* the self: a participatory universe. In Buddhist terms, the integration of self implies reintegration into Self, interpenetration with that "other" from which one is never really separable.

The highly orchestrated first three sections of the collection are followed by poems that are very different in structure, although they are also concerned with patterns of metaphoric correspondence. The poems in "Long Hair" involve a movement outwards from the climactic personal intensity of those in "Regarding Wave." The first, "Revolution in the Revolution in the Revolution" proposes an essential connection between interbirth and revolutionary consciousness, at the center of which are the mantric "seed syllables" of the previous poem. By connecting the relations that have already been established between Vak (waveness, energy, power) and the rather different expectations one is likely to have about the power of revolutionary liberation, the concluding lines suggest that their origin is, in an important sense, the same: "& POWER / comes out of the seed-syllables of mantras." Given its position in the sequence of the collection, the transvaluation of both religious and political terminology that the poem explores is significant. The linguistic fusion in "True Communionism" provides an important context for the earlier descriptions of "personal" epiphany.

In the poems that follow, grain and wave are recalled, their repetition remaining the basis of the metaphoric structure. But since the "Regarding Wave" poems explicitly celebrated a sense of the personal correspondence with these, such correspondences are now implicit. It seems to be enough to describe the "Running Water Music" itself:

> Clear running stream
> clear running stream
>
> Your water is light
> to my mouth
> And a light to my dry body

> your flowing
> Music,
>       in my ears, free,
>
> Flowing free!
> With you
>       in me.   (RW 74)

The poems in "Target Practice," the final section of *Regarding Wave*, are not haiku, but they do show the apparently effortless condensation that is characteristic of the form, and for the same reasons. (According to Blyth, "Haiku are an expression of the joy of our reunion with things from which we have been parted by self-consciousness" 260.) Like much of Snyder's early poetry and its Oriental models, these poems depict a reunion with "those things we take to be outside ourselves." As in other Zen poems, this is done by pointing without explanation at the material thing itself and so reducing the opposition of subject-object. In this collection, however, the reading of these brief metonymic pieces is informed by the more extended descriptions of intensely perceived correspondences in the poems that have preceded them. Given the sense of interdependence of things which the other poems in the collection suggest—with metaphoric patternings, repetitions, parallels—it is now enough to return with delight to any apparently insignificant fragment. As Suzuki puts it: "When an object is picked up, everything else, One and All, comes along with it" (Blyth 256). By attending in this way to minute particulars, the necessarily declimactic and apparently inconclusive last section returns the reader to the metonymic detail of experience on which, as in Williams' poem about the red wheelbarrow, "so much depends."

## II

Following *Regarding Wave*, *Turtle Island* makes explicit the political implications of the idea of sacramental interdependence, or the interpenetration of the self, or individual organism, and the community of objects ostensibly external to it. In contrast with the recurrent correspondence of wave-wife, the central image here is of the Earth as Mother, and the enormity of her destruction by patriarchal-technological culture. The concerns are, nevertheless, a continuation of the earlier ones. The present ecological crisis is shown to be a direct consequence of "otherworldly" (and often patriarchal) metaphysics, and the Cartesian oppositions with which these are linked. Assuming that religious or mystical positions may not be ideologically neutral, Snyder examines the political meaning of religious doctrines, in particular those which promote potentially exploitative attitudes towards whatever is conceived as "other."

With respect to form, *Turtle Island* is obviously very different from the metaphorically patterned *Regarding Wave*. It also differs from Snyder's early poetry, with its tendency to avoid metaphor and symbol. Here the political, spiritual, personal concerns of the poetry are informed by several important metaphors, what Altieri would probably call "myths." These include "Amerika," "Turtle Island" and "the Great Family," and involve repeated references to a symbolic feminine. As the Introductory Note indicates, the book's title works as a focusing metaphor. In identifying the turtle with the serpent-of-eternity, Snyder establishes from the beginning its identity with primal creative energy that precedes differentiation: the ouroboros biting its tail. "The poems speak of place, and the energy-pathways that sustain life. Each living being is a swirl in the flow, a formal turbulence, a "song." The land, the planet itself, is also a living being—at another pace" (TI 1). The relation established here between the turtle, "place" and "energy-pathways" is significant. Whereas in *Regarding Wave* the energy of Vak is omnipresent, vibrating in "every hill," "every leaf," *Turtle Island* suggests that this resource is largely hidden, the energy buried within the land, beneath the recent accretions of civilized culture. In proposing ways of access to this buried power, the poems attempt to regain those aspects of experience that Western culture has tended to deny. In this context, "a sense of place" means being "grounded" to the maternal Earth, and perception of the complex interdependencies of things involves a sense of oneself as being part of her family.

Making this critique of culture explicit produces poetry that is fairly unambiguous, often didactic and generalizing, and which does therefore sometimes justify the adverse criticism the collection has received. Altieri, for example, has argued that Snyder's assumption of a prophetic voice in *Turtle Island* has meant the generalization and interpretation of his images (transforming them into "myths") in order to make them more accessible. This tendency is somewhat contradictory for Snyder since it runs counter to the basic terms of his vision (Altieri, "Seer and Prophet" 769).[9] Molesworth responds more positively to the same features. He argues that the innovations which Altieri criticizes are appropriate in that they indicate an attempt to find new forms for the lyric, and alternatives to the privatized reader (Molesworth 92–107). My own view is that the collection is best seen as a transitional one. It raises questions and initiates new forms which the later work will address and develop.

## III

In the nine years between the publication of *Turtle Island* and that of *Axe Handles*, Snyder seems to have evolved a style that is not as vulnerable to the kinds of critical objection which the earlier collection raised. Like *Regarding Wave*, then, this collection is more obviously homogeneous than *Turtle Island*. However, in contrast with the high degree of metaphoric patterning that was evident in the former, many of the poems in *Axe Handles* recall Snyder's earliest poetry, through the use of metonymy. They are to this extent, like those that Kern discussed, "focused metonymically on things contiguous in the world, and not on language in the poem" (Kern, "Open Form" 188). Clear examples of this are poems such as "Fence Posts," "So Old" and "Removing the Plate of the Pump on the Hydraulic System of the Backhoe."

However, this tendency is not uniform, and the informing structure of the book as a whole is metaphoric. The title, cover picture ("The Snow Goddess") and the suggestive naming of the book's three sections ("Loops," "Gaia," "Nets") make this clear. These function as the controlling metaphors which define the context in which the "metonymic" poems are to be read. More importantly, these are very explicit metaphors for a perception of the world and of history which is itself (in Jakobson's terms) metaphoric. Each of the key metaphors refers to patterns of correspondence and interrelatedness—the sort of "mythic" thinking that Lévi-Strauss identified with the metaphoric pole of discourse. The effect of this is similar to that in the later sections of *Regarding Wave*. In each case the metaphoric structure of the collection as a whole conditions the way in which individual, metonymic poems are to be read. In so doing, these metaphors develop on those in *Turtle Island*, in a more explicit attempt to "go beyond" dualistic thinking. In what follows I will discuss each of the three central metaphors which structure the collection and within which the poems in *Axe Handles* take shape.

The first section of the book is called "Loops." If the poems in *Turtle Island* communicated a "sense of place," of the buried energies within the land itself, then *Axe Handles* proposes a particular sense of *time* or *timing* and of tradition. This is contrasted with the pace and "ungroundedness" of contemporary American civilization. The alternative modes are conveyed either syntactically, phonetically, or by means of the arrangement or "scoring" of the words on the page.

Snyder has frequently used the idea of "looping back" to indicate a recursive sense of history and tradition. The metaphor implies at many levels a reconnection with origins, "the old ways," and a recognition of continuity with ancient tradition. This sense of being a participant in and bearer of culture or tradition is one consequence of the recognition that the individual is necessarily a participant in a collective system. The view is intrinsic to Snyder's sense of role as a poet, as the title poem and this collection, more than his previous work, acknowledge. From one point of view this orientation involves the attempt to use poetry as a vehicle to "get back to the Pleistocene" (TRW 57), as a connecting "loop" to the roots of poetry in song and ritual observance. From another point of view, Snyder frequently writes that ecological sanity, and therefore political sense, require reassessment of our cultural roots, and attempting to relearn some of the "Old Ways" by which people lived for thousands of years before the comparatively recent accretion of high technology culture.

Many of the poems (and not only in the "Loops" section) are concerned in different ways with "looping back": a return to Japan, to Piute mountain where he worked twenty-five years before, the looping back of plant and animal life to their origins. The loops to Snyder's own past recall a time of relative solitude, in contrast with the family and other concerns in which he is now involved: "Today at Slide Peak in the Sawtooths / I look back at that mountain / twenty-five years. Those days / When I lived and thought all alone" (AH 29).

The title poem, "Axe Handles," is a record of a significant epiphany arising from a response to manual work on one fairly ordinary occasion. Its placing is important in several ways. As in *Turtle Island* and *Regarding Wave*, the first poem in the collection informs the reading of the others. In this case, the epiphany arises in the recognition that the axe is at once a real tool, and a powerful metaphor by which the interdependence of old and new may be perceived.

> And I see: Pound was an axe,
> Chen was an axe, I am an axe
> And my son a handle, soon
> To be shaping again, model
> And tool, craft of culture,
> How we go on. (AH 6)

In the course of the poem the axe becomes metaphoric. A semantic transfer of some kind is certainly taking place, but this is not quite the kind that one usually expects. The process whereby a new handle is shaped from an existing one, works here as a metaphoric vehicle which is used to clarify something about the transmission of culture (here the tenor). In this poem, however, the metaphor is one where the vehicle is not separable from the tenor. This is because the shaping of the axe handle (and the father's communication of this to the son) is itself an example of the sort of process for which it is a metaphor: in this sense both "model and tool." This is rather similar to what happens in a number of the poems (compare, for example, "Wave" in *Regarding Wave*). The device seems to be a meaningful feature of the poetry, representing an attempt to avoid the dualistic split that other sorts of metaphor may imply, where the tenor and vehicle are clearly separable domains.

As the title of the collection indicates, the metaphor suggests a way of reading the poems that follow—as "axe handles." As such they are artifacts that may work as tools in their own right, as well as models for what is to follow. This is because they themselves have been "shaped" from and are connected to numerous precedents.

Clearly then, "Loops" represents the possibility of a cyclic sense of time which belongs to the metaphoric or mythic way of thinking— as opposed to the linear abstraction that Lévi-Strauss calls "historicism" (Altieri, "Objective Image" 104).[10]

The final section of *Axe Handles* is called "Nets." Even more so than "Loops," the metaphor "Nets" is a multivalent word for Snyder, and for the subculture by whom his work has been received.[11] It appears in his work as early as *Earth House Hold*, where the "jewelled net" of INDRA is used as a metaphor for the mythic or metaphoric notion of "interbirth" or "Communionism." *Axe Handles* resumes the explicit attention to this perception of things that *Regarding Wave* initiated. "Nets" as it is used in *Axe Handles* recalls the central metaphor in "Shark Meat," where the shark that had fouled the fishermen's nets is eaten by the islanders (RW 39). In this context, given the appropriate rituals—enough time, attention, reverence— activities like hunting, fishing and eating other animals are not problematic. If "the real work is eating each other," then the meaning of "net" as that by which animals are trapped is clearly significant. The relation it implies between man and animal is shown to be one instance of the phenomenon of interdependence, the web of reciprocity. Elsewhere Snyder calls it "the shimmering foodchain."

This attitude towards "those things we take to be outside ourselves" is illustrated in the poem "Geese Gone Beyond." As in *Turtle Island*, hunting as it is described here is accompanied by ritual behavior, recalling ancient practice: "I kneel in the bow. . . ." This prepares the reader for the shooting itself, in which there is no sense of violation, or personal animosity—"A touch across, / the trigger . . ." (AH 66). The function of these lines is to diminish the sense of *personal* responsibility: the syntax works to give the action a very different status from what it would have had in, say, "I pull the trigger." It seems, too, as though the first bird is in some sense a conscious participant. The bird flies up, as though acknowledging what is to happen: "The one who is the first to feel to go." This interpretation is reinforced by the poem's title, "Geese Gone Beyond" which alludes to an idea of "Gone Beyond Wisdom" introduced on the flyleaf of *Regarding Wave*. Its use here suggests that in shooting the geese the narrator is acting as a vehicle for *their* transcendence, and thereby (to the extent that he has "become one" with them) for his own as well. As in "Shark Meat" and "The Hudsonian Curlew," the human is understood to be a necessary agent in the animals' cycle of birth and death: killing in this way for food is an acknowledgement of our interdependence, human and non-human, in the living web.

As early as his B.A. thesis in 1951, with its fascination with the Muse and the Mother Goddess, Snyder gives emphasis to a theme which has been continuous in his work. This theme is the mythic significance of Woman as *"the totality of what can be known"* [my emphasis] (Snyder, *Haida Myth* 71). As Snyder indicated in a letter, the goddess as metaphor represents more for him than the reverse image of a patriarchal deity. It is rather a crucial metaperspective on oppositional or dualistic epistemology:

> We only divide the world up into two sets—such as essential and karmic, or noumenal and phenomenal, or wisdom and compassion, temporarily for arriving at certain kinds of clarity. But in the uncompromisingly non-dualistic Buddhist view which is an experiential view, not merely abstract and philosophical, these divisions are really just means and the world is one. Or as Yamada Roshi says, "not even one." There are such terms in esoteric Buddhism as the garbha (womb) realm and the vajra (thunderbolt) realm. But all of these are studied to the point of dissolving the dualism, even while maintaining a healthy understanding of the multiplicities by which things function. Prajna paramita is the "perfection" of a kind of wisdom that goes beyond such distinctions as being / nonbeing yin / yang essential / phenomenal or even wise / ignorant, or even enlightened / unenlightened. The wisdom that has done this is the wisdom that has "gone beyond". . . . But to make the circle interesting, the esoteric Buddhist tradition represents the wisdom that goes beyond all dualisms as . . . a goddess. I find this charming. For "wisdom that has gone beyond," "illusion and wisdom both have been left behind." (Letter 8/20/84)

This sense of "woman" or the goddess as symbolic of totality needs to be spelled out in this way because it is confusing for obvious reasons. A similar difficulty arises with Snyder's use of "nature" to signify, not an alternative to "culture," but the whole biosphere, the whole earth. In the later work, the culminating expression of this theme is the goddess Gaia—a metaphor for the attempt to go beyond dualistic oppositions, and for a metaphoric view of the world. In Gaia, "the great biosphere being," both "woman" and "nature" as *totality* are simultaneously evoked.

The metaperspective this represents is wholly fitting to the character of this ancient divinity. In Greek mythology, Gaia is the primal Earth Goddess, the Great Mother, and in terms of the idea of "looping back," she is clearly appropriate in Snyder's symbolic system. As the oldest Greek deity, both in mythic and probably in historical terms, she stands firstly for the earth and for values contrary to those associated with patriarchal religion and culture. Secondly, however, as mother of Uranus, existing before the discrimination into sexes, she is, symbolically, the mother out of whom these contrary values are born.

In addition, the name of Gaia has come to be associated with the concept of the "network" in recent years. Two environmental scientists, James Lovelock and Sydney Epton, have in the last ten years evolved a fairly influential model which they call The Gaia Hypothesis. In this model (from which Snyder borrowed the name) "Gaia" is the name for "a complex entity involving the earth's biosphere, atmosphere, oceans and soil; the totality constituting a feedback or cybernetic system which seeks an optimal physical and chemical environment for life on this planet" (Lovelock 11). It follows that in whatever sense she is understood, Gaia represents both "the whole network," and the originating source of its life. Consequently the energy she embodies is both primarily undifferentiated and an image of the transcendence of oppositional relations.

In *Axe Handles*, "Little Songs for Gaia" is centered between "Loops" and "Nets," serving to emphasize the role of Gaia as the one who binds these elements together: a net is made of loops, while it is mythically the work of the goddess to weave the disparate threads of the net or web together. The songs in this central section, rather like those in "Target Practice" (RW), evoke the simplicity of a state of consciousness "beyond transcendence" (EHH 128). The following poem is a good illustration of the sense of correspondence this characteristically involves for Snyder.

> 24.IV.40075, 3:30 PM,
> n. of Coaldale, Nevada,
> A Glimpse through a Break
> in the Storm of the Summit
> of the White Mountains
>
> O Mother Gaia
> sky cloud gate milk snow
> wind-void-word
> I bow in roadside gravel (AH 71)

The moment of its occurrence carefully documented, the epiphany which this poem records is an intense recognition that "at one level there are no hierarchies of qualities in life" (TRW 17). For this reason the monosyllabic elements in the second line are equally weighted— evenly paced with equal spaces between. This is followed by a characteristic hyphenating of words, conveying a paradoxical interrelation of "wind," "void," and "word." Contrary to what might have been expected, neither the first line (invocation) nor the last (ritualized response) are separated from the rest: weaver of the net of correspondences, "Mother Gaia" is wholly immanent in the world of interpenetrating phenomena—they are in fact one and the same. At the same time she represents that which transcends and is beyond the particular scene. Similarly, the human perceiver's awed response is to a world in which he is participant as well as observer: the ritual bow "in roadside gravel" is an indication at once of a delighted recognition of the goddess "out there," and at the same time of his own part in the magic system. In *The Old Ways* Snyder alludes to this order of experience, with regard to its scarcity in contemporary "civilization": "Not that special, intriguing knowledges are the real point; it's the sense of the magic system; the capacity to hear the song of Gaia at *that* spot, that's lost" (TOW 65). The body of Snyder's work suggests that momentary epiphanies of the kind the poem (and others in *Axe Handles*) presents are valuable. But this value depends on the extent that they are seen to be surrounded not, as in Eliot or Stevens, by "waste sad time" or its equivalent. The context is rather an everyday one, in which the Goddess, and the sacramental metaperspective she represents, continue to be accessible in the rhythm of the most everyday activities.

## IV

This essay began with Gregory Bateson's questions about what he calls "the pattern which connects." His book *Mind and Nature: A Necessary Unity* is based on the premise that "we are parts of a living world" (27) and examines some of the complex patterns of information and energy by which all living things are connected. As the title suggests, the purpose of his discussion is a radical reconsideration of the mental habit which opposes self and other, mind and nature, us and them. Snyder's project is a similar one. His response to the problem of "other" is Buddhist and ecological. As other critics have noted, his work proposes a mode of perception that transcends or "goes beyond" dualism. For this reason the earlier poetry notably avoided metaphor and symbol. Surprisingly, however, metaphor and structures of metaphoric pattern and correspondence are used in the later work for precisely the same purpose: to suggest a necessary interdependence between the individual and "those things we consider to be outside ourselves." In the collections I have discussed, metaphor works to reveal Snyder's sense of the pattern which connects, producing a context of complex correspondences in which the individual, often metonymic, poems are to be read.

This makes for poetry that contradicts some of the critical observations that have been made about it. Altieri, for example, sees some of the poems in *Regarding Wave* as an extension of Williams' objectivism ("Process as Plenitude" 150). Elsewhere he discusses the main features of this orientation. Using Jakobson's model of metaphor and metonymy, he argues that two main traditions in modern poetry derive from different strategies for approaching the metonymic image and transcending its limits. The first, essentially symbolist, tradition ("mythmakers" like Yeats, Eliot, Stevens) assumes that the mind requires informing universals if it is to be satisfied in experience, and so it finds in metonymy a cause for despair. For the second tradition (Williams, for example) metonymy is a step in the right direction because "the source of despair is not metonymy itself but the dream that consciousness can find unifying structures" (Altieri, "Objective Image" 108–9).

There is, however, a crucial difference between Snyder's use of metaphor and metonymy and either of the trends which Altieri describes. In his case, the context in which a wheelbarrow (or anything else) is perceived in a universe of necessary correspondences, mutual interpenetration, in which all things are wave-patterned, an expression of the Goddess: all things, even the inanimate, have Buddha-nature. Given this, it is irrelevant for the human perceiver to construct "unifying structures." As Molesworth's comment about metaphor suggested (89), the poet's work is rather to recognize and make explicit a metaphoric connection which *already exists* between the various elements.[12] Instead of being a "mythmaker," s / he is a "myth handler-healer," restoring the connections that have been disrupted by divisive mental habit.

The social and political implications of recognizing the pattern which connects are extensive, as writers in other fields have shown. Snyder's work draws attention to the ideological consequences of our habitual binary thinking, and the poetry returns again and again to examples of this in Western technological culture. This political incentive is certainly a crucial aspect of his spiritual, ecological, personal perspective. But problems do seem to arise from putting the poetry to work for political ends. I would agree with other commentators that this is most evident in *Turtle Island*, although my sense of the problem is slightly different. I also think that the problems are not confined to *Turtle Island*.

In rejecting a dualistic model, Snyder's project is to write poetry that proposes an alternative to binary thinking. And yet, to the extent that it involves placing the self in opposition to an exploitative, oppressive ideology, the "alternative" view is in danger of becoming its mirror-image. This becomes particularly clear in the choice of metaphors. So for example the angry depiction of "Amerika" in *Turtle Island* is a rather two-dimensional oversimplification, and some of the "natural" metaphors verge on sentimentality, as Kern and Altieri have shown. Wilden states the problem in general terms as follows: "We cannot destroy the master simply by taking his place; we have to make him irrelevant—and that means to reduce his mastery by transcending the oppositional relationship in which we find ourselves in a negative identification with him. To destroy exploitative mastery we must do more than become the negative complement of the master, his mirror-image. . . ." (Wilden 30).

The most significant area in this respect for Snyder is the metaphoric complex he calls "the Goddess"—which includes Vak, "Mother Earth" and Gaia. Snyder's Goddess connects nature, woman, and all the other unfortunates that appear on the wrong side of the divide in a binary epistemology. The intention in this focus is clearly very different from that which has motivated the simultaneous exploitation of women, nature, other races, animals, etc. It is, quite explicitly, an attempt to heal the damage caused by these attitudes and to propose the mythic feminine as an image of totality. This image of the feminine achieves its clearest expression in *Axe Handles,* with its celebration of Gaia and of the world in which she is perceived. As metaphor, Gaia represents a perspective that is clearly of a higher logical type than those which either welcome or bemoan an identification of the "feminine" with "nature," and represent the goddess as the reverse image of the "masculine," "patriarchal" god (Daly; also Dickason). As such, the metaphor is a powerful image of totality. Even so, the post-feminist reader is likely to ask whether it is possible to associate woman and nature metaphorically without calling up the patriarchal-technological viewpoint which made this connection an exploitative one. Although I do find Gaia an effective metaphor, I think that the poetry shows very little self criticism on this subject, and little sense of the problems inherent in making such connections.

I have argued that in the later work the use of metaphor, and specifically metaphors associated with the Goddess, is an important way of pointing to the jewelled network of connecting pattern. And yet the poems themselves insist on their provisional nature: even at its best, poetry remains a kind of pointer, since the Way to the Pattern must finally be one that has no map. Snyder's version of the Buddhist idea of the Pathless Path, the Gateless Gate appears in *Regarding Wave* in the poem "The Way Is Not a Way." In this context, hitting the target or finding the pattern must involve, paradoxically, "Looking for Nothing"—as the first poem in "Target

† In parenthetical references, titles of works by Snyder will be abbreviated as follows: AH—*Axe Handles* (North Point Press, 1983); EHH—*Earth House Hold* (New Directions, 1969); RW—*Regarding Wave* (Fulcrum, 1970); TI—*Turtle Island* (New Directions, 1974); TOW—*The Old Ways* (City Lights, 1977); TRW—*The Real Work: Interviews and Talks 1964–1978* (New Directions, 1980).

Practice" indicates. Significantly, this point of view reveals the Goddess after all:

> Look in the eye of a hawk
> The inmost ring of a log
>
> The edge of the sheath and the
> Sheath—where it leads—
>
> River sands.
> Tārā      "Joy of
> Starlight"
>        thousand—
>        eyed. (RW 79)

## Appendix

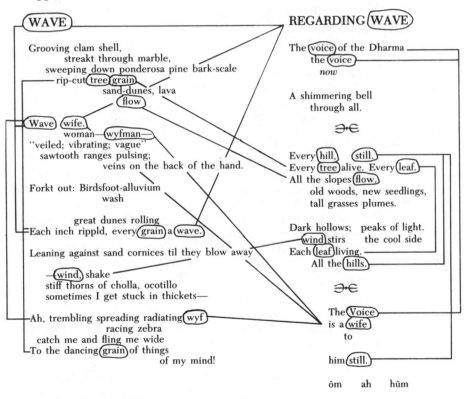

The purpose of this diagram is to give simple visual confirmation
of the highly patterned metaphoric structure of the poems "Wave"
and "Regarding Wave," and to show how the use of parallels and
repetition draws connections between the two poems. The function
of this structure is a formal mimesis of the poems' subject. The

reader's attention is drawn to the marked repetition of certain pho-
nemes, in particular those derived from seminal words like "*wave*,"
"*regarding*," "*Wife*" and "*still*." Where complete words are repeated,
these have been circled. The vertical lines connect those which are
repeated in the same poem, and the horizontal / diagonal lines connect
those which occur in both poems.

## Notes

1. One thinks in particular of the work by Robert Kern and Charles Altieri.

2. See also Marilyn Ferguson on the metaphor of the net in *The Holographic
Paradigm* 25.

3. This attention to Western thought is not to suggest that Snyder considers
Oriental models always to have been an improvement.

4. See for example Anthony Wilden (207).

5. See the works by Jakobson and Lodge listed below.

6. The notion of mystical sound or Vak has a Western correlative in the concept
of the creative Logos, and derives from the experience of many mystics that all things
are composed of sound according to their nature (Woodroffe 4f).

7. The three syllables in this particular mantra correspond to the Buddhist
Three Mysteries (Govinda, *Tibetan Mysticism* and *Creative Meditation*).

8. As such, it is an extreme form of the tendency Altieri perceives: "Snyder is
trying to create potentially not so much a system of references that articulate 'The
Way,' as an emotional consciousness of what it feels like to know oneself as part of
such a system" (*Enlarging the Temple* 144).

9. Kern makes a similar point ("Silent Form" 48).

10. This is clearly in agreement with the Buddhist understanding of the Wheel
of DHARMA, according to which certain experiences must be repeated until the
necessary conditions have been fulfilled.

11. In her book *The Aquarian Conspiracy*, Marilyn Ferguson describes the in-
creased use in the last decade or so by this subculture of the word "networks" to
denote the remarkable burgeoning of interrelated "underground" social formations.
One consequence is the emergence of "networking" as a verb. The "Conspiracy" is
the name she gives to this leaderless network of networks. Acting from a similar
incentive, some forms of eco-feminism have adopted the web as their identifying
symbol—another expression of the conviction that, as one lapel button has it, "everything is connected."

12. It should be clear that, while making use of Jakobson's model of metaphor
and metonymy, this essays rejects the idea that these features are necessarily binary
alternatives.

## Works Cited

Altieri, Charles. "Gary Snyder's *Turtle Island:* The Problem of Reconciling
    the Roles of Seer and Prophet." *Boundary* 2, 4, No. 3 (1976), 761–775.
_____ "Objective Image and Act of Mind in Modern Poetry." *PMLA*, 91
    (1977), 101–114.

_____ *Enlarging the Temple: New Directions in American Poetry during the 1960's*. Lewisburg, Pa.: Bucknell Univ. Press, 1979.

Bateson, Gregory. *Mind and Nature: A Necessary Unity*. London: Fontana, 1980.

Blyth, R. H. *Haiku*. Vol. 1 of *Eastern Culture*. 1949; rpt. Tokyo: Hokuseido Press, 1973.

Daly, Mary. *Beyond God the Father*. Boston: Beacon Press, 1974.

_____ *Gyn / Ecology: The Metaethics of Radical Feminism*. Boston: Beacon Press, 1978.

Dickason, Anne. "The Feminine as a Universal." In *Feminism and Philosophy*. Ed. Mary Vetterling-Braggin, et al. 1977; rpt. Totowa, New Jersey: Littlefield, Adams & Co., 1978, 79–100.

Ferguson, Marilyn. *The Aquarian Conspiracy: Personal and Social Transformation in the 1980's*. 1981; rpt. London: Granada, 1982.

Fox, Matthew. "Meister Eckhart and Karl Marx: The Mystic as Political Theologian." In *Understanding Mysticism*. Ed. Richard Woods. New York: Image Books, 1980, 541–563.

Govinda, L. A. *Foundations of Tibetan Mysticism*. 1960; rpt. London: Rider & Co., 1975.

_____ *Creative Meditation and Multi-Dimensional Consciousness*. London: Unwin, 1977.

Jakobson, Roman. "Two Aspects of Language and Two Types of Linguistic Disturbance." In R. Jakobson and M. Halle, *Fundamentals of Language*. 2nd ed. 1956; rpt. The Hague: Mouton, 1971, 55–82.

_____ "Linguistics and Poetics." In *Poetry of Grammar and Grammar of Poetry*. Vol. 3 of *Selected Writings*. Ed. Stephen Rudy. 1958; rpt. The Hague: Mouton, 1981, 18–51.

_____ "Poetry of Grammar and Grammar of Poetry." *Lingua*, 21 (1968), 597–609.

Kern, Robert. "Toward a New Nature Poetry." *Centennial Review*, 19, No. 3 (1975), 198–216.

_____ "Clearing the Ground: Gary Snyder and the Modernist Imperative." *Criticism*, 19, No. 2 (1977), 158–177.

_____ "Recipes, Catalogues, Open Form Poetics: Gary Snyder's Archetypal Voice." *Contemporary Literature*, 18, No. 2 (1977), 173–197.

_____ "Silence in Prosody: The Poem as Silent Form." *The Ohio Review*, No. 26 (1981), 34–52.

Lodge, David. *The Modes of Modern Writing: Metaphor, Metonymy and the Typology of Modern Literature*. London: Edward Arnold, 1977.

Lovelock, James E. *Gaia: A New Look at Life on Earth*. New York, 1979; rpt. London: Oxford Univ. Press, 1982.

McLeod, Dan. "Some Images of China in the Works of Gary Snyder." *Tamkang Review*, 10 (1980), 369–384.

Molesworth, Charles. *Gary Snyder's Vision: Poetry and the Real Work*. Columbia: Univ. of Missouri Press, 1983.

Parkinson, Thomas. "The Poetry of Gary Snyder." *Southern Review*, 4 (1968), 616–632.

Snyder, Gary. *He Who Hunted Birds in His Father's Village: The Dimensions of a Haida Myth*. Grey Fox Press, 1979.

———— Letter to author. August 20, 1984.

Wilber, Ken, ed. *The Holographic Paradigm and Other Paradoxes*. Boulder: Shambhala, 1982.

Wilden, Anthony. *System and Structure: Essays in Communication and Exchange*. London: Tavistock, 1972.

Woodroffe, Sir John. *Garland of Letters*. 4th ed. 1922; rpt. Madras: Ganesh & Co., 1963.

Yip, Wai-Lim. "Aesthetic Consciousness of Landscape in Chinese and Anglo-American Poetry." *Comparative Literature Studies*, 15, No. 2 (1978), 211–242.

# Alternation and Interpenetration: Gary Snyder's *Myths & Texts*

Patrick D. Murphy°

Gary Snyder's *Myths & Texts* has been critically neglected.[1] The few articles that do discuss it usually analyze the structure because of its tantalizing complexity, while others dip into it for allusions, poetics, and biography.[2] Structural analyses fall into two main categories: one, Snyder structures the sequence as a quest; two, he structures it as a three-part progression. These two theories of structure, monomyth and triptych, promote linear conceptions of the sequence's development that describe only its outer skeleton. While one may say that *Myths & Texts* loosely follows a quest motif based on the monomyth, such a statement does not explain how the sequence is internally structured. Yet statements such as this have, for the most part, substituted for close critical examination of one of America's most important post–World War II sequences. One recent exception is Sherman Paul's meditation on the poem in which he remarks that the structure of the poem is "not a growth model, as in economics, but a steady-state model."[3]

A look at Snyder's undergraduate honors thesis provides some clues for understanding *Myths & Texts*.[4] In *He Who Hunted Birds in His Father's Village*, Snyder states: "Original mind speaks through little myths and tales that tell us how to *be* in some specific ecosystem of the far-flung world."[5] Snyder surmises: "Myth is a 'reality lived' because for every individual it contains, at the moment of telling, the projected content of both his unarticulated and conscious values: simultaneously ordering, organizing, and making comprehensible the

° This essay was written specifically for this volume and appears here for the first time by permission of the author. Quotations from *Myths & Texts*, © 1960 Gary Snyder, reprinted by permission of New Directions Publishing Corporation.

world within which the values exist. One might even reformulate the statement to say 'Reality is a myth lived' " (109–110). Myth, then, places people in a cultural and physical matrix, providing them with a coherent presence in place and time. Snyder also defines the role of the poet in modern society, tying it into this conception of myth: "The poet would not only be creating private mythologies for his readers, but moving toward the formation of a new social mythology" (112). Clearly, by "private" Snyder does not mean privy only to the poet, but personally developed by the poet for his readers. As Snyder understands it, the poet acts as vehicle for a social mythology that seeks to reintegrate individual, society, and ecosystem.

He thus brings to the creation of *Myths & Texts*, begun a year or so after his thesis, a strongly developed sense of the social role of myths, the responsibility of the poet, and the kind of consciousness that myth must help create, integrate, and maintain in the contemporary world. This complex sensibility enables Snyder to employ aspects of the monomyth motif and adopt a metaphorical triptych without limiting his structure to either of these extrinsic forms. He employs, instead, an alternation and interpenetration of "myth" and "text" fragments to structure the internal dynamics of the forty-eight passages, as well as to produce the governing structure for the work as a whole.[6] *Myths & Texts* produces a dialogic interplay of mutual explication and interpretation between these two kinds of fragments, "the two sources of human knowledge" (vii), until at the end they become complementary descriptions of one experience.

The "texts" consist of sensory experiences undergone by speakers in the poem as well as previous experiences undergone by historical figures who are either speakers or the subjects of little stories, with both presented as equally existent: "The purpose of Snyder's telegraphic style is to give everything from sensation to rumination the clarity of present, direct vision."[7] Similarly, one finds two kinds of "myths" in the poem: 1) allusions to and brief stories about primitive and ancient myths of previous cultures; 2) little stories and mythopoeic elements—figures, events, locales—that contribute to "the formation of a new social mythology," a task of the poem explicitly stated in "Hunting 1." For Snyder, as William Jungels notes, "it is probably generally true that myths serve as much to sustain and encourage a culture in its practices and values as to simply reflect them."[8] In addition, myths serve as a means for presenting a new spiritual perception of the contemporary world. In this context, then, what may have been or may be at the moment a "text," an external sensory experience, may become through the work of mythopoeia part of a little "myth" that will "tell us how to *be* in some specific ecosystem." "Myths" enable the poet and the reader to interpret individual and group "texts," while such "texts" contribute to and provide the foundation for great and little "myths."

The first passage of *Myths & Texts*, "Logging 1," opens with "The morning star is not a star." This line functions as a text fragment making a factual statement about Venus, while suggesting that the mind can misinterpret sense impressions. It also functions as a myth fragment alluding to *Walden* as American myth and alluding to the mythological name of Venus as "Lucifer" when it appears as a morning star. The negation itself, implying false vision, and the subtle allusion to Lucifer begin the section on an ominous note, one prefigured by the epigraph from Acts 19:27, which refers to Christian attacks on the worship of the goddess Diana.

> 1
> The morning star is not a star
> Two seedling fir, one died
> > Io, Io,
>
> Girdled in wistaria
> Wound with ivy
> > "The May Queen
> Is the survival of
> A pre-human
> Rutting season"

The second line presents another text fragment, while the third presents a refrain alluding to a myth of wandering and to the "Great Mother."[9] This too responds to the epigraph by referring to another form of goddess worship. The next two lines describe the initial garbing for a mythic celebration. The quotation then produces a textual gloss of the myth. In these few lines myth as the religious story about a universal cultural experience and text as the record of actual experience intermix.

The second stanza of "Logging 1" reads:

> The year spins
> Pleiades sing to their rest
> > at San Francisco
> > dream
> > dream
> Green comes out of the ground
> Birds squabble
> Young girls run mad with the pine bough,
> > Io

The first line presents a text fragment connecting human conception of time with earth's physical cycles. The next line mixes myth and text: a constellation setting is described by means of its accompanying myth. The reader is given a physical location, but the invocation of "dream / dream" suggests the sensory realm of the collective unconscious, the locus for mythic vision. Then spring is indicated through descriptions of animal and plant life, and this text is linked to the myth of that season by the following line, which describes "the thyrsus, carried by maenads worshipping Dionysus," who is the son of Io.[10] But the physical location of the Pleiades indicates the season as autumn with spring existing only as a dream. Jungels interprets this juxtaposition of seasons in this way: "With the goddesses retired and the earth devastated it is only in dream that spring and Io . . . can be conjured.[11] The passage closes with "Io," who, linked with Dionysus and Diana, suggests a favoring of anti–Christian, archaic rituals. At the same time, the autumnal setting suggests that the matrifocal/Earth-worshipping values are waning, which prepares for the transition to the quote from Exodus that opens "Logging 2."

> 2
> But ye shall destroy their altars,
> break their images, and cut down their groves.
> —Exodus 34:13
>
> The ancient forests of China logged
> and the hills slipped into the Yellow Sea.
> Squared beams, log dogs,
> on a tamped-earth sill.

The Exodus quote historically prefigures the poem's epigraph. "And cut down their groves" links the two, both being attacks on matrifocal, nature-worship religions. Use of the quote indicts the Judeo-Christian idea of dominion over the things of the earth. The next line describes China's denuding its forests with consequent erosion. This juxtaposition links the destructive character of widely divergent "advanced" civilizations, indicating Snyder recognizes that the antiecological drive is not limited to the West but has occurred and continues to occur worldwide.[12]

To present a contrast to the simple houses of ancient days, which still took their toll of the forests, Snyder describes the housing of San Francisco and the plunder it requires. The third stanza is a text fragment with myth introduced into it:

> San Francisco 2×4s
> were the woods around Seattle:
> Someone killed and someone built, a house,
> a forest, wrecked or raised
> All America hung on a hook
> & burned by men, in their own praise.

The use of "killed" in relation to the forests asserts the living quality of trees and "in their own praise" places the entire description within a religious, mythic framework. The metaphor of the Cross as a tree also lurks here. In addition to intertwining myth and text, Snyder foreshadows the other two sections of the sequence. "Someone killed and someone built, a house" foreshadows the reverent and sacrilegious ways of killing addressed in "Hunting," as well as the felled tree as home in "Logging 8." The line "& burned by men, in their own praise" foreshadows by contrast the poem "Burning." In "Burning," the fire is part of nature's cleansing, regenerative cycle of growth and decay and is an offering to the universal regenerative force. In "Logging 2," the fire is an unnatural form of self-worship, one which denies cyclical balance by consuming without regenerating.

The narrator comments in stanza four: "I wake from bitter dreams," a contrast with the invocation of "dream / dream." Snyder follows this bitter stanza with one that again interweaves myth and text:

> "Pines grasp the clouds with iron claws
> like dragons rising from sleep"
> 250,000 board-feet a day
> If both Cats keep working
> & nobody gets hurt

Although the pines and Cats form part of the experiential text of logging, they also comprise referents conducive to symbol-making in the formation of a logging myth. An essential difference exists, though, between the pines-as-dragons myth, with its Chinese fertility symbolism,[13] and any logging myth in that the "iron claws" grasp but do not devour the clouds, while the Cats devour the pines as dead "board-feet."

"Logging 3" opens with a quotation describing the lodgepole pine. In juxtaposition to the preceding mythopoeic quote, this one is a textbook definition, but one which provides a phoenixlike archetypal symbol: a tree whose new life arises from seed cones living in the ashes of the tree consuming fire. This contradicts the destructive burning of "Logging 2," and encourages an optimistic rather than pessimistic reading of that earlier line, "two seedling fir, one died."[14] The second stanza describes the process of hooking felled trees, the experiential text for the earlier mythic line, "All America hung on a hook." Snyder follows this with a mythic tale of Hsu Fang who lived a life diametrically opposed to the destructive one that demands the rape of forests.[15] He follows this with another story describing the unnaturalness of farming recently logged-off land. It concludes with a regenerative remark: "The kids grow up and go to college / They don't come back. / The little fir-trees do."

"Logging 3" ends:

> Rocks the same blue as sky
> Only icefields, a mile up,
> > are the mountain
> Hovering over ten thousand acres
> Of young fir.

This text of sensory experience contains essential elements for Snyder's mythopoeia. The mountain plays a crucial role in "Burning" as its height provides the physical opportunity for a different perception of the world, duplicating the opportunity for a changed psychological perception that dreaming can provide and support. The word "Hovering" animates the mountain, reinforcing the image of living earth (similar images appear in the "Bubbs Creek Haircut" section of *Mountains and Rivers without End*[16]). The stanza concludes by reiterating the image of natural regeneration that began it.

The tonalities in these first three passages of "Logging" deserve some comment. The work begins with that ominous opening note. It seems to be undercut by the lighter tone of dream and celebration in the rest of "Logging 1." The ecstatic end of that passage is undercut by the opening of "Logging 2." Snyder reinforces the tone of this injunction through the next two stanzas. "Logging 2" contains a strong emotional intensity with its description of destruction and the narrator's bitterness. The description in "Logging 3" presents the power of nature and provides an emotional lift after the gloom of 2, with the cyclical regularity of regeneration posited as a living force in the world. The second stanza undercuts that feeling, but it is in turn reversed by the brief presentation of an alternative in the person of Hsu Fang. Another lifestyle follows, one that is dying out and thereby enabling future regeneration. Yet a tone of sadness enters, a poignant counterpoint that accepts such dying as positive but also registers the emotional ambivalence of one who knew it as a child. Like the earlier recognition that the denuding of forests has not been limited to modern countries, this recognition of mixed emotions over the disappearance of a familiar way of life demonstrates the complexity of Snyder's thought. It prevents the poem from falling to the level of diatribe. The final stanza of "Logging 3" presents a meditation on nature that links internal awareness and external interconnectedness.

The rest of "Logging" continues these patterns. Passages 4 and 5 produce an intermixing of myth and text similar to the first three passages. Sections 6 and 7 produce stories from the recent past that are already beginning to take on aspects of "little myths," with 6 being "the voice of Snyder's father, taken down without his awareness."[17] It tells of the natural profundity of second-growth regeneration. "Logging 7" tells of the Wobbly days in Washington and how these experiences have led to slogans that have their own symbolic, and potentially mythic, characteristics. Sections 8 and 9 focus almost exclusively on individual physical experiences, but from "Logging 10" to the end, the mythic elements begin to increase in proportion, with the exception of a lull in 13.[18]

In "Logging 13," the narrator describes a natural forest fire and observes it as lookout rather than as logger. He concludes: "The crews have departed, / And I am not concerned." This passage, like the last stanza of "Logging 3," uses natural description to develop the reader's awareness of a state of mind. The narrator's lack of concern suggests a changing perception of natural activity.[19] The fire also foreshadows the almost entirely mythic fire imagery of "Logging 15," the closing passage of the section. From this psychological vantage point—that mountain position suggested in "Logging 3"—"Logging 14" looks back through history at all the destruction wrought by various societies, each with its own myths, and brings it up to the present of the Protestant-capitalist myth governing America. It also specifically condemns the destruction of Native American societies.[20] This passage closes with an experience rendered as myth, contrasting regenerative and destructive fires:

> Sawmill temples of Jehovah.
> Squat black burners 100 feet high
> Sending the smoke of our burnt
> Live sap and leaf
> To his eager nose.

This stanza serves as both a mythic representation of a text experience and as an experiential evaluation of the results of a still-functioning myth guiding American society.

"Logging" concludes with a passage entirely composed of myth fragments. "Logging 15" proposes a different source for society's guiding myths than the Judeo-Christian tradition. It draws on Hinduism and Buddhism for its perception of the interpenetrating movement of natural life and human social life and culminates by seeking solace in the Hindu teleology of the kalpa cycle; but this seeking produces a multiplicity of tonalities, which suggests the conclusion's tentative character. Just as the way of life portrayed proves insufficient to cope with the relationship of society and nature—the contradiction of texts—so too the culmination of insights—lessons of the myths—proves insufficient to resolve the contradictions of that relationship.

"Logging 15" has its share of conflicting interpretations. Charles Molesworth misquotes the third stanza, turning "Let them lie" into "Let them die," and then criticizes Snyder for defeatism and pessimism.[21] Other critics tend to emphasize either an apocalyptic or a regenerative interpretation.[22] Both tones exist within the passage. But rather than the final quotation from Pa-ta Shan-jen playing a reassuring role by asserting that art preserves, it expresses a conflict the narrator cannot resolve simply through seeking solace in cyclicity.[23]

> Lodgepole
>> cone/seed waits for fire
> And then thin forests of silver-gray.
>> in the void
>> a pine cone falls
> Pursued by squirrels
> What mad pursuit! What struggle to escape!
>
> Her body a seedpod
> Open to the wind
> "A seed pod void of seed
> We had no meeting together"
>> so you and I must wait
> Until the next blaze
> Of the world, the universe,
> Millions of worlds, burning
>> —oh let it lie.

In the first half of "Logging 15" the lodgepole pine stands as a symbol of earth's regenerative cycles, including fiery destruction. The pursuit of the squirrels followed by the line from Keats's "Ode on a Grecian Urn" produce both a lighthearted tone and an emphasis on sexuality and fecundity.[24] The second stanza, though, abruptly reverses the tone, embedding a text fragment of unfulfilled pairing between myth fragments of sterility and cleansing. Snyder intensifies the reversal through the diametrically opposed uses of "void." Hope lies in the mythic cycle of rebirth, not in the physical regeneration of the society depicted in "Logging." In contrast to the exclamation of the first stanza, the second closes with a dejected ejaculation.

The third stanza picks up the end of the kalpa image initiated in the previous stanza:

> Shiva at the end of the kalpa:
> Rock-fat, hill-flesh, gone in a whiff.
> Men who hire men to cut groves
> Kill snakes, build cities, pave fields,
> Believe in god, but can't
> Believe their own senses
> Let alone Guatama. Let them lie.
>
> Pine sleeps, cedar splits straight
> Flowers crack the pavement.
>> Pa-ta Shan-jen
> (a painter who watched Ming fall)
>> lived in a tree:

> "The brush
> May paint the mountains and streams
> Though the territory is lost."

The first two lines state the mythic apocalypse of the world's body. The next lines denounce modern society and its Judeo-Christian antecedents. But the narrator pulls himself up short. He mildly, and perhaps fatalistically, sighs, "Let them lie." He has condemned, but he has not as yet offered an alternative. Further, his own seeking of solace in the cycles beyond humanity's meddling encourages passivity. The resignation of the second stanza, emphasized by the repetition of "let them lie," deflates the anger of the third.

The opening lines of stanza four present a text of natural activity, but one of mythic proportions. In opposition to the cutting of groves, "flowers crack the pavement." These images return to the mood of the opening stanza. The quotation that closes the passage, however, questions nature's ability to succeed in its regeneration, providing no reassurance that the "territory" will not "be lost."

The question stands at the end of "Logging": can the damage of modern society be undone, or will humanity so damage the system that it must collapse before regenerating? And its corollary, addressed to both poet and reader: can we do anything about it, or must we merely wait, watch, and record the death? The quotation suggests some reassurance in the word "may," but it provides no promise. The teleological process may be clearly announced in "Logging 15" as an antidote for bitterness, but it leaves the narrator and the reader ambivalent about their own activities in the meantime. Such ambivalence spurs the reader to follow the narrator into "Hunting."

"Hunting" opens with the "first shaman song," which provides the beginning of a response to "Logging." If "Logging" exemplifies by means of Judeo-Christian capitalism that "Myth is a 'reality lived,'" then "Hunting" by means of primitivism and shamanism exemplifies that "Reality is a myth lived." Or, as Jungels puts it, "Snyder sees hunting, meditation, and shamanism as all part of the same complex of human perception."[25] "Hunting 1" ends:

> I sit without thoughts by the log-road
> Hatching a new myth
> watching the waterdogs
>                 the last truck gone.

According to T. S. Eliot's *Four Quartets*, to "wait without thought" is a prerequisite for vision. Snyder uses the participle "hatching" with precision. Throughout "Hunting" humanity's life will be intimately tied to the life cycles of animals and the myths surrounding such cycles. Furthermore, "Hunting" does not produce a new myth;

instead, it shows the unfolding process of old myths informing the living of reality, providing a basis for the next culture's mythmaking. Jungels has uncovered the old myths behind "Hunting," "those of the coastal Salish."[26] This background of Native American hunting and food-gathering myths, with their attendant shamanistic beliefs, bolsters the narrator in his own hunting and gathering of the mythic material the next culture needs.

"Hunting 3" and "Hunting 4" focus on birds. Passage 3 begins:

> Birds in a whirl, drift to the rooftops
> Kite dip, swing to the seabank fogroll
> Form: dots in air changing line from line,
>     the future defined.

Snyder defines the text of living birds, then describes their role in divination and links that religious role with writing: "Form: dots in air changing from line to line." The narrator is linked with the seer or shaman in the role of preserving the myths of animals. The end line also suggests not only that myths define the future through ritual but also that the birds, metonymically representing nature, determine humanity's future.

The second stanza begins with a description of Native American ritual and then moves to physical description:

> Brush back smoke from the eyes,
>     dust from the mind,
> With the wing-feather fan of an eagle.
> A hawk drifts into the far sky.
> A marmot whistles across huge rocks.
> Rain on the California hills.
> Mussels clamp to sea-boulders
> Sucking the Spring tides

The last two lines contrast with "Hunting 1," in which "Soft oysters rot now, between tides." The following two-line stanza of 3, "Rain soaks the tan stubble / Field full of ducks," names another bird and further develops the rainstorm description. The long concluding stanza first adds to that description, then develops the color imagery as the gray of the passage darkens in the storm. The "Black Swifts" assume a mythic divinatory role in the closing two lines: "—the swifts cry / As they shoot by, See or go blind!" An ambiguous imperative, it warns that humanity must change its perception to "See," which has a visionary sense given the divinatory context. As Paul notes, "the reason for augury is cosmological; seeing is always a matter of seeing relationships."[27] Further, the narrator must go forward—if as yet without vision, then blindly.

"Hunting 4" opens with an animal-medicine myth and animal-song myths. Snyder interjects a historical event about the eating of bird eggs in San Francisco in the 1850s.[28] He then moves more deeply into bird myths, concluding with "Brushed by the hawk's wing / of vision." The narrator has apparently gone on "blind," but the birds help him to gain vision. Implicit within the bird imagery is the metaphor of rising above the ground of "Logging" to see the real earth from a new height. The next stanza relates a story of the Flathead tribe migrating, which is linked to a bird myth. As Jungels argues, this story may serve to emphasize the importance of accurate naming both in terms of "a fidelity to the text of objects" and "a correspondence to the inner world of myth."[29] Section 4 closes by following this story with a description:

> Raven
> on a roost of furs
> No bird in a bird-book,
> black as the sun.

The narrator of "Hunting," through his increasing perception of birds as mythic creatures, gains an understanding of the limitations of book-knowledge and, by extension, "texts" in general. Snyder ties this perception to a recognition of the most notorious mythic bird in American literature, warning the reader of the necessity both to read the skin textually as the reality of physical appearance and to read the entrails mythically as the reality of spiritual essence. Viewing Snyder's physical and mythic portrayals of the Raven in terms of Native American lore, Jungels states that "the result of these associations, both visual and mythic, is to merge Raven and sun as reciprocal aspects of a single reality embodying both the object and source of vision."[30] The reality of physical appearance remains a useful source for information, but one limited to historical and individual sensory experience. The reality of spiritual essence, on the other hand, contains "unarticulated and conscious values" available to individual and society from the universal racial memory of all the cycles of human life. For the text of individual and historical experience, then, to be understood and properly acted upon, it must be contextualized by the mythic consciousness of spiritual knowledge.

At the same time that Snyder has carried the poem tonally into a storm's darkness, the blindness of humanity, and the sinister blackness of mythic birds, he has also prepared the reader emotionally for a strong response to the regenerative ritual of "Hunting 5," "the making of the horn spoon," which is drawn from Kwakiutl ritual.[31] Here blackness has a positive value. This action shows respect for dead animals by using all their parts, with its ritual character reinforced by the passage closing with an untranslated chant.

"Hunting 8" opens with a myth-song sung by "deer," a sacred animal. The second stanza describes a hunting experience without redeeming ritual. After missing a buck, the narrator kills a rabbit without taking it for food, a sacrilegious act.[32] He and his cohorts are pursued by the sacred deer, "howling like a wise man," because the deer recognizes the hunter's violation of ritual. The identity of deer and rabbit is implied by Snyder's drawing the deer song here from the same source, a Cowlitz tale, that supplied the rabbit song in "Hunting 7."[33] The second part of 8 describes someone driving home drunk, catching a buck in his headlights, and shooting it while it is blinded, ironically echoing the swifts' warning. The gutting of the deer by the roadside is a debased ritual. The "hot guts" of the animal juxtaposed to the rapid chilling of its skin and horns reiterates the divinatory role of animals and the textual skin / mythic entrails relationship. It also presents the dark side of "the future defined." The description ends with "the limp tongue," which refers to the loss of the deer's singing voice. One danger of "the future defined" is that it may produce the permanent loss of this voice, both in its physical and mythic roles.

In reading this passage one needs to distinguish the individuals who narrate it. Nothing indicates that the narrative "I" of "Hunting" as a whole is necessarily the same person who kills the rabbit or the one who kills the buck. If they are the same person, these incidents are recollections from before his end-of-logging days. Elsewhere in "Hunting" there occur similar narrative shifts suggesting that the narrator of *Myths & Texts* as a whole has begun in "Hunting" to move beyond the individual ego in his sense of identity, not only in a recognition of his relationship with the men of "Logging" but also with the Native Americans of "Hunting," who appear as historical and contemporary figures. In terms of the text/myth relationship, he is expanding his consciousness beyond his own ego-based experience, his personal text, toward the boundaries of the race's collective experience, the archetypes of which are articulated through myth.

The two descriptions of wanton murder are followed by a brief epilogue:

> Deer don't want to die for me.
> I'll drink sea-water
> Sleep on beach pebbles in the rain
> Until the deer come down to die
> in pity for my pain.

This promise of penance describes a type of shamanistic journey into the wilderness to seek vision, based on coastal Salish practices.[34] It also suggests the proper relationship between hunter and hunted, which Snyder discusses some years later in *Earth House Hold* as "hunting magic."[35] The vision achieved during this penitential journey is described in "Hunting 9" and "Hunting 10," while "Hunting 11" compares it with the myth of Prajapati, " 'Lord of Creatures' Brahma as Creator."[36]

While 11 is almost entirely myth and part of a developing process of interpenetrating shamanistic and Hindu-Buddhist myth elements, 12 is entirely text, ostensibly describing the "I" who opens "Hunting" coming out of the mountains after being purified through his wandering. The exact character of this narrative "I" remains problematic with its referential multiplicity. Through the course of "Hunting" he changes from the one who sits by the log-road into a variety of historical and mythical figures. As part of the narrator's growing sense of identity beyond ego, these figures represent different aspects of his changing perception of humanity's relationship with nature, a key element of his developing consciousness.

Although most of "Hunting" focuses on Native American and shamanistic myths and rituals, "Hunting 11" introduces Prajapati and 14, 15, and 16 expand the integration of Hindu-Buddhist myth elements, linking the two belief systems. This linkage prepares the reader for the predominantly Hindu-Buddhist references in "Burning." "Hunting 16" closes this second major section of *Myths & Texts* with an explicit statement of thematics:

> Meaning: compassion
> Agents: man and beasts, beasts
> Got the buddha-nature
> All but
> Coyote.

Uncompassionate Coyote is a savior-figure alternative to Christ who will return to play his role near the end of "Burning." Closing "Hunting" with Coyote serves to carry over the mythic beliefs of "Hunting" into the next section, in contrast to the end of "Logging." Jungels correctly notes that "in spite of past doubts it is possible to affirm birth and humanness for these are the conditions of compassion."[37] Here the narrator needs to keep rather than discard the section's belief system.

"Burning 1" continues the references to shamanistic experience.[38] The first stanza ends: "Seawater fills each eye," reiterating the theme of vision. The second stanza introduces the Hindu-Buddhist concept of karma, while the third stanza ends: "River recedes. No matter." The distinction between myth and text, ritual and real experience, is undercut by a series of evolutionary and empathetic images in "Burning 1." Humanity has arisen from the mineral and animal life of the planet and must also empathetically return to the swamp to "see" the world of which it is *a part*, but from which it seems *apart*. Paul claims that "self-transformation is the work proposed by 'Burn-

ing,' " but this falsely overvalues individual achievement.[39] The shaman and the poet are *public* figures, whose transformations serve the
community, as emphasized by "Burning 10," subtitled "Amitabha's
Vow."

"Burning 2" provides a philosophical gloss of "Burning 1" in its
opening stanza:

> One moves continually with the consciousness
> Of that other, totally alien, non-human:
> Humming inside like a taut drum,
> Carefully avoiding any direct thought of it,
> Attentive to the real-world flesh and stone.

The last line suggests an ironic rejoinder to the word "consciousness."
The other within exists with or without consciousness of its presence.
The "consciousness" that sees *only* "the real-world flesh and stone"
prevents a person from seeing that "other" within oneself. This
prevents people from seeing themselves as part of a larger whole,
and prevents them from being "attentive" in ways beyond rational
consciousness. This stanza serves as a response to the reader's anticipated recoil from the identity of "I" and "other" presented in
"Burning 1" and presents one philosophical position on the relationship of humanity and nature, self and other.

The second stanza presents a second philosophical position:

> Intricate layers of emptiness
> This only world, juggling forms
>                    a hand, a breast, two clasped
> Human tenderness scuttles
> Down dry endless cycles
> Forms within forms falling
>                          clinging
> Loosely, what's gone away?
>                          love

In response to the rational consciousness that posits the dichotomy
of self and other, this stanza posits that the two sides and their
dichotomy are "forms" lacking permanence. The error that produces
the dichotomy of consciousness is that of "clinging" to appearances
as if they were permanent. The final stanza reinforces this recognition
through a series of texts demonstrating impermanence: the avocado
tree shedding its leaves; cherry trees blossoming and birds "at this
moment" rattling through them. Then, Snyder intrudes the line, "All
these books," which pivots the stanza away from the cyclical, non-
conscious actions of trees and birds to the conscious actions of people,
which in turn lead to thoughts of death, the most conscious reminder
of physical impermanence.

"Burning 3," "Maudgalyayana saw hell," has two stanzas. The

first relates the myth of that Buddha's descent into hell. Reinvoking sight imagery, line three states: "The mind grabs and the shut eye sees." Snyder uses "mind" rather than consciousness, and the shut eye alludes to the mystical "third eye." The mind moves beyond and below consciousness to gain spiritual vision. The second stanza comments on humanity's general experience in the world. It ends:

> Day-to-day got vision of this sick
> Sparkling person at the inturned dreaming
> Blooming human mind
> Dropping it all, and opening the eyes.

The opening of the eyes does not block out what "the shut eye sees" but rather unites the two visions, completing the learning process begun in "Hunting." The two forms of vision enable the narrator to recognize both the "forms" of the physical world and the "intricate layers of emptiness" of the spiritual world.

"Burning 4" looks to the future as a mythic piece on "Maitreya the future buddha." Although brief, this celebratory passage directly replies to the pessimistic aspect of "Logging 15." Rather than focusing on the cataclysmic end of the kalpa as the solution to the world of "Logging," 4 focuses on a spiritual rebirth embodied in the promise of a future Buddha, and begins, as Paul notes, a series of Tantric connections.[40]

"Burning 8" quotes an experience of enlightenment John Muir had when he ceased trying to solve a mountain-climbing crisis through conscious analysis: "I seemed suddenly to become possessed / Of a new sense." He has experienced a *kensho*, a brief moment of enlightenment in Zen terminology,[41] enabling him to unite with the rock rather than fight it. The excerpt concludes: "My limbs moved with a positiveness and precision / With which I seemed to have / Nothing at all to do." The last line suggests both *wuwei*, the action of nonaction, and the letting go of consciousness, that release of the self from the limitations of rationality and will that enables Muir to breach the self/other dichotomy. This text embodies the unity of inner and outer vision mythically propounded in "Burning 3" and demonstrates the interpenetration of physical and spiritual realities. It also embodies the contrasting attitudes in "Burning 4." Muir initially views the crisis fatalistically, but then he experiences a sudden rebirth.

"Burning 10" presents a haibun-style sequence of updated Bodhisattva vows and depictions of physical observations. The last lines echo "Hunting 12," which describes the narrator coming out of the mountains. Here the "we" decide not to "come down" but to continue ascending, having crossed some boundary of perception and having committed themselves through their vows to a path toward "Buddhahood."[42] "Burning 10" marks a transition in the poem, a commitment to a way of perception that will culminate in the epiphany of "Burning 17" in which the dichotomy of myth and text dissolves.

"Burning 11" and "Burning 12" treat the difficulties of embarking on this path. Section 11 imitates koan study in which the student tries to answer the question, "What is the way of non-activity?" The answer begins describing the meditation posture then blossoms into myth fragments, initially beautiful but increasingly presented in terms of pain and fire. It closes with a myth fragment of a Coyote-as-savior legend in which he and Earthmaker contemplate rebuilding the world. And Jungels notes that in regard to such rebuilding, "Snyder, I think, believes we need both the Coyote and Earthmaker, who though logically contradictory, are psychically complementary."[43] Part 12 begins with the narrator describing a nightmarish meditation reiterating the impermanence of the body addressed in "Burning 2." The second stanza tells of "The City of the Gandharvas," a beautiful story, but it is, as Snyder notes, "an Indian trope for 'a mirage.' "[44] The passage closes with a reference to birds: "Hoarse cry of night-hawk / Circling & swooping in the still, bright dawn." These lines underscore the difficulty of achieving enlightenment along the path of meditation, reiterate the hope that nature will assist in achieving vision, and foreshadow the tranquil state of knowledge presented in "Burning 17."

"Burning 13" returns to the more unsure tone opening "Burning 12." The first stanza presents the difficulties of gaining release from the distraction of the senses. The second contrasts the experience of writing poetry, of constructing "little myths," with the text of life in which that writing took place (Snyder refers here to the writing of the poems in Riprap[45]). The third briefly intermixes text and myth fragments, while the fourth begins with a myth of Emperor Wu putting an end to war. This story is brutally undercut by the lines:

> Smell of crushed spruce and burned snag-wood.
> remains of men,
> Bone-chopped foul remains, thick stew
> Food for crows—

The first line alludes to the world of "Logging," while the pun on "foul" and the reference to "crows" call into question the vision gained from birds in "Hunting." The rest of the passage confronts this deepening doubt by acceding that conditions are bad, then responding: "As long as you hesitate, no place to go"—a gloss on the John Muir vignette. After casting doubt on meditation, poetry, and politics, the narrator then defies the darkness:

> it's all vagina dentata
> (Jump!)

"Leap through an Eagle's snapping beak"

Actaeon saw Dhyana in the Spring.

He calls on the reader to leap beyond the living of reality to the living of myth, turning the latter into the former to gain a glimpse of the world beyond appearance. The use of the "vagina dentata" and "Dhyana" emphasizes not only the danger of such a leap[46] but also the power of myth in its ability to concentrate the essence of experience if a person opens oneself to such perception, as is possible through meditation. Snyder punningly alludes to meditation through spelling "Diana" as "Dhyana," which is a transliteration of Sanskrit meaning "absorption; the form of meditation."[47] The passage ends with a haikulike description of a moment of enlightenment, written in the style of Zen humility. This haiku closure reinforces the turning point of "Burning 10."

"Burning 14" also returns to "Burning 10," providing a text of the experience in which the narrator marries. Passage 15 returns this married narrator to civilization. Paul emphasizes correctly that this unity with the "other" is predicated upon an adoption of matrifocal values.[48] The return occurs through a series of locations expanding outward from a farm to the mythic center of the universe, "Mt. Sumeru L. O." Text and myth alternate until the closing lines, "The hot seeds steam underground / still alive," in which they come together as a description of physical reality and as seed for a new mythic vision. After this foreshadowing of "Burning 17," "Burning 16" briefly relates a set of songs of different cultures, then reiterates the invocation of "Logging 1": "Dream, Dream, / Earth!" This passage speaks of a human transformation from living a superficial physical reality to living a deep spiritual reality, and closes with the signature of Coyote, the Native American equivalent of Maitreya.[49] Also, Jungels points out that in many Native American stories Coyote renders the "vagina dentata" no longer deadly to men.[50] Both the "vagina dentata" and Coyote are components of the mythic realization of what the future has in store. This strongly contrasts with the fatalistic resignation that made the narrator look to the immolation of the kalpa cycle in "Logging" as a possible cure for the world's ills.

"Burning 17," the final section of "Burning" and of *Myths & Texts*, brings the alternation of myth and text fragments together. It consists not of two stanzas, although initially appearing so, but of three. The first is labeled "the text," the second "the myth," while the third has only three lines: "The sun is but a morning star / Crater Mt. L. O. 1952-Marin-an 1956 / end of myths & texts." The first stanza presents a text of fighting a forest fire, one which is extinguished by the predawn rain. The second retells the text as a myth, one which evokes the end of an age: "Fire up Thunder Creek and the mountain— / troy's burning!" and then, "The cloud mutters / The mountains are your mind." The link is made between physical experience and psychological experience, between myth and reality, demonstrating the unity of Snyder's remark: "Myth is a 'reality lived' . . . . Reality is a myth lived."

The myth stanza does not replicate the text stanza. To do so the line "The sun is but a morning star" would need to end it to maintain a parallel with "The last glimmer of the morning star," but Snyder sets this line apart. It returns the reader to the start of this experience of changed perception, the opening line of "Logging 1." In terms of emotional power, the offsetting of this line, taken directly from *Walden*, reverses the ominous tone of the opening and posits unlimited possibility before the reader. The myth presents an awareness the reader can have by recognizing that "the mountains are your mind." This identity is further reinforced by the location line, "Crater Mt. L. O. 1952-Marin-an 1956." The poem has been written as a wandering journey, a Zen trek toward enlightenment rather than a Western quest for a tangible boon, with the poet as vehicle for the song. The first location, while a physical place, alludes to the Mt. Sumeru of "Burning 15," the "mountain" location foreshadowed as early as "Logging 3." It is a mythical, mystical vantage point. "Marin-an 1956" presents the text equivalent, the physical place of mythopoeic completion, Marin County, California; the use of "an," however, allies the location with Zen Buddhism, further reinforcing the allusion to Mt. Sumeru.[51]

The argument for including this location line as part of the sequence is based on considering the poem's final line to be the "end of myths & texts." The closing of the sequence represents the end of myths and texts because, with their identity as one interpenetrating process, the reader can no longer view them as separate, dichotomous categories of experience or perception. Snyder's "little myth" of *Myths & Texts* can help readers to learn to recognize the two "sources of human knowledge" as one *myths 'n' texts* so they can learn "how to *be* in some specific ecosystem of the far-flung world." In this sense, *Myths & Texts* is both mythopoeic and metamythopoeic, creating a myth and commenting on that process of mythmaking. Creation and commentary interpenetrate as do myth and text elements to engender a dialogical, but not dichotomous, unity of alterity that is neither linear nor cyclical but more spiral. Rather than creating a closure, the completion of the poem opens up another arm of the spinning galaxy of experience.

## Notes

1. Gary Snyder, *Myths & Texts* (New York: Totem Press, Corinth Books, 1960; New York: New Directions, 1978). Further references to this work are cited in the text.

2. See Lee Bartlett, "Gary Snyder's *Myths & Texts* and the Monomyth," *Western American Literature* 17 (1982): 137–48; Bob Steuding, *Gary Snyder*, Twayne United States Authors Series, no. 274 (Boston: Twayne, 1976); and Sherman Paul, *In Search of the Primitive: Rereading David Antin, Jerome Rothenberg, and Gary Snyder* (Baton Rouge: Louisiana State University Press, 1986). These authors provide the most developed analyses of the poem's structure. Also see Bert Almon, *Gary Snyder*, Western Writers Series (Boise: Boise State University, 1979); Charles Molesworth, *Gary Snyder's Vision: Poetry and the Real Work* (Columbia: University of Missouri Press, 1983); and James Wright, "The Work of Gary Snyder," in *Collected Prose*, ed. Anne Wright (Ann Arbor: University of Michigan Press, 1983), 105–19. Probably the best work to date on *Myths & Texts* remains virtually inaccessible, contained in a variety of theses and dissertations, the findings of which curiously tend to remain unpublished.

3. Paul, *In Search of the Primitive*, 226.

4. As William Jungels notes in "The Use of Native American Mythologies in the Poetry of Gary Snyder" (Ph.D. diss., SUNY at Buffalo, 1973), 7, Snyder himself has expressed the basis for such a reading of *He Who Hunted Birds:* "It's curious how in my thesis I mapped out practically all my major interests," as quoted by David Kherdian in *A Biographical Sketch and Descriptive Checklist of Gary Snyder* (Berkeley, Calif.: Oyez, 1965), 9.

5. Gary Snyder, *He Who Hunted Birds in His Father's Village: The Dimensions of a Haida Myth* (Bolinas, Calif.: Grey Fox Press, 1979), x. Further references to this work are cited in the text.

6. I do not claim this as an original idea. Other critics, such as Almon and Wai-lim Yip, in "Classical Chinese and Modern Anglo-American Poetry: Convergences of Language and Poetry," *Comparative Literature Studies* 11 (1974): 21–47, have also suggested the idea; but to my knowledge no one else has worked it out as the major structuring device for the entire sequence.

7. Jungels, "Native American Mythologies," 186.

8. Jungels, "Native American Mythologies," 214.

9. Robert Graves, *The White Goddess* (1949; amended and enlarged, New York: Farrar, Straus & Giroux, 1966), 50.

10. Howard McCord, *Some Notes on Gary Snyder's "Myths & Texts"* (Berkeley, Calif.: Sand Dollar, 1971).

11. Jungels, "Native American Mythologies," 17.

12. For a later remark on this point, see Gary Snyder, *The Old Ways: Six Essays* (San Francisco: City Lights Books, 1977), 34–35.

13. Jungels, "Native American Mythologies," 26.

14. See Paul, *In Search of the Primitive*, 227.

15. McCord, *Some Notes*.

16. Gary Snyder, *Six Sections from Mountains and Rivers without End Plus One* (San Francisco, Calif.: Four Seasons Foundation, 1970).

17. Jungels, "Native American Mythologies," 32; McCord, *Some Notes*.

18. See Jungels, "Native American Mythologies," 37–47, for a discussion of the Native-American myths to which Snyder alludes in "Logging 12."

19. Compare Paul, *In Search of the Primitive*, 233.

20. See Jungels, "Native American Mythologies," 22.

21. Molesworth, *Gary Snyder's Vision*, 34.

22. Almon and Bartlett emphasize the apocalyptic, while Steuding emphasizes the aspect of rebirth, pointing to the lodgepole pine as a phoenix symbol and the cyclical rather than cataclysmic character of the kalpa cycle.

23. Compare Steuding, *Gary Snyder*, 79; Paul, *In Search of the Primitive*, 233–34.

24. Compare Jungels, "Native American Mythologies," 54–60.

25. Jungels, "Native American Mythologies," 61.

26. Jungels, "Native American Mythologies," 68.

27. Paul, *In Search of the Primitive*, 236.

28. McCord quotes Snyder's explanation of this passage.

29. Jungels, "Native American Mythologies," 80.

30. Jungels, "Native American Mythologies," 80.

31. Jungels, "Native American Mythologies," 82.

32. See Jungels, "Native American Mythologies," 103 and 109.

33. Jungels, "Native American Mythologies," 108.

34. Jungels, "Native American Mythologies," 111.

35. Gary Snyder, *Earth House Hold: Technical Notes and Queries to Fellow Dharma Revolutionaries* (New York: New Directions, 1969).

36. McCord, *Some Notes.*

37. Jungels, "Native American Mythologies," 123.

38. See Jungels, "Native American Mythologies," 130–31.

39. Paul, *In Search of the Primitive*, 241.

40. Paul, *In Search of the Primitive*, 244.

41. Robert Aitken, *Taking the Path of Zen* (San Francisco: North Point Press, 1982).

42. Compare Jungels, "Native American Mythologies," 157–58.

43. Jungels, "Native American Mythologies," 161; see also 159–61.

44. McCord, *Some Notes.*

45. Gary Snyder, *Riprap, & Cold Mountain Poems* (San Francisco: Grey Fox Press, 1980).

46. Jungels, "Native American Mythologies," 167.

47. Aitken, *Taking the Path*, 139.

48. Paul, *In Search of the Primitive*, 247.

49. Snyder has commented in correspondence that the second half of "Burning 16" and its use of Coyote is, as he recalls in the mid-1980s, "framed from the language of Smohalla's 'Dreaming' religion—a later 19th-century messianic movement of the middle Columbia River peoples—Coyote as coming Messiah." This remark about Coyote as a messiah figure also pertains to his appearances in "Hunting 16" and "Burning 11."

50. Jungels, "Native American Mythologies," 168.

51. See Lok Chua Cheng and N. Sasaki, "Zen and the Title of Gary Snyder's 'Marin-An,'" *Notes on Contemporary Literature* 8.3 (1978): 2–3.

# How to Be in This Crisis:
# Gary Snyder's Cross-Cultural
# Vision in *Turtle Island*                    Katsunori Yamazato°

I

For Gary Snyder, Buddhism was and is not merely a system of faith
and worship; as he succinctly summarizes, "Buddhism is about existence."[1] Buddhism teaches one how to be in this "impermanent"
world, and this is one of the aspects of Buddhism that Snyder especially
deepened and solidified during his Japanese years (1956–68). Despite
persistent skepticism toward traditional, institutionalized Buddhism,
he gained valuable insights into its strengths and weaknesses during
his stay in Japan, and these insights grew into an ontological vision.
"How to be" is the central question that Snyder asks and tries to
answer throughout *Turtle Island*, as in "What Happened Here Before":

> *now,*
>
> we sit here near the diggings
> in the forest, by our fire, and watch
> the moon and planets and the shooting stars—
>
> my sons ask, who are we?
> drying apples picked from homestead trees
> drying berries, curing meat,
> shooting arrows at a bale of straw.
>
> military jets head northeast, roaring, every dawn.
>
> my sons ask, who are they?
>
> WE SHALL SEE
> WHO KNOWS
> HOW TO BE
>
> Bluejay screeches from a pine.[2]

As he states in his essay "Energy is Eternal Delight," the question
of "how to be" is closely related to his vision of an alternative culture:
"The return to marginal farmland on the part of longhairs is not
some nostalgic replay of the nineteenth century. Here is a generation
of white people finally ready to learn from the Elders. How to live

° This essay was written specifically for this volume and appears here for the first time
by permission of the author.

on the continent as though our children, and on down, for many ages, will still be here (not on the moon). Loving and protecting this soil, these trees, these wolves. Natives of Turtle Island" (*TI*, 105). In 1970, two years after his return from Japan, Snyder and his family moved to Kitkitdizze—a name he gave the wild land that he bought in 1967. They were joined by others settling roots on the San Juan Ridge, Nevada City, California, and a community began to emerge, a group of people determined to live as "natives of Turtle Island," seeking ways of "how to be." The answer to his sons' question, "who are we?", cannot be separated from the answer to the question of "how to be," and one of many things that makes Gary Snyder a distinguished poet and thinker is that he seeks answers to this perennial compound question by actually experimenting in the heart of Turtle Island, Snyder's mythic, alternative name for North America (*TI*, "Introductory Note"). He rejects an easy answer, for the question is based on his quest for an alternative culture. In the heart of Turtle Island, he has tested his conviction that "Buddhism is about existence," and Buddhism has been effective in finding an answer to his radical question.

To understand fully Snyder's cross-cultural vision in *Turtle Island* we need to explore the Buddhist elements that pervade the book. Among the teachings of Buddhist sects that he studied in Japan, Zen Buddhism naturally constitutes his basic attitude, as he suggested in a 1979 interview.[3] In that interview, Snyder laughs away conventional and stereotypic images of Zen Buddhism, and the laughter is indicative of the depth and sophistication that he attained during his rigorous training at the Daitoku-ji in Kyoto. Zen became fundamental for the poet—a way of seeing and working through life—and as such, it manifests itself in such unlikely places as "Why Log Truck Drivers Rise Earlier Than Students of Zen" (*TI*, 63). At this point, Zen has become so fundamentally embodied in his works that it is difficult to pinpoint particular "Zen aspects" in the poems collected in *Turtle Island*—as difficult, in fact, as isolating water from the cells of a plant. Zen has become the basis of Snyder's everyday life.

Moreover, it is dangerous to discuss *Turtle Island* and other works written after the poet's return to the United States solely in terms of Zen, for Snyder also studied and incorporated teachings of other Buddhist schools in Japan, bringing these into play in his work.[4] In *Turtle Island*, he uses some teachings of other Buddhist sects in his attempt at a "cross-fertilization of ecological thought with Buddhist ideas of interpenetration."[5] Since the Buddhist ideas that Snyder drew on to "cross-fertilize" with ecological ideas have received little critical analysis, a discussion of the Buddhist concept of interpenetration, a key metaphor in *Turtle Island*, is well in order.

## II

Buddhism holds that every being in this universe is interrelated. According to Junjiro Takakusu, "The universe is not homocentric; it is a co-creation of all beings."[6] In the Buddhist universe, nothing can exist separately from other beings, and "everything is inevitably created out of more than two causes."[7] This is called "Dependent Production or Chain of Causation," or, in Japanese, *engisetsu,* and, as Takakusu explains it: "From the existence of *this, that* becomes; from the happening of *this, that* happens. From the non-existence of *this, that* does not happen."[8] Everything in the universe is mutually related, and, as Takakusu succinctly puts it, "all is . . . a product of interdependence."[9]

In Buddhism, there are two ways of explaining the universe. Seen in terms of time, all things contained in the universe are depicted as "impermanent"; but in terms of space, the things in the universe become "interrelated." Snyder occasionally refers to the impermanence of life in this world, yet we should note that he tends increasingly to emphasize the spatial aspect in Buddhism, that is, the interpenetration of all things.

The theory of causation or the idea of universal interpenetration has been developed by various schools of Buddhism. Among these, the Kegon school, which upholds the Avatamsaka sutra, is said to have developed the idea of interpenetration to its climax.[10] The idea of interpenetration, according to D. T. Suzuki, is "the ruling topic of the sutra,"[11] and the central image in the sutra is "the world of all realities or practical facts interwoven or identified in perfect harmony."[12] This word is called, in Japanese, *jijimuge-hokkai,* and the sutra introduces "Indra's net" to illustrate the magnificent image of interpenetration. As Takakusu puts it, it is "a net decorated with bright stone on each knot of the mesh," and the jewels reflect each other endlessly, reflecting "the real facts of the world" mutually interpenetrating.[13] Interpenetration is the fundamental insight of the Avatamsaka sutra, and, by using the image of "Indra's net," the sutra illustrates, in D. T. Suzuki's words, a "perfect network of mutual relations."[14]

From the beginning of his career, Snyder has repeatedly referred to the Avatamsaka sutra and its key image. In "Lookout's Journal," for instance, he writes: "—shifting of light & cloud, perfection of chaos, magnificent *jijimu-ge* / interlacing interaction."[15] In "Buddhism and the Coming Revolution," an essay first published in 1961, he points out that "Avatamsaka (Kegon) Buddhist philosophy sees the world as a vast interrelated network in which all objects and creatures are necessary and illuminated" (*EHH,* 91–92). And in "Poetry and the Primitive," an essay later published in *Earth House Hold,* Snyder sketches the idea of interpenetration in a more elaborate context, foreshadowing its full development in *Turtle Island*: ". . . every person, animals, forces, all are related via a web of reincarnation— or rather, they are 'interborn.' It may well be that rebirth (or interbirth, for we are actually mutually creating each other and all things while living) is the objective fact of existence which we have not yet brought into conscious knowledge and practice. "It is clear that the empirically observable interconnectedness of nature is but a corner of the vast 'jewelled net' which moves from without to within" (*EHH*, 129).

Continuing in the same vein in a 1973 interview given in New York, Snyder refers again to the fundamental Buddhist idea of interpenetration: "I find it always exciting to me, beautiful, to experience the interdependencies of things, the complex webs and networks by which everything moves, which I think are the most beautiful awarenesses that we can have of ourselves and of our planet."[16] In his lecture, "Reinhabitation," delivered at the Reinhabitation Conference held at San Juan Ridge County School in August of 1976, Snyder continues: "The Avatamsaka ('Flower Wreath') jewelled-net-interpenetration-ecological-systems-emptiness-consciousness tells us, no self-realization without the Whole Self, and the whole self is the whole thing."[17] Even a cursory survey of the poet's references to the nets and webs imagery in the Avatamsaka sutra tells us that Snyder gradually developed and incorporated the key image of this sutra into his own system. We also notice how the idea of interpenetration becomes deepened, refined, and finally solidified as a vital element in the poet's consciousness—as seen in the growth of his ontological vision.

Buddhism and ecology "cross-fertilize" each other well. Coined by the German biologist Ernst Haeckel in 1869, the term *ecology* has since gained a wide popularity only a century later, and its key concept has been a common assumption of nature-conscious people in the second half of the twentieth century: "All units of the ecosystem are mutually dependent. This is a good point to keep in mind when we are tempted to extol the importance of some group of organisms in which we happen to be especially interested."[18] Humankind is "a part of 'complex' biological cycles" dependent on the food web of eating and being eaten.[19] Snyder was well aware of this key concept of ecology in his early stage, as in "Japan First Time Around," in which he sketches the link in the chain: "salts—diatoms—copepods— herring—fishermen—us. eating" (*EHH*, 31).

It is clear, then, that Snyder in Japan deeply realized that Buddhism and ecology shared a vision of the world in terms of the interrelatedness of all beings. The former is a picture of a spiritual world caught in the Eastern religious vision, and the latter a model of the natural world presented by the rational thinking of Western science. During his first sojourn in Japan (1956–57), he discovered the connection between Zen and the Avatamsaka teachings: "So, Zen being founded on Avatamsaka, and the net-network of things" (*EHH*, 34), and three short months later, the shared imagery of the Avatamsaka sutra and the principles of ecology were fused in his mind: "Indra's net is not merely two-dimensional. . . .—two days contemplating ecology, foodchains and sex" (*EHH*, 38).

Science, for Snyder, does not "murder to dissect." Ecology with its ethical and spiritual dimension is "divine" (*EHH*, 112), and he writes that "science walks in beauty" (*TI*, "Toward Climax," 84). Unlike many visionaries, he does not reject rational thought, and he is attempting to fuse science and religious teachings to create a guiding principle by which to live on Turtle Island. This is a daring new American synthesis, perhaps not feasible in the vision of traditional Buddhists, as Snyder himself is aware: "Traditional orthodox Buddhists are not concerned with building new cultures any more than they are interested in natural religion or girls. Poets must try to get them together—playing a funny kind of role, today, as pivot-man, between the upheavals of culture-change and the persistence of the Single Eye of Knowledge."[20] In Snyder's continuing synthesis, ecology helps him see his position clearly and concretely in exploring the heart of Turtle Island, and his life there is given a spiritual depth by his acute awareness of the interrelated existence of all beings in the universe. As I shall show, this double structure serves as the basis for most poems in *Turtle Island*.

Further, the Mahayana belief in *busshō*, which teaches that all beings are endowed with "Buddha-nature" (the inherent capacity to become a Buddha), demands—along with ecology—that people treat other beings responsibly. The human, in Snyder's words, is "an animal that was brought into being on this biosphere by these processes of sun and water and leaf."[21] Endowed with "Buddha-nature," other beings demand a radically different treatment. Snyder writes that "as the most highly developed tool-using animal, [people] must recognize that the unknown evolutionary destinies of other life forms are to be respected, and act as gentle steward of the earth's community of being" (*TI*, "Four Changes," 91). Thus, the insights from the Avatamsaka sutra and other Buddhist teachings merged with an ecological consciousness, to become a guiding principle in living on Turtle Island.

This guiding principle, moreover, involves an attempt to restore "life" to other beings that modern civilization has tended to regard as "dead matter." In his criticism of modern civilization, Snyder writes that "at the root of the problem where our civilization goes wrong is the mistaken belief that nature is something less than authentic, that nature is not as alive as man is, or as intelligent, that in a sense it is dead, and that animals are of so low an order of intelligence and feeling, we need not take their feelings into account" (*TI*, "The Wilderness," 107). Writing in "Four Changes," he goes further, aiming at "transforming" a civilization that he has long found destructive: "We have it within our deepest powers not only to change our 'selves' but to change our culture. If man is to remain on earth he must transform the five-millennia-long urbanizing civilization tradition into a new ecologically-sensitive harmony-oriented wild-minded scientific-spiritual culture" (*TI*, 99). His quest in Japan reaches a climax here, and we understand that his is a vision that, by combining East and West, deeply urges the reader to reconsider the validity of traditional cultural paradigms.

## III

To support and guide one's behavior by a religious vision provided by Buddhism, and to be deeply aware of the ecological reality of Turtle Island, and to learn at the same time from the Native American cultures, all these have offered parts of the answer for the poet's question of "how to be." The poems in *Turtle Island* reflect Snyder's exploratory life and his pursuit of the perennial question in the heart of the mythic American land. The Buddhist concept of interpenetration, "cross-fertilized" with classical Western ecology, runs beneath the poems collected in *Turtle Island* and enriches the poetic world depicted there. Solidified in the poet's consciousness during his years in Japan, the Buddhist-ecological matrix manifests itself in various modes in his poems. Some poems in *Turtle Island* are candidly satiric and political, and Snyder's attack on problems inherent in modern civilization is based on his conviction of the interrelatedness of all beings. In "Front Lines," for instance, the poet depicts the destructiveness in contemporary society. When rain continues and the log trucks are unable to work, "The trees breathe." But the destruction of nature continues: "Every pulse of the rot at the heart / In the sick fat veins of Amerika / Pushes the edge up closer—." A bulldozer is "grinding and slobbering / Sideslipping and belching on top of / The skinned-up bodies of still-live bushes." The trees and bushes, depicted thus, are not just dead matter. For Snyder, they share "Buddha-nature" with human beings, all belonging to "the great community of living creatures," and their lives must equally be respected (*TI*, "Four Changes," 97). Yet, for the greediness of "a man / From town," trees are suffocated and bushes are destroyed.

Snyder's attitude is not merely that of "a nature lover"; he is indicting a civilization, devoid of sensibility of and respect for other life forms, mindlessly engulfed in its own destructiveness. He goes a step further. As he concludes, we perceive clearly that the interplay of Mahayana Buddhism and his ecological consciousness implies, perhaps even demands, social activism:

> Behind is a forest that goes to the Arctic
> And a desert that still belongs to the Piute
> And here we must draw
> Our line (*TI*, 18)

The poet's criticism of a destructive civilization and his compassion for "all other members of the life-network" are sometimes expressed as "spells" against destructive forces, incantations that will arrest and convert negative energy (*TI*, "Four Changes," 97). "Spel against Demons" (first printed in *The Fudo Trilogy*, 1973) is a poem that attempts to exorcise the demonic forces inside the civilization by introducing a powerful figure from Buddhism, "ACHALA the Immovable" (*Fudōmyō-ō*, in Japanese). *Fudōmyō-ō* is a deity that belongs to the *Shingon* school (also known as *Mikkyo*; literally, the secret teachings), a branch of Mahayana Buddhism in Japan. The *Shingon* teachings are said to have originated in second-century India, and, after transmission to China, were systematized in Japan by the Japanese Buddhist priest Kukai (774–835).[22] According to Shōkō Watanabe, *Fudōmyō-ō* in *Shingon* is regarded as an incarnation of the Mahavairocana Buddha or the Great Sun Buddha,[23] whom Snyder also refers to in "On 'As for Poets' " (*TI*, 114). Originally a Hindu deity, *Fudōmyō-ō* became an object of popular worship in Japan after its incorporation into the *Shingon* teachings.

*Shingon* or *Mikkyo* comes into the poet's work through his interest in the *Shugendō* (or *Yamabushi*) tradition in Japan (*Yamabushi* is a Japanese term for those priests who discipline themselves in the mountains). *Shugendō* originally was a nature-worship religion that borrowed its theoretical basis from *Shingon; Fudōmyō-ō*, a deity originally belonging to *Shingon*, also became a powerful deity for the *Shugendō* tradition. Snyder's penchant for the tradition manifested itself earlier in his essay, "Anyone with *Yama-bushi* Tendencies," printed in *Zen Notes* in 1954. His interest in the tradition persisted throughout the Japanese years, and he did a pilgrimage to Mt. Ōmine, a sacred mountain for the *Yamabushi* tradition, and was initiated as a *yamabushi* ("a mountain priest") in 1961.

In "Spel against Demons," the poet introduces *Fudōmyō-ō*, hoping to exorcise "demonic energies" in society:

> *Down* with demonic killers who mouth revolutionary
> slogans and muddy the flow of change, may they be
> Bound by the Noose, and Instructed by the Diamond
> Sword of ACHALA the Immovable, Lord of Wisdom, Lord
> of Heat, who is squint-eyed and whose face is terrible
> with bare fangs, who wears on his crown a garland of

severed heads, clad in a tiger skin, he who turns
Wrath to Purified Accomplishment,

whose powers are of lava
of magma, of deep rock strata, of gunpowder,
and the Sun.

He who saves tortured intelligent demons and filth-eating
hungry ghosts, his spel is,

NAMAH SAMANTAH VAJRANAM CHANDA
MAHAROSHANA
SPHATAYA HUM TRAKA HAM MAM (TI, 17)

As we see above, Fudōmyō-ō (Fudō meaning "Immovable" in Japanese) always holds a sharp sword in his right hand, which subdues devils or evil spirits. The rope, "the Noose," held in the diety's left hand, is used to capture, bind, and lead evil spirits into enlightenment.[24] The facial expression of the deity is fierce and contorted with bare fangs, and his halo is aflame. According to Watanabe, the word achala originally means "something immovable," that is, "mountain," and hence it also represents "nature in general."[25] The mantra, "his spel," that Snyder quotes, is called jikunoshu in Japanese, and it is the most famous among the mantras attributed to Fudōmyō-ō.[26]

"Spel against Demons" clearly shows that Snyder's studies in Buddhism enlarged beyond Zen, and in the comic and now-famous "Smokey the Bear Sutra" (not included in Turtle Island), he again incorporates Fudōmyō-ō's mantra, comfortable enough in his Buddhist work to be at once playful and serious:

Wrathful but Calm, Austere but Comic, Smokey the Bear will
illuminate those who would help him; but for those who
would hinder or slander him,

HE WILL PUT THEM OUT.

Thus his great Mantra:
Namah samanta vajranam chanda maharoshana
Sphataya hum traka ham mam

"I DEDICATE MYSELF TO THE UNIVERSAL
DIAMOND BE THIS RAGING FURY DESTROYED"[27]

"Smokey the Bear" unfolds with a discourse given "about 150 million years ago" by "the Great Sun Buddha," in which the Buddha predicts he will enter a new form in America of the future "to cure the world of loveless knowledge that seeks with blind hunger; and mindless rage eating food that will not fill it." The Great Sun Buddha then reveals himself "in his true form of SMOKEY THE BEAR." A *Fudō* figure, Smokey the Bear holds a shovel in his right paw "that digs to the truth beneath appearances; cuts the roots of useless attachments, and flings damp sand on the fires of greed and war." The left paw, continuing the *Shingon* symbology, is "in the Mudra of Comradely Display—indicating that all creatures have the full right to live to their limits and that deer, rabbits, chipmunks, snakes, dandelions, and lizards all grow in the realm of Dharma." Thus, for the poet, Smokey the Bear is an American incarnation of *Fudōmyō-ō*, an earlier incarnation of the Great Sun Buddha. "Smokey the Bear Sutra" is both a spell against destructive forces and an invocation for, among others, "the age of harmony of man and nature." The "official" image of Smokey the Bear is transformed, and, in Snyder's alternative vision, becomes a guardian deity, protecting not only the oppressed human beings but also the interpenetrating beings from "a civilization that claims to save but only destroys."

## IV

While *Turtle Island* introduces a strong political and satirical tone to Snyder's work, it contains compassionate and sometimes elegiac elements as well. "The Uses of Light," for example, extends his compassion for other beings to include inanimate "stones," and, contrary to its surface simplicity, reflects a deeper harmony:

> It warms my bones
> say the stones
>
> I take it into me and grow
> Say the trees
> Leaves above
> Roots below
>
> A vast vague white
> Draws me out of the night
> Says the moth in his flight—
>
> Some things I smell
> Some things I hear
> And I see things move
> Says the deer—
>
> A high tower
> on a wide plain.
> If you climb up
> One floor
> You'll see a thousand miles more. (*TI*, 39)

As the source of energy in the solar system, the sun draws out various reactions from the beings in the poem, and the second stanza is fundamentally ecological. The solar light is pervasive in the world, giving each being energy to live by. But how do people react to this world of light? Unlike other beings given only a limited sight (or no sight, as in the cases of "the stones" and "the trees"), humans climb "a high tower" of vision and wisdom. Their awareness of the idea of interpenetration renders them compassionate, not exploitative, toward other beings—sentient and nonsentient—and the poet implicitly advises readers to use their superior sight both for a harmonious whole and for their function as a "gentle steward of the earth's community of beings." People need "to always look one step farther along" to gain a deeper and clearer vision for "the life-network" (*EHH*, 34)—an attitude that Snyder sharpened during his rigorous training in Zen in Japan.

"The Uses of Light" also reflects Snyder's respect for the "Buddha-nature" in other beings, and, in this context, the "light" takes on a spiritual dimension. The principal Buddha in the Avatamsaka sutra is Vairocana (the Sun Buddha), who is depicted in that sutra as the center of the universe. Takakusu explains both the causation theory and the world depicted in the Avatamsaka sutra: "The causation theories particular to this school mean general interdependence, universal relativity, causes and effects being interwoven everywhere. Thus it makes from the beginning one perfect whole without any single independent thing—all comprehensive *mandala* (circle) and the Cycle of Permanent Waves illumined throughout by the great Sun-Buddha (Vairocana)."[28]

Thus, at a deeper level, "stones," "trees" "moth," "deer," and people in this world are all interrelated and constitute a harmonious whole while *illumined* by the spiritual light that emanates from the Sun Buddha. The stanzaic arrangement gives the impression that both the sentient and nonsentient beings depicted are separate and independent, and yet one must say that the spiritual light pervades the space between the stanzas, connecting at a deeper level humans and other beings into "one perfect whole."

"Light"—spiritual and ecological—is one of the dominant images in *Turtle Island*, and another poem, "Two Fawns That Didn't See the Light This Spring," shares a spiritual dimension with "The Uses of Light." The poem consists of two anecdotes told by the poet's friends. First, "a friend in a tipi in the / Northern Rockies" hunting whitetail shoots by mistake a doe carrying a fawn. The friend is not wasteful, and he expiates his mistake by performing a "ritual": "He cured the meat without / salt; sliced it following the grain." The second anecdote is told by a woman in the Northern Sierra. She hits a doe with her car, and the poet's friends perform an impromptu "ritual" of death and birth. Butchering the doe, they discover a fawn:

> "—about so long—
> so tiny—but all formed and right.
> It had spots. And the little
> hooves were soft and white." (*TI*, 58)

In Snyder's Buddhist-ecological vision, to be born permeated with "light" is basically joyful; we do not "wawl and cry" coming into this world. As he suggests in the Buddhist detachment in "Night Heron," the joy of birth and death arises from the fact that one becomes interrelated with and serviceable to other beings in the network illumined by the spiritual-ecological "light":

> the joy of all the beings
> is in being
> older and tougher and eaten
> up. (*TI*, 36)

In "Two Fawns That Didn't See the Light This Spring," Snyder expresses his controlled sorrow for the two fawns that missed being part of the joyful, interdependent world permeated by the "light" that emanates from one compassionate Buddha. Snyder does not explicitly lament, and yet his sorrow and sense of loss take on an elegiac tone.

"The Hudsonian Curlew" is one of the most successful poems in *Turtle Island* in depicting interdependency between humans and other animals. It involves "killing" birds, but is an affirmative poem based on the poet's idea of the Buddhist-ecological interpenetration of beings in this world. What we see in the poem is the ritual of the food web, of eating and being eaten. The eating has a spiritual significance arising from Snyder's veneration for the life of other beings.

The poem unfolds with an image of "the Mandala of Birds." Amid the gathering of various birds, the human being is simply another animal engaged in hunting for food:

> we
> gather driftwood for firewood
> for camping
> get four shells to serve up steamed snail. (*TI*, 54)

The hunters then shoot two curlews, and the poet dwells on the concrete preparation of the birds for eating. It is a long passage, but the whole is worth quoting:

> The down
> i pluck from the

neck of the curlew
eddies and whirls at my knees
in the twilight wind
from sea.
kneeling in sand

warm in the hand.

ooo

*"Do you want to do it right? I'll tell you."*
he tells me.
at the edge of the water on the stones.
a transverse cut just below the sternum
the forefinger and middle finger
        forced in and up, following the
        curve of the ribcage.
then fingers arched, drawn slowly down and back,
forcing all the insides up and out,
toward the palm and heel of the hand.
firm organs, well-placed, hot.
save the liver;
finally scouring back, toward the vent, the last of the
        large intestine.

the insides string out, begin to wave, in the lapping
        waters of the bay.
the bird has no features, head, or feet;
        he is empty inside.
the rich body muscle that he moved by, the wing-beating
        muscle
anchored to the blade-like high breast bone,
is what you eat. (*TI*, 55–56)

The "i" in this poem is drastically different from the dwarfed, passive "i" seen, for instance, in the works of e. e. cummings. Snyder's humble but joyfully monistic "i" is aware of his place in the inter-penetrating web, and the "i" recognizes the potentialities of other beings and their "Buddha-nature." This perhaps is a radically new "i" in modern poetry written in English. The traditional, "anthro-pocentric" modern "I" cannot assert its superiority in the world of this poem, and gratitude, not guilt or aggressiveness, is the central attitude in this food web of eating and being eaten. Moreover, the minute and concrete depiction of the preparation and cooking of the bird, combined with the poet's neatness, accuracy, and reverential attitude—"kneeling in sand"—in the process suggests a spiritual depth; depicted thus, eating finally becomes a joyful ritual of the food web. In "Japan First Time Around," the poet asks: "just where am I in this food-chain?" (*EHH*, 32). This is 1956, and Snyder, in a sense, disciplined himself in Japan to find an answer for this ontological question. By combining Buddhism and ecology (and perhaps through a Native American model for hunting), he found an answer for the question, offering it to his reader.

As I mentioned earlier, Zen is pervasive in *Turtle Island*, and, in addition to the underlying Kegon (Avatamsaka) philosophy, we detect an unmistakable Zen attitude in this poem. It reflects the poet's ritualistic neatness and attention to small details sharpened in his Zen training; as Snyder records in "Japan First Time Around," "the Zen Master's presence is to help one keep attention undivided" (*EHH*, 34). Further, the Zen attitude is reflected in the central act of this poem, that is, eating. As Snyder points out in *The Wooden Fish* (a manual of Zen that Snyder and Kanetsuki Gutetsu, a Japanese colleague, compiled), "Eating is a sacrament in Zen training. No other aspect of ordinary human daily life is treated with quite such formality or reverence in the Sōdō [a training hall for monks]."[29] That eating is a sacrament is also evidenced in the verses that monks recite before meals. I quote below a representative verse from *The Wooden Fish*:

> First, let us reflect on your own work, let
> us see whence this comes;
>
> Secondly, let us reflect how imperfect our
> virtue is, whether we deserve this offerings [sic].
>
> Thirdly, what is most essential is to hold
> our minds in control and be detached from
> the various faults, greed, etc.
>
> Fourthly, that this is taken as medicinal
> to keep our bodies in good health;
>
> Fifthly, in order to accomplish the task of
> enlightenment we accept this food.[30]

This verse is called, in Japanese, *Shokuji gokan* ("The Five Reflections"), and it clearly shows the Zen attitude toward eating. Although the passage quoted from "The Hudsonian Curlew" does not show metaphysical elaboration, its reverential and sacramental attitude toward the birds is convincing and renders the poem one of the most successful in *Turtle Island*.

## V

Since the Buddhist-ecological interpenetration is best rendered concretely and specifically, a number of poems focus on home life at Kitkitdizze. These poems directly reflect the poet's earliest exploration of the literal land and a quest for its mythical element, essential parts of his attempt to establish a sense of place, and—ultimately— to find answers for the question of "how to be." To develop a sense of place means to live as a native of the land, not as a sojourner, and the life of the land at the same time is a quest for a vision of a new, alternative culture as it flowers.

Snyder's life at Kitkitdizze as reflected in *Turtle Island* is exploratory; he wants to know accurately where he is, and, as he states in a 1974 lecture, it is "a work to be done," and essentially "the old American quest . . . for an identity."[31] He had envisioned such a life during his long sojourn in Japan—he bought the land in 1967, a year before his permanent return—and, with his vision for an alternative culture, his life at Kitkitdizze reflects the work of exploration in the forest of North America.

"The Wild Mushroom," for instance, shows the poet exploring the forest at Kitkitdizze. He and his son Kai go mushrooming with "A basket and a trowel / And a book with all the rules," and the father gives the following instruction:

> Don't ever eat Boletus
> If the tube-mouths they are red
> Stay away from the Amanitas
> Or brother you are dead. (*TI*, 46)

These instructions are directed not only to his son but also to the reader and the poet himself, and thus, mushrooming is a way of knowing Turtle Island. This exploration is full of joy, and the poem becomes a praise for the interpenetrating web, acknowledging the identity of a mushroom family that, "Shining through the woodland gloom," coexists with the poet's family in this place in North America.

The exploration of Turtle Island continues, bringing in the process the poet and his family closer to the land. "The Bath" depicts the love and harmony in the family, and the poem ultimately becomes a praise for our body and the earth on which we live, perhaps Snyder's most ecstatic vision of harmony. We see the family settling deeper into the land, and the familial harmony depicted in the simple act of bathing reflects the larger web of beings:

> Clean, and rinsed, and sweating more, we stretch
>      out on the redwood benches hearts all beating
> Quiet to the simmer of the stove,
>      the scent of cedar
> And then turn over,
>      murmuring gossip of the grasses,
>      talking firewood,
> Wondering how Gen's napping, how to bring him in

    soon wash him too—
These boys who love their mother
    Who loves men, who passes on
    her sons to other women;

The cloud across the sky. The windy pines.
    the trickle gurgle in the swampy meadow

    *this is our body*

Fire inside and boiling water on the stove
We sigh and slide ourselves down from the benches
    Wrap the babies, step outside,

black night & all the stars. (*TI*, 13–14)

Instead of depicting a tension between human and nature, the passage arrests and asserts a harmonious moment in which every being in this cosmos contributes tenderly to sustain each other. The sky, winds, trees, waters, grasses, animals, children, men, and women are the members of "great / earth / sangha" (*TI*, "O Waters," 73). The poem implies an answer for the question of "how to be," and the poet affirms, laughing with his family on "the Great Earth" (*TI*, 14), the life that he and his family are creating on Turtle Island.

The knowledge gained in living everyday life on the land and the spiritual attitudes that underlie such a life must be transmitted, as Snyder in "Energy Is Eternal Delight" implies, to community, to society, and to posterity as a legacy if one is to continue fruitfully to live in a place as a native of it. In this sense, Snyder increasingly becomes a "teacher" in his poetry and essays; his is not only one person's vision but is directed to humanity at large. By his reverential and attentive attitude toward nature, and by actually living close to a devastated territory—an aftermath of hydraulic gold mining and logging (*TI*, 79)—he seeks a way of healing it, which in turn teaches his reader and audience how to live in this world of ecological crisis.

In "Pine Tree Tops," Snyder depicts the interpenetrating natural world that is almost mythic and sacred beyond people's meager knowledge:

            in the blue night
            frost haze, the sky glows
            with the moon
            pine tree tops
            bend snow-blue, fade
            into sky, frost, starlight.
            the creak of boots.
            rabbit tracks, deer tracks,
            what do we know. (*TI*, 33)

The beauty of the interpenetrating nature that the poet captures this night is awesome, and he characteristically avoids asserting his presence in the world—a typical Snyder poem that places "human tracks" next to "rabbit tracks" and "deer tracks." The last line is almost an ecstatic statement, telling the reader that dissecting, dichotomizing knowledge is unnecessary and that this holistic nocturnal beauty arising from the interpenetration of all beings is just enough.

Continuing in the same vein, in "By Frazier Creek Falls," Snyder shows that people are not separate from nature, that finally "We *are* it":

> This living flowing land
> is all there is, forever
>
> We *are* it
> it sings through us—
>
> We could live on this Earth
> without clothes or tools! (*TI*, 41)

Earlier in his career, Snyder referred to Japanese literature to show human inseparability from nature[32]; by this stage of his development, however, such literary allusions are no longer necessary. He finds new values through his direct contact with the interpenetrating land on Turtle Island, and those values are offered, along with his discoveries, to the reader, to the larger society, and to posterity. Thus, the merging of Buddhism and ecology has become an essential element in Snyder's exploratory poems on Turtle Island, and, beyond enriching the poetic world, these poems are didactic, directing poet and reader to answers for the question of "how to be."

Snyder believes that, in its anthropocentric view of the world, modern industrial civilization—East and West—has tended to ignore the lives of other beings that coexist with humanity. From this general tendency, it has earned the ecological crisis that we witness today. *Turtle Island* offers the reader not only a sense of "how to be" in a world with just such an ecological crisis but also, in Charles Molesworth's words, "a new sense of what it means to be human."[33] Gary Snyder blends the insights gained in his cross-cultural quest in Japan and Western traditions (including the indigenous American cultures) to create a vision that transcends the mythic American land. By creating the myth of Turtle Island and unfolding it to the reader in his poetry and prose, he urges the reader to reconsider the validity of the old myths on which modern civilization is based. His cross-cultural quest begun in the mid-1950s thus results in a new ontological vision.

## Notes

1. Gary Snyder, *The Real Work: Interviews & Talks, 1964–1979*, ed. William Scott McLean (New York: New Directions, 1980), 83.

2. Gary Snyder, *Turtle Island* (New York: New Directions, 1974), 80–81. Further quotations from *Turtle Island*, designated *TI*, will be cited in the text.

3. Snyder, *The Real Work*, 153.

4. Hisao Kanaseki, in his *Amerika gendaishi techo (Notes on Contemporary American Poetry)* (Tokyo: Kenkyusha, 1977), 249, states that while in Japan Snyder studied Zen, Hinduism, and *Shingon Mikkyo* (esoteric Buddhism).

5. Snyder, *Turtle Island*, back cover.

6. Junjiro Takakusu, *The Essentials of Buddhist Philosophy*, ed. Wing-tsit Chan and Charles A. Moore, 3rd. ed. (1947; Honolulu: Office Appliance Co., 1956), 29.

7. Takakusu, *Essentials*, 29.

8. Takakusu, *Essentials*, 30.

9. Takakusu, *Essentials*, 193.

10. Takakusu, *Essentials*, 113.

11. D. T. Suzuki, *Essays in Zen Buddhism*, 3rd series (London: Luzac and Co., 1934), 77.

12. Takakusu, *Essentials*, 119.

13. Takakusu, *Essentials*, 121.

14. Suzuki, *Zen Buddhism*, 87.

15. Gary Snyder, *Earth House Hold* (New York: New Directions, 1969), 16. Further quotations from *Earth House Hold*, designated *EHH*, will be cited in the text.

16. Snyder, *The Real Work*, 35.

17. Gary Snyder, *The Old Ways* (San Francisco: City Lights Books, 1977), 64.

18. Eugene P. Odum, *Fundamentals of Ecology* (Philadelphia: W. B. Saunders, 1953), 79.

19. Odum, *Fundamentals*, 12.

20. Snyder, *The Old Ways*, 54.

21. Snyder, *The Real Work*, 55.

22. Takakusu, *Essentials*, 147.

23. Shoko Watanabe, *Fudōmyō-ō* (Tokyo: Asahi Shimbunsha, 1975), 38.

24. Watanabe, *Fudōmyō-ō*, 164.

25. Watanabe, *Fudōmyō-ō*, 134.

26. Watanabe, *Fudōmyō-ō* 205. Watanabe notes that the mantra appears in the Mahavairocana sutra, one of the three sutras of the *Shingon* school.

27. Gary Snyder, *The Fudo Trilogy* (Berkeley, Calif., Shaman Drum, 1973).

28. Takakusu, *Essentials*, 124.

29. Kanetsuki Gutetsu and Gary Snyder, *The Wooden Fish: Basic Sutras & Gathas of Rinzai Zen* (Kyoto: First Zen Institute of America in Japan, 1961), 25.

30. Gutetsu and Snyder, *The Wooden Fish*, 30.

31. Snyder, *The Old Ways*, 79.

32. See, for example, "Poem 4" in the "Logging" section of *Myths & Texts* (1960; New York: New Directions, 1978), 6.; and "Kyoto Born in Spring Song" in *Regarding Wave* (New York: New Directions, 1970), 18–19. Also see my article, "A

Note on Japanese Allusions in Gary Snyder's Poetry," *Western American Literature* 18 (1983), 143–48.

33. Charles Molesworth, *Gary Snyder's Vision* (Columbia: University of Missouri Press, 1983), 109.

# Poetic Composting in Gary Snyder's *Left Out in the Rain*    Jack Hicks°

In a 1977 interview, Gary Snyder distinguishes between poets "who have fed on a certain kind of destructiveness for their creative glow," and those closer to his own energies (like Wendell Berry and Robert Duncan) "who have 'composted' themselves and turned part of themselves back in on themselves to become richer and stronger . . ."[1] *Left Out in the Rain: New Poems 1947–1985*, Snyder's most recent collection, is, in the richest sense, an extended instance of poetic composting, a mingled cycle of 154 poems, some more than forty years old, some freshly harvested, serving as a personal, cultural, and poetic recapitulation, offering glimpses of new turns on the trail.[2]

It is a risky book: one danger—of which Snyder and his North Point publishers had to be aware—was that it would be seen as merely a collection of juvenilia, ephemera, and poetic turnings swept up from the workshop floor. And some of the poems do fall into those categories.

But read properly, it is an intriguing collection: it is a corrective volume, restoring some of the dimensions of the man and the mature poet, revealing him first as apprentice working through influences, experimenting with verse forms and techniques. In the later poems, Snyder finds in the process of working with his first work—indeed, in the poems themselves—this principle of poetic composting, a source of poetic energy. He sets a dialogue with his own past in motion, a shuttling that invigorates the recent work and promises to energize that of the future.

"I wanted to finish publishing all my shorter poems—those worth seeing print—to date," he says in a recent interview. He picks up the metaphor: "Having accomplished this digestion, the *composting* of the material, I didn't have to work on it anymore. The cycle is complete."[3]

Appropriately, both the title of this volume and the physical text are recycled. The title derives from no poem herein, reaching back to *Myths & Texts* (1960). Near the end of the opening "Logging"

° This essay was written specifically for this volume and appears here for the first time by permission of the author.

section, as the poet and a fellow logger eat fresh oysters at the American rim of the Pacific, "looking off toward China and Japan," the friend wisecracks, silenic: "If you're gonna work these woods / Don't want nothing / That can't be left out in the rain—".[4]

The early manuscript itself was packed in orange crates and stored with friends (Bob and Jean Greensfelder) in Marin County when Snyder left for Japan in 1956. In 1969, having returned with wife Masa Uehara Snyder and son Kai a year earlier, building what would become Kitkitdizze, he moved the crates in a pickup truck to the rugged site north of Nevada City, California. Busy raising a house, he stashed them "outdoors under some oak trees, covered with black plastic. Literally left out in the rain—and the snow and the sun and the wind, too."[5]

In winter, 1971, Kitkitdizze well-established, he uncovered his cache to find his early work had become a home. "Woodrats had eaten into the boxes," he laughs. "They nested, chewed up some manuscripts, shit in there, generally made themselves a little home in my poetry."[6]

Repacked, the files went to the loft of the main house, where they remained until 1982. Working through his papers (they were deposited later as the Snyder Collection at the University of California, Davis), he rediscovered the early poems and moved them to his office in a nearby wood. After *Axe Handles*, Snyder had planned to return to *Mountains and Rivers without End*, hoping to complete that cycle. And he planned as well to work on a prose book on nature in China and Japan, a project that is taking shape slowly as *The Great Clod*.[7] But the pre-Kyoto poems lingered in his mind (about forty poems survive in *Left Out in the Rain*) and took precedence.

The last five years have been distinctly transitional for Gary Snyder's life and writing. After a long, healthy suspicion of formal American institutions and academies, he joined the English / Creative Writing faculty at the University of California, Davis, a choice providing a base for his intellectual life. At Kitkitdizze, his dream of a Zen community in the Sierra foothills—a grafting of East and West—has come to flower with the building of the Ring of Bone Zendo (named in honor of poet Lew Welch, who vanished nearby) and the growth of that community. And after a time of family and "reinhabitation" in a region ravaged by hydraulic gold mining in the 1870s, he set off on two major turns. The first is his separation from his former mate of twenty years, Masa Uehara Snyder, who continues her life in the community. The second is a series of voyages in apparently diametric landscapes: in once-hostile cityscapes like New York City (the basis for his recent "Walking the New York Bedrock: Alive in the Sea of Information") and in Beijing, in which "The Persimmons" is rooted.[8]

In the same period, he has traveled extensively in Alaska and the northern wilderness, to see through "an invigorating window into the essential nature of planetary normal, the diversity and richness of wildlife and terrain and people as it ought to be—and was, up until recently."[9]

Five Alaskan treks to date percolate through his work, a body of poems that constitute "a mind of tumbling water," as it is termed in "Raven's Beak River at the End," a projected sequence for *Mountains and Rivers without End*.[10] The poems are new, but they recycle through familiar figures, as in "The Sweat," which echoes "The Bath" (*Turtle Island*) two decades later.[11] And some archetypes are redis-covered, as in "The Bear Mother:"

> She veils herself
>    to speak of eating salmon
> Teases me with
>    "what do you know of my ways"
> and kisses me through the mountain
>
> Through and under its layers, its
>                gullies, its folds;
> Her mouth full of blackberries,
> We share.[12]

But deeper, the urban and wild are not opposing: the "com-posting" of *Left Out in the Rain* turns him back on himself, to see the wild in New York. It is a mind, an ecosystem, that is alive, especially with predators and scavengers. A "—Peregrine sails past the window / . . . and stoops in a blur on a pigeon." And street people are "bottom feeders."[13] And he finds worldly in the wild, as on remote Baranoff Island (Alaska), in which the women of "The Sweat" are fully in the 1980s, talking of returns to college, running businesses, careers, "science, writing, values, spirit, politics, poems—".[14]

The work begun in organizing *Left Out in the Rain*, then, and expressed in the later poems, has invigorated his sense of interpe-netration, set him on a course which "is attempting to deconstruct the dichotomy between nature and human culture."[15]

As his vision matures, Snyder has become less rigidly "anti-" and more "alternative-," embracing apparent contradiction and paradox— not unlike Coyote who shows up as a cosmic gunfighter to end gunfights in "Coyote Man, Mr. President, & the Gunfighters" (206–209). In Snyder's imagination by metamorphosis and transfor-mation, city and wilderness each become a system charged with the same energy, as filled with life as a single drop of water from the Bering Sea.

He views the forthcoming *Mountains and Rivers without End* as "a highly intuitive and unpredictable exercise."[16] But the composition is powered by the poet's walking the doab between wilderness and the city, imaging the weave between natural weft and urban or cultural warp—and looking at the vast hieroglyphics of those two places on earth, watching for clues to the state of the single and social spirit, the buried structure of mind.

So *Left Out in the Rain* is part of a series of demarcations, the decision to compile and publish the book marking "a period of fresh directions . . . a real turn in my strategies . . . like recomposting—turning the soil over one more time."[17] What began in the earliest manuscripts grew to a larger undertaking, and Snyder finally saw a six-part chronological cycle that would reveal all early work worthy of publication, adding recent major poetry, appending two sections of jeux d'esprit, "Tiny Energies 1970–1984" (155–178) and "Satires, Inventions & Diversions 1951–1980" (181–209).

His intent was to bring the early poems into print faithful to the original texts, with little revision. Only a few were reworked—most notably, "Longitude 170° West, Latitude 35° North" (59–61). Revision strengthened this night-sea meditation, a series of the poet's suspensions between worlds: East and West, sky and water, waking and dreaming, past and future, illusion and the Void.

Some poems he had simply lost track of. Eight or ten had been overlooked, especially "Crash" (97), an etched narrative speaking to the dangers of inattention, alive even in the practice of concentration in Kyoto. The search also led him back to his voluminous journals and notebooks. He retrieved "Straits of Malacca 24 October 1957" (76), an excellent study of the move from perception to poem (by selective excision and compression) from a notebook. And "First Landfall on Turtle Island" (115) was a whole-cloth journal "finding" depicting his first glimpse of America on returning from Japan in 1968.

As the concept grew, Snyder also pruned, working the folders through which his writing sifts, disposing of many poems, setting aside sixty to seventy others he will hold but not publish. What results lengthens the span of his poetic career at each end. "Elk Trails" (5–7) was written at age seventeen, "The Persimmons" (159–61) at fifty-three, and they give us a richer sense of the origins and dimensions of the corpus.[18]

This is Gary Snyder's most directly autobiographical volume, chronicling key moments in the life of a poet and a generation. As one of the nation's most closely attended literary figures, he has learned to steward carefully aspects of his private life and those of his friends, choosing when and how to yield his pith. Thus some of the poems in *Left Out in the Rain* were withheld previously because they were too personal, too autobiographical, or depicted the living too graphically. "Ballad of Rolling Heads" (192–94) gave him greatest pause. It is a winey reminiscence drafted at Shokoku-ji temple, "the Shavehead Roshis put to bed / Like babies simple in the head" (192). The poet recalls a last Beat Generation debauch in which names are named (Kerouac, Whalen, Ginsberg, Orlovsky, Cassady, lesser lights), "the whole wild tribe on the vag" (193).

He acknowledges the "hot and cool" strains of the Beats, warning last that "squares and fools will be revealed / By Whalen's calm and classic dance, / Allen Ginsberg's naked dance" (194).

Similarly, "On Vulture Peak" (170–73) is primarily of cultural, historical interest, recording in rhymed couplets the poet and his confreres, some drunk, some hung over, roistering at McClure Beach. Kerouac and Snyder feast on fresh mussels, squat naked in the sand, "a pair of drunk Siwash starting a shellmound" (70).

"Alabaster" (116), composed in 1970, a celebration of the women carpenters who helped build Kitkitdizze, working bare-chested in the summer heat, was also held back out of respect to individual privacies. Prior to publication here, Snyder sought and received permission from each of the five women depicted.[19]

The early "Atthis" sequence (20–31)—inspired by Ezra Pound's figure in *Personae* and trimmed to ten from an original eighteen or twenty poems—was also withheld because Snyder felt it "too personal, too close to the people involved."[20] The published sequence is a good corrective to the flattening of Snyder's personae, and here we see the young poet groping painfully through a lost love, ending nine years later on a sailor's hornpipe, but one more melancholy than rollicking:

> Now if we'd stayed together,
> There's much we'd never've known
> But dreary books and weary lands
> Weigh on me like a stone.
> ("Seaman's Ditty," 31)

Held back, as well, were the "Three Poems for Joanne" (91–93), limning the growth and death of the marriage between Snyder and poet Joanne Kyger. The poems move from a Western celebration outdoors "in loving words" of two poets who also love words, to bitter lees in a cold Japanese bed, "fights and the frown / at dawn" (93). This harshness flares even brighter in the "tiny energy" of domestic hell, where "some lovers wake one day" (160).

So, too, was "Versions of Anacreon" in Part VIII, "Satires, Inventions, & Diversions 1951–1980" (197–99), which is not merely an exercise in anacreontics, but offers, as well, a more explicit glimpse of the poet as sexual figure than he wished earlier in his life.

This energy burns most intensely in "April" (55), a fevered glimpse of "brief, doomed love" between the poet and an unnamed woman, pregnant with her husband's third child. The poem is charged with dangerous solar and human heat, and it serves a corrective function, as does the whole body of sensual, sexual, erotic, and bawdy poems in *Left Out in the Rain*, restoring to us the yang of the passionate, appetitive man of, say, "The Song of the Taste."[21] Too often, his readers—followers and detractors—reduce him, imagine him a pristine Zen priest of fish and blossom. Such sexual poems counter this reading.

Based on work I have seen recently, I suspect this tapping of the range from the sensual through the erotic and bawdy (see "Fear Not," 142)—poems Snyder terms "in the line of delight in the flower of the body. More to follow."—will surface strongly in *Mountains and Rivers without End* and coming work.[22]

Other poems were withheld for broad aesthetic reasons. Through *Axe Handles*, Snyder has composed collections not merely to offer his strongest individual works, but with an eye to defining "a path," at once a poetic aesthetic and a way of living in the world. "Once I had established my aesthetic clearly," he explains, "a good *track*, then I could play around the edges by bringing this book out."[23]

"Playing at the edges" is often a corrective impulse in *Left Out in the Rain*. Snyder's personae assert their sexuality and eroticism, and they restore other dimensions to our readings. The voice of the youth in "Elk Trails" (5–7) is stern, sapwood adolescent, and that of the young man in "Atthis" (20–31) embraces the pain of rejection and lost love. A sequence of poems in IV and V enriches our sense of the Kyoto period, one his readers tend to see through a romanticized haze of plum blossom and delicate kimonos. Being a foreigner and a seeker via templed discipline entails periods of drudgery and complex doubt, and "Dullness in February: Japan" (64–65), "Riding the hot electric train" (100), and "In Tokyo: At Loose Ends" ("me on my feet through the town. / liking it, / ready to leave," 104) all suggest this.

Grant, then, the sterner energies here, but note also the sense of play, a tone of relaxed, bemused acceptance that grows as poet and poetry mature. "Lots of play / in the way things work" ("Lots of play," 17), he advises, and one face of play here is pleasure in baring early sources and influences, a willingness to offer poems that show the apprentice at work as well as those of the mature craftsman.

Gary Snyder's Eastern and American Indian influences and his assimilation of their spiritual and poetic modes have been well-established, but in *Left Out in the Rain* he demonstrates his debts to Western traditions and individual talents. His approach to influence and the "anxiety of influence" is direct: "Harold Bloom's position is very patriarchal, very Occidental, and very Jewish. The Chinese have been happy poetically for millennia to refer, adopt whole lines, to nourish their poetry with the speech of others. And they certainly don't have any anxiety about that. My feeling is that the artist is a shameless thief. You know, the raven flies over and anything left out gets picked up. It's not a problem for me."[24]

Snyder has acknowledged the poetic influences of European and American Modernists in earlier interviews ("Stevens, Eliot, Pound, Williams and Yeats"), and the poems in this collection clearly show such "picking-up."[25]

"Elk Trails" (5–7), his earliest published verse, establishes a figure ripening in his work more than forty years later, but it originates in the poet's reading Robinson Jeffers.[26] There is a flinty disdain of modern life and mind ("man-made trails, / Precise-cut babies of the mountain / Ignorant of the fine, high-soaring ridges," 6). Jeffers courses through the poem, in sound, diction, line, and metaphor, but mainly by the rocky, antihuman vision, fiercely adolescent, that conjures the spirits of the Elk *trails* (*not* the Elk), an "ancient, coarse-haired, / Thin-flanked God" who laughs "at man, and all his trails" (7).

The shade of William Butler Yeats also looms large in the apprentice poetry, in what Snyder terms "his special sense of symbol and imagery."[27] The "Atthis" sequence (20–31) opens with an Eliotic invocation far too obvious to miss, but the vision and craft of Yeats— in image, line, sound, and rhythm—is remarkable in poems three and four, as it is elsewhere in the roughly contemporaneous "Message from Outside" (15).

More surprising is the influence of Alexander Pope, shown in Snyder's satiric imitation, "The Elusiad, or Culture Still Uncaught" (183–84), and elsewhere in the final two sections. "I've always had a funny, closet fondness for eighteenth century verse, especially Pope and Swift," he admits.[28] And his playing with Pope (one serious work of the apprentice) is evident. Composed in his early twenties, the poem was submitted as a graduate paper for a course in "Anthropology and Culture" at the University of Indiana in 1952. The imitation traces, in rhyme, meter, image, and ironic vision, Pope's influence, as "*Culture's* net unseen" tangles "man in folly all his days" (183).[29]

Snyder's sense that one real work of the poet originates in play expresses itself in several other ways. If we see a "trying on" of earlier poets, we also see an interest in formal structures; echoing and imitation are tools of the apprenticeship. *Left Out in the Rain* offers us heroic satires ("The Elusiad," 183–84), sestinas ("Sestina of the End of the Kalpa," 187), villanelles ("Villanelle of the Wandering Lapps," 181), and a wide range of exercises with couplet, quatrain, and metered rhyme.

If the poet's work is often serious play, play is also fun, funny, even frivolous. Snyder's most recent collection mirrors this sense of the shuttle at work, in one sense by a recurrent interest in trickster figures, shape-shifters, transformers, and metamorphosers. Coyote— merely invoked in the early "Message from Outside" (15) but comically potent in the closing "Coyote Man, Mr. President, & the Gunfighters" (206–209)—is the clearest instance, and "the ugly infant" and "Greasy Boy" of "The Professor as Transformer" (182) and "Fox-girls" who "switch from / humans to fox-form / right during the party!" ("Fear Not," 142) are also metamorphosers. Such figures insist that the serious can be silly in an instant.

Most basically, they manifest Snyder's sense of the illusion of a dualistic universe. Han-Shan was first a crazy, wandering drunk, the Yamabushi deity Fudō Myō-ō is a "punk or street-Buddha," a marauder who "forcibly rescues folks from hell whether they want it or not."[30] All of these shape-shifters and transformers feed on apparent contradiction and paradox. Good and evil, the pure light and drunken folly, moments of sexual heat and bad practical jokes—all are convenient dualistic separations to be dissolved.

Thus play is at once "serious" work and "frivolous," which conclusion led Snyder to append the final two sections of *Left Out in the Rain*. His intent, once again, was corrective: "I had questions about them. They'd previously been too frivolous to publish. Then, I thought, why not let frivolity show? Show the 'goofy' side as well— what I'm really like at times. And one power of such figures 'at play' is that we cannot easily contain them."[31]

Such thinking is undeniably seductive, and readers do tend to overlook the comic strain in the poetry, the delight in language, puns, wordplay, arcane echoes, but taken to the extreme, it yields such ephemera as "Smog" (204), an instance of concrete verse which is surely the nadir of this collection and probably of Snyder's entire poetic career.

Finally, the metaphor of composting implies that the past is alive and feeding the present and future, that Gary Snyder derived impetus from the process of retrieving and publishing his earliest poetry, used it as an energy source, a fuel for his most recent work. The structure of the poem *Left Out in the Rain* (Snyder's collections are carefully arranged extended poems) is one of a series of arcs, starting with "Elk Trails" (5–7) and "Out of the soil and rock" (8), brought to close in "At the White River Roadhouse in the Yukon" (148) and "The Persimmons" (149–51). Thus opening and closing sets of poems are end-pieces, framing a series of arcs that bend outward from Pacific Coast wilderness, to California and Beat life, to Asia, back to home and family, back to the Northwest (Alaska), finally striking a series of complex balances in "The Persimmons" (149–51), one of Snyder's most resonant poems in many years.

These arcs—seen as oppositions to, movements away from—are set off in the persona of "Elk Trails" and "Out of the soil and rock," a young, stern, solitary seeker of exotic bedrock. He burns on a summer eve for the destruction of cities, disdains all forms of human civilization and culture. Gazing first at Mt. St. Helens and Spirit Lake and then New York, he is Western youth and egoism personified.[32] Abstract and strained in language and image, seeing mainly death in the elements of life before him, he is unable to engage the present, yearning, instead, for the ancient wisdom of an unknown memory that may offer a radically transformed future.

The texts suggest that Snyder writes in response to this earliest poetic self in "At White River Roadhouse . . ." and "The Persimmons," turns back in on himself to conduct an implied dialogue. He composts from that stern, dichotomized, arcing self, transforming to the mature, mellowed persona who gathers arcs into cycles. For this second self, the past is alive, and the future is charged with potential, yet he stands fully realized in the present, no longer stranded, redeemed in the concrete moment of ripe fruit. The boy abstractly imagines the steel and cement of New York ephemeral; the man responds in his own specific vision, a dream in which a ringing bell links him to both the solitary and the social, a Buddhist temple and wayfarers on an Alaskan highway. He radiates into "The Persimmons," first a traveler in winter Alaska, then voyager in October China, and he dissolves, heals the arcs spoken and implied in the mind of the earliest poems, to balances, cycles: God and men, the ancient wild and the city of the 1980s, harsh spirit and failing matter, the freedom of the single self and the prisons of family, culture and history, life and death. These are all connected in the mind of the poem.

And so the mature "I" of "The Persimmons" composts himself from "Elk Trails," turns back in on himself for new energy, just as he recycles the energy of the universe in the simple act of eating a persimmon ("each orb some life left from summer," 149). He recalls an afternoon walk on The Great Wall and a descent into a deep Ming tomb, in which he saw a ripe Tamopan persimmon on a plaited tray. And now, on an adjacent Beijing street filled with travelers and other persimmon vendors, he gathers the arcs set off in his young persona's mind. He composts from it with a simple, delighted gesture, the purchase of a fruit from an old man, a balance that entitles him, as well, to join "the people and the trees that prevail" (151). Doing so, the mature man rises from life in the boy (his poetic father), composts him in a cycle, "richer and stronger."[33] From physical text to title to conceptual evolution to the emergence of the mature persona from the chrysalis of his past, *Left Out in the Rain* speaks of the transformation of poetic composting.

## Notes

1. Gary Snyder, "The *East West* Interview," interview by Peter Barry Chowka, in *The Real Work: Interviews and Talks 1964–1979*, ed. William Scott McLean (New York: New Directions, 1980), 123.

2. Gary Snyder, *Left Out in the Rain: New Poems 1947–1985* (Berkeley, Calif.: North Point Press, 1986). Subsequent references to poems in this collection appear parenthetically in the text.

3. Gary Snyder, interview by Jack Hicks, tape recording, Davis, California, 23 August 1987.

4. Gary Snyder, *Myths and Texts* (New York: New Directions, 1978), 14.

5. Snyder-Hicks interview.

6. Snyder-Hicks interview.

7. Three chapters of *The Great Clod* are complete to date. A subsequent prose book, *Practice of the Wild*, of which six chapters have been privately circulated, is approximately three-fourths complete.

8. Gary Snyder, "Walking the New York Bedrock: Alive in the Sea of Information," in *The Best American Poetry 1988*, ed. John Ashbery (New York: Collier Books, 1988), 175–80.

9. Snyder-Hicks interview.

10. Gary Snyder, "Raven's Beak River at the End," *Sulfur* 22 (Spring 1988): 118–19.

11. Gary Snyder, "The Sweat," privately circulated, June 1987. See also "The Bath," *Turtle Island* (New York: New Directions, 1974), 12–14.

12. Gary Snyder, "The Bear Mother," *Sulfur* 22 (Spring 1988): 115.

13. Snyder, "Walking the New York Bedrock," 179–80.

14. Snyder, "The Sweat," 2.

15. Snyder-Hicks interview.

16. Snyder-Hicks interview.

17. Snyder-Hicks interview.

18. Snyder-Hicks interview.

19. Snyder-Hicks interview.

20. Snyder-Hicks interview. See also Ezra Pound, "Atthis," in *Personae* (New York: New Directions, 1926), 112.

21. Gary Snyder, "Song of the Taste," *Regarding Wave* (New York: New Directions, 1972), 17.

22. Gary Snyder, letter to Jack Hicks, 20 October 1987.

23. Snyder-Hicks interview.

24. Snyder-Hicks interview.

25. See Gary Snyder, "The Real Work," interview by Paul Geneson, in *The Real Work*, 57–58.

26. Snyder makes a major distinction between "path" and "trail" in "On the Path and Off the Trail," *Practice of the Wild*, privately circulated, September 1988.

Here *trail* is a utilitarian concept, implying destination, quantification, and mastery over the wild. To be on the *path* is to have a spiritual "way."

27. Snyder, *The Real Work*, 58.

28. Snyder-Hicks interview.

29. Snyder-Hicks interview.

30. Gary Snyder, *Riprap & Cold Mountain Poems* (San Francisco: Four Seasons Foundation, 1965), 33–60. Fudō Myō-ō is described at length in the fourteen-page catalog, *Contributions to the Ring of Bone Zendo Dharma Art Exhibit*, privately circulated, September 1987.

31. Snyder-Hicks interview.

32. "Elk Trails" was composed during the summer of 1947; the New York poem, in the summer of 1948.

33. Gary Snyder, *The Real Work*, 123.

# Practicing the Wild—Present and Future Plans: An Interview with Gary Snyder                David Robertson*

DAVID ROBERTSON:    Let's begin by talking about the writing projects you have planned for the winter.

GARY SNYDER:    For the past three years most of my writing has been in prose, researching, thinking out, and now, since last winter, the writing of a series of essays that I am going to call *The Practice of the Wild*. This is the first extended prose undertaking I've done for some time. It grew out of the workshops I've given during the last ten or twelve years dealing with ecology, environmental problems, native peoples, as well as spiritual, cultural, and literary interrelationships. I thought I should bring together a whole lot of territories that I've worked in, such as bioregionism, Native American spirituality, the Buddhist quest for environmental values, deep ecology, my own rising interest in Occidental literature—for example, my rereading in the last few years, since I've been at Davis, of Emerson and Thoreau. I have found a lot of pleasure in learning how to write prose better; it's been very interesting and challenging. I also have a number of other writing projects.

DR:    For the moment let's continue with *The Practice of the Wild*. Have you projected the subject matter of the various chapters?

GS:    I have quite a clear picture of the book now. You saw the first four chapters, which were circulated in the graduate class I

* This interview was conducted specifically for this volume on 6 July 1989 and is published here for the first time by permission of David Robertson.

taught this spring. In addition, there is the essay already out called "Good, Wild, Sacred." Another essay that fits in is called "On the Path, Off the Trail." And about three or four more essays that are in the works right now. I would say that the book is two-thirds finished. I have blocked out most of the fall to complete it.

DR:    Why don't you go back and describe in more detail the first four chapters. The initial chapter is entitled "The Etiquette of Freedom."

GS:    Yes. It deals with some basic definitions, of such words as *nature, wild,* and *wilderness.* Then, having defined *wild* in terms of natural order and self-maintaining systems, I take another look at human beings not just as animals, but wild animals. Also I take some phenomena that are commonly taken as cultural, such as language, and consider them as wild systems. That's in the first chapter. The second chapter is about how we place ourselves. I start with the most immediate context of our existence, our localness, our childhood sense of place, and consider how that expands as we grow. Not to have been rooted in place is to have missed a fundamental aspect of human education. That leads into a discussion of regionalism and bioregionalism. The third chapter is called "Tawny Grammar." It grows out of conversations I've had with Alaskan natives about problems of culture and teaching in the modern age. There is also more exploration of the wild side of language, borrowing Thoreau's phrase, "tawny grammar." The fourth chapter is a retelling of the story of the girl who married a bear from the bear's point of view. Then will come "Good, Wild, Sacred" and "On the Path, Off the Trail," followed by "Fear of Bears," which I've already written, but it will have to be integrated into the book.

DR:    And you expect to finish . . .

GS:    My target date is winter solstice; that's to get it to the publisher, North Point Press.

DR:    One of the things I like so much about your prose writing is your ability to lay out a vision of life as it ought to be, at the same time recognizing very hardheadedly that actual life is rooted in ambiguity and frustration over uncompleted goals. This quality is quite evident in the chapters of the book I've already read. I feel encouraged to strive and simultaneously helped to deal with my own inadequacies. Not only that, but taught that daily routine, which I so often see as getting in the way, is part of my "real" work. What about your other writing projects?

GS:    After I complete *The Practice of the Wild,* I'm going to finish "Mountains and Rivers without End," my long poem project. Also, either sequentially or simultaneously, I'm projecting a volume of essays on Zen, poetry, and love. I've written about a third of it already. Another project I have about sixty percent completed is a history of Chinese environmentalism. So there are two books of prose and one of poetry after *Practice of the Wild.*

DR:    Where does "Mountains and Rivers without End" stand at this point?

GS:    It is not easy to say where it stands. I have written some new sections for it in the past few years, like the New York and Los Angeles city poems, but I don't know what shape it will take until I lay it all out again. I have a lot of notes, and semiwritten stuff, as well as finished stuff. I want to mull over where I want it to go and what it will take to finish it. I shouldn't make any predictions. I feel that it is going to take a new shape, it's going to show me some new things when I really look at it again, when I hold it all in mind at once.

DR:    I take it you don't plan to finish it anytime soon, that is, in the near future?

GS:    Oh, I expect to finish it within a year or two from the time I start back to work on it. I will go at it hammer and tongs until it is done. Probably I will work on it that way instead of doing several projects parallel. I feel that it is ready to be finished. I've had a lot of fun with it because it is so weird. I've given myself so much freedom. It is rather different from a lot of my other poetry, which is rather minimal, stripped down, pointed in rather careful, intense directions. This is a poem where I allow myself to use much more information and a lot more mythological and symbolic material. It is a different order of poetic, and it is nice to do that kind of writing also.

DR:    And there are the two other projects. One is the history of the environment in China.

GS:    Yes, that is going to be called *The Great Clod.* One of the questions is why Buddhist and Taoist worldviews are inadequate to halt environmental degradation in China and Japan. It is a study of the relationship between the effects of a society and that society's own value system, how, for example, the Japanese can continue to call themselves great lovers of nature and at the same time do such horrendous things to the land. My conclusion is, basically, that religious and philosophical value systems are small potatoes in the dynamics and thrust of a civilization, where the real power lies in the mercantile sector. Ideologies are never much more than window dressing.

DR:    Are you taking a Marxist point of view here?

GS:    No, not really. My use of Marxism is really my own use of it. Any historical analysis can benefit from an application of Marxist ideas. The class struggle is not the only reality of history, but it certainly is one of the bigger ones. I'm far from being any kind of orthodox Marxist. I don't really have a historical theory that I work from, or, if I do, it is informed more by anthropology than anything else. Two real flaws in Marxist thought are its neglect of the environment and its failure to grasp the importance of ethnic minorities and primitive peoples. I am also interested in the question of how civilization arises.

DR:    And you mean by civilization?

GS:    Class structure, centralization, metalworking, a military class, and a priesthood. That cluster of phenomena. I take the Chinese state as a reference point. Some really interesting work has been done by a Chinese scholar named Kwang-chih Chang. Independently, we have arrived at the conclusion that the Chinese state served no useful function and that it comes into existence as an extortion racket, as a device to siphon wealth off from a large number of people and concentrate it in the hands of a few, with no benefits whatsoever accruing to the masses. Apparently civilization arises in China without any major technological advances. Tools used by the peasants were the same before and after. It is not as if a new mode of production called into being a new institution. The state seems to be a function of the discovery that with the right kind of organization and a few weapons you can enforce your will on others. It's raiding, essentially. The institution of raiding becomes the Chinese state.

DR:    At the present time does the Neolithic play a crucial role in your thinking? How do you characterize the Neolithic anyway?

GS:    The Neolithic is characterized by localism, village-level self-government, virtually no specialized military, and a much more vernacular and unspecialized religious system. It is stable and self-governing, with a modest amount of wealth and comfort. The way to understand the Neolithic is to realize that self-sufficient, autonomous villages for the last twelve to fifteen thousand years have been the life of the world, that the governments of China and Japan up until recently were just that. On the local level the Chinese and Japanese have been essentially self-governing, and that self-governing capacity is a transmission directly from the Neolithic. In Southeast Asia even today what is government is the village council. In India village life goes on uninterrupted from the Neolithic.

DR:    Our modern conceptions of the Neolithic seem to play a very large role in your notions about how human groups ideally ought to be organized.

GS:    Actually, the Paleolithic, and especially the upper Paleolithic, is in a sense more critical to me.

DR:    What is the difference between the Paleolithic and the Neolithic as it figures in your present thinking?

GS:    The Paleolithic, blending into the Mesolithic, is economically nonagricultural, that is, hunting and gathering. It is a very viable lifestyle. A number of scholars, including Marshall Sahlins, have argued rather convincingly that agriculture is a step down in terms of the ratio of the energy put out to the energy coming in. It is an era of greater mobility and independence in comparison with the Neolithic, and possibly more and better food, not to speak of a more intimate relationship with the natural region. The distinction between cultivated and wild lands is not made. There is a much broader territory of interaction with wild animals and plants, a very broad species consciousness. With the development of agriculture gradually people's knowledge of plants and animals is narrowed down to a very small spectrum.

DR:    In terms of your work in the immediate future, how do you see your association with the University here at Davis fitting in?

GS:    On a very concrete level, it puts me back in touch with students, who are able to give me feedback in both realms of writing, poetry and prose. Access to a library, that's basically it, along with the possibility of working ideas through consistently with people over a period of time. In the last decade and a half I have done a lot of teaching, but it was usually one-weekend workshops, or at the most two or three days on a campus. There is a real collaborative effect that happens when you are a member of a faculty. The longer commitment and engagement with people is very stimulating.

We are entering into a really critical age. Things are bad, and they are going to get worse. The territory to address problems we face is not the purely scientific. All the scientific information in the world will not do any good unless it is applied, and for it to be applied you have to have people who have a broad cultural and political understanding of how societies work. The people who take the type of classes I and others here at Davis are beginning to teach will be prepared to go into areas of environmental policy-making and enlighten legislators and the like about how we have come to the present crisis. Several points need to be made clear. One is the interlocking nature of all systems. Another is the area of how we get good information about these systems. Still another is the disparity between the needs of natural systems and public policy, the discrepancy between what is taken as common wisdom by people who run counties, cities, and states, by developers and planners, on the one hand, and the facts of the planetary situation, on the other.

DR:     One area that we might cover briefly is politics. Do you contemplate any new moves in the political arena?

GS:     I plan to continue my involvement on the local level, with matters on the San Juan Ridge, but actually, because of my writing, I am not doing much at present. It is a pleasure and an obligation to keep in touch with local activists, but the forestry issue leads right into world deforestation, and that leads into questions about the World Bank and multinational corporations. As the Soviet Union and China, each in their own way, seem to be going in some sort of reformist direction, people are saying that socialism has failed and free-market economies are more practical. People are saying that the world is moving toward democratic capitalism. So far so good. But if so, then thinkers of the capitalist world had better get their act together and figure out how it can be restrained. How do you set limits? How do you shape it? Can capitalism put its own house in order, and not be simply driven by the market and by profits? If it is driven by nothing but the market, then the defeat of socialism will not be much of a victory, for capitalism will go on to wreck the whole world and its resources. Here is a new direction and a new challenge. The challenge that comes from below is the rise of the green movements all over the planet. We seem to be on the edge of an era when the green movements will be the counter party to that of democratic capitalism, or at least the ecological and social conscience of democratic capitalism. So I expect that I will be engaged in the international green movement.

What shape a green movement in the United States will take is hard to guess. It is not likely that it will become a viable third party. It might be something more like Common Cause, a powerful caucus of a special territory of interests that would cut across the right and left of traditional American politics. You might have Democratic green people and Republican green people who would unite on green-related issues.

DR:     If a green movement of some viability came into existence, it might embody what you mean by the "practice of the wild."

GS:     To some extent. I hope that the book I am now writing will be stimulating to a broad range of people and provide them with historical, ecological, and personal vision all at the same time. I would like to see the book be political in the sense of helping people shape the way they want to live and act in the world.

# INDEX

263